AFRICAN CULTURE AND MELVILLE'S ART

For Edward Blum —

It is good to have
contact with you.

Sterling Stuckey

To Marjorie Craig Benton and Harle Montgomery

and in memory of
W. Haywood Burns

AFRICAN CULTURE AND MELVILLE'S ART

The Creative Process in Benito Cereno and Moby-Dick

Sterling Stuckey

OXFORD
UNIVERSITY PRESS
2009

OXFORD
UNIVERSITY PRESS

Oxford University Press, Inc., publishes works that further
Oxford University's objective of excellence
in research, scholarship, and education.

Oxford　New York
Auckland　Cape Town　Dar es Salaam　Hong Kong　Karachi
Kuala Lumpur　Madrid　Melbourne　Mexico City　Nairobi
New Delhi　Shanghai　Taipei　Toronto

With offices in
Argentina　Austria　Brazil　Chile　Czech Republic　France Greece
Guatemala　Hungary　Italy　Japan　Poland　Portugal　Singapore
South Korea　Switzerland　Thailand　Turkey　Ukraine　Vietnam

Published by Oxford University Press, Inc.
198 Madison Avenue, New York, New York 10016

www.oup.com

Oxford is a registered trademark of Oxford University Press

Library of Congress Cataloging-in-Publication Data
Stuckey, Sterling.
African culture and Melville's art : the creative process in Benito Cereno and Moby-Dick / by
Sterling Stuckey.
p. cm.
Includes bibliographical references and index.
ISBN 978-0-19-537270-0
1. Melville, Herman, 1819–1891—Criticism and interpretation.　2. Melville, Herman, 1819–1891—
Knowledge—Africa.　3. Melville, Herman, 1819–1891. Benito Cereno.
4. Melville, Herman, 1819–1891. Moby Dick.　I. Title.
PS2387.S78 2008
813'.3—dc22　　　2008007992

1　3　5　7　9　8　6　4　2

Printed in the United States of America
on acid-free paper

Acknowledgments

Research assistant John Neff was superb. Helpful in a variety of ways, perhaps his most outstanding contribution was to find an illustration of the Lord Nelson statuary in Liverpool that is described by Melville in *Redburn*. That statuary casts new light on the opening pages of *Benito Cereno*'s recurring symbols. Christian Trajano, in "Research Seminar in American History," uncovered crucial aspects of Melville's creative process in relation to Atufal, a discovery that, moreover, helped me solve, in some degree, the important problem of how Melville arrived at the symbolic fate of Babo in *Benito Cereno*. For several years, Jennifer Hildebrand offered various forms of technical assistance and read most of the chapters of the book.

Owing to the presence of colleague Ray Kea, a distinguished student of African history, I was able to hone certain insights regarding the Ashantee cultural past. Kea's responses to questions were unfailingly helpful. French critic and Melville scholar Viola Sachs offered wonderful insights when, on two occasions, I met with her in Paris. Moreover, Professor Sachs, then teaching at Paris VIII, sponsored a number of gatherings in Paris that I attended in an atmosphere that was entirely open and charged with intellectual excitement. Christina Georcelli, Itala Vivan, Agnes Derail, Michel Imbert, Dominique Marçais, Celestine Makouta, Shelly Fisher Fishkin, Janine Dove, David Lionel Smith, Hortense Spillers, Carroll-Smith Rosenberg, Carolyn Karcher, Bernard Vincent, and Emory Elliott were among the scholars participating in conferences in which there was always some attention given to Melville. Like Viola Sachs, Michel Imbert was a particular influence on my Melville work. Professor Christina Georcelli, moreover, invited me to publish some of my developing ideas on Melville in her journal, *Litterature d'America Revista Trimestralei*. The hospitality of Dominique and Pierre Marçais added elegant charm to more than one conference.

Robert S. Levine read each of the chapters of this book. All benefited from his editorial advice. Charles Long's extended and intriguing conceptual and analytical comments, particularly on Hegel, are especially appreciated. James Alan McPhersen, Samuel Floyd, Jr., Robert Hill, Olly Wilson, Henry McGee, Jr., James W. and Almarie Wagner, John Ganim, Kenneth Barkin, Martin Kilson, Peter Carroll, Brian Lloyd, David Joravsky, Lisa Dembling, Clarence Ver Steeg, Hans and Jenne Panofsky, David L. Easterbrook, Miriam DeCosta-Willis, Frank Crossley, and poet and critic Samuel W. Allen read chapters and offered encouragement. So did David Roediger. Moreover, Roediger, a talented student of Melville, was quick to call to my attention *proof* of Melville's familiarity with Hegel, a thesis pioneered in relation to *Benito Cereno* and *The Bell Tower* by Joshua Leslie. E. D. Hirsch, Jr., read a portion of the manuscript and was a source of inspiration. And medievalist Piotr Gorecki and I, on countless Saturdays and Sundays, were on the sixth floor of the Humanities and Social Sciences Building holding down offices on our respective corners. Our numerous conversations were sustaining as I worked on Melville. While doing so, I could not have benefited more from the History office staff. I shudder to think how protracted my work would have been except for the amazingly prompt technical assistance of Connie Young. Knowing that her support was forthcoming made it possible for me to face remaining work with a calmness that otherwise would have been impossible.

At the otherworldly Center for Advanced Study in the Behavioral Sciences, Stanford, I was able, in 2002–2003, to glimpse from my study the waters of the bay, which provided the kind of spiritual renewal that Melville points to in the opening pages of *Moby-Dick*. While at the Center, I wrote a chapter of this manuscript. Kathleen Much provided fine editorial assistance during that year and later.

I'll always be indebted to a student in a seminar at Northwestern, almost certainly a student of Ivor Wilks, an eminent Ashantee authority, who provided the source on the dance and song of Ashantee women that relates to acts of military valor. That contribution as much as the revelations of R. S. Rattray led me to begin compiling an extensive list of Ashantee sources, a precondition for understanding major dimensions of Melville's creative process in *Benito Cereno* and *Moby-Dick*.

It was at Northwestern that I first taught *Benito Cereno* in a freshman seminar. The fire generated in that course never went out. I express gratitude to Todd Jacobs, Robert Neustadt, Chantal Sanchez, and Rebecca Purnell for sharing the excitement of first discovery. In addition, I remain indebted to Michael Capuzzo, who, in another course at Northwestern, researched and copied for me all of the articles that had been published on *Benito Cereno* up to the early 1980s!

For a period of two years, the last years of work on this book, the intensity of the work each day was matched by exhilaration. In fact, intensity and exhilaration seemed endlessly to feed into each other, causing me to wonder if it would ever end. Through it all, Harriette's loving support was crucial. Without it, the book could not have been written.

Contents

Introduction 3

CHAPTER I
The Tambourine in Glory 21

CHAPTER II
Benito Cereno and *Moby-Dick* 41

CHAPTER III
The Hatchet-Polishers, Benito Cereno, and Amasa Delano 63

CHAPTER IV
Cheer and Gloom: Frederick Douglass and Herman Melville
on Slave Music and Dance 81

APPENDIX
Chapter XVI from Captain Amasa Delano's
A Narrative of Voyages and Travels 99

Notes 125

Index 143

AFRICAN CULTURE AND MELVILLE'S ART

Introduction

Like the paintings in the Ajanta caves, the beauty of Moby-Dick *can be known only to those who will make the pilgrimage to it, and stay within its dark confines until what is darkness has become light, and one can make out, with the help of an occasional torch, its grand design, its complicated arabesque, the minute significance of its parts.*
—*Lewis Mumford,* Herman Melville, *1929*

To an astonishing extent, what Mumford says of *Moby-Dick* applies to *Benito Cereno*. Indeed, his reference to particular angles of light, as from a torch, illumining previously dark areas of understanding applies to both masterpieces. By warning us that much of *Moby-Dick* remains to be understood, Mumford posits a great animating principle of Melville's art, that neither the sweep of his creative imagination nor the depth of his probing of the human condition are meant to be exhausted in particular lifetimes. That Melville searches out and examines cultural resources that appear least likely, when transmuted, to garland his art deepens the darkness and extends the time required for much of it to be cast aside. But he is equally good at taking that which is before our eyes and working a subtle magic that long makes it invisible.

Attention is directed at criticism that at times denies Melville's skills as a novelist. In such instances, critics who view his work unfavorably are responded to because they touch on areas of Melville's alleged inadequacies that are, in light of new findings, greater strengths than critics, past and present, have imagined. These findings illuminate so much about the works themselves that they enable us to answer questions never before posed about Melville's creative process. To this end, my purpose is to show how he used sources never before read by critics to fashion strikingly intricate and subtle techniques of craft, heretofore unexplored, in creating two of his greatest works, *Benito Cereno* and *Moby-Dick*.

The introduction sets the stage for sustained consideration of how Melville used such sources to form his aesthetic. What follows is a chapter-by-chapter *demonstration* that he was a far more subtle and inventive writer than even the most fervent admirers of the works under consideration claim. In other words, what is at issue is the degree of Melville's indebtedness to previously unknown sources for extraordinary technical advances that expanded both the range and depth not only of particular works but of the aesthetic that gave birth to them. Put another way, because most critics now agree that Melville was a great novelist, that criticism, except in rare instances, is not under examination in this work.[1] Rather, this work is almost exclusively about veins of Melville's art, subterranean and interconnected, that are being examined for the first time.

I emphasize, especially, the book's attention to aspects of Melville's aesthetic in *Benito Cereno* and *Moby-Dick* that have gone unexamined. How the one work relates to the other, not a particular concern of previous criticism, is a principal concern of this book. Moreover, the novella and *The Encantadas* are joined in ways never before written about and bear an interconnectedness similar to what the novella bears to *Moby-Dick,* which means that these works, taken together, reveal exquisitely subtle—and broadly resonating—qualities of Melville's art. In both *Moby-Dick* and *Benito Cereno,* larger structures of creation than previously imagined are now perceived.

[I]

So inventive is Melville's creative process that, to be believed, it must indeed be *demonstrated,* which is the challenge before me here. He repeatedly and dazzlingly inverts historical reality for artistic effect, sometimes leaving no trace of his sources. Moreover, when there are few or no clues to how he created, no answer to that "problem" in criticism, the solution might be found continents away, or in places at home where one would least expect to find it. This means that numerous problems are first known *after* they have been identified and solved, accounting for the length of time it has taken for us even to consider them. No other writer risked hiding vital aspects of his creative process, and thereby affecting his critical reception, to the extent Melville did. One wonders why he decided on this strategy of creation.

A classic feature of Melville's art is its astonishingly layered nature. One or more cultures may be concealed, contributing to the formation of symbols, characterizations, and scenes on the printed page. Even with an understanding of much of this process, such features of his art, though widely appropriated, shine through as entirely of his own making. The skill with which he carries out this layering does not prepare the reader to expect it repeatedly, heightening the wonder of the process. For this reason, much that is vital in his work is not the object of discussion, and his very talent can militate against the admiration his gifts merit. Nevertheless, as problems are identified and solutions reached, new and radiant light is cast on otherwise familiar features of *Moby-Dick* and *Benito Cereno*. On occasion, entirely new symbols appear before us.

Much that would be forgettable in the hands of a less talented writer glimmers thanks to Melville's genius. We may especially savor small details that result in unforgettable artistic triumphs, such as Babo being dragged to the gibbet and the use of the Rimac Bridge in the last sentence of *Benito Cereno*. A certain fluidity of cultural thought and practice occurs when Melville relates one culture to another, enabling him to imagine the flow of influences, to layer one beneath, or above, the other. His is not universality as abstraction, devoid of cultural specificity and content, but the reverse: particular human beings from different parts of the world, at times nameless, are lifted from the mundane circumstances in which Melville finds them to the dazzling heights of his art. A curious sort of immortality results from his artistry as he works from most of the world's continents.

But Melville's skill at characterization is profoundly revealed when one is examining principal figures in his work. In ways that catch one completely off guard, that can be stunningly impressive, the discovery is made that he has, in the act of creating, actually fused characters into being, both in *Moby-Dick* and *Benito Cereno*. Especially in *Benito Cereno,* this genius at characterization is revealed, and one wonders, for this alone, if he has received anything like the credit he deserves as an avant-garde artist. Once again, questions about this method of characterization, certainly in *Benito Cereno,* were not posed because Melville's method, in this realm, is but now being recognized in relation to the novella. Accordingly, what was not considered a problem is identified today as one after its solution has been carried through.

Melville appropriated and transformed material from writers who were well known in his time but not previously thought to have influenced him artistically. This form of intertextuality, of which the reader is innocent, is pivotal to his method of creating. And there are resonances between his own works: for example, between *Moby-Dick* and *Benito Cereno,* between *Moby-Dick* and *Omoo,* between *The Encantadas* and *Benito Cereno,* and between *Redburn* and *Benito Cereno*. The depth of the interplay is still more pronounced for *Moby-Dick* and *Benito Cereno,* for they are anchored by a common source on which Melville, creating art largely through the prism of history far more than previously thought, forever links his two greatest works in characterizations, symbolism, and the theme of slavery. *The Encantadas* fits in here as well.

Charles Dickens was a writer of Melville's own time, and Melville drew on him in writing *Moby-Dick*. His presence in America, and in Melville's hometown of New York City, might have motivated critics to look further than they have at Melville's writing for ways in which he might have been stirred to still more creative effort, especially because it was said that Melville admired Dickens and was influenced by him.[2] Even though "New York," a chapter of Dickens's *American Notes for General Circulation,* figures prominently in the creation of "Midnight, Forecastle" of *Moby-Dick,* critics have not noticed dance and other connections in that work with Melville's art.

When looking at *American Notes,* instead of trying to determine how Dickens may have influenced Melville's writing, critics have focused elsewhere—on how, for example, Dickens conducted himself while he was in America. Concern about how Dickens related to Americans continues to have primacy, even in relation to Melville, when *American Notes* is discussed. This critical stance is taken in Hershel Parker's *Herman Melville:* "At least Charles Dickens, the ungrateful author of *American Notes,* had behaved politely as long as he was in the United States."[3] Not even Melville's considerable interest in and mastery of dance was enough of a clue to bring the two together.

A principal reason it has taken time to discern the literary value of dance and music in Melville's work is that those forms are at a discount in literary criticism despite the fact that Melville has used them skillfully. But this has gone virtually unnoticed in his work, and one is not likely to go to American fiction expecting music and dance, or the two together (which is Melville's style), to greatly aid in understanding a particular work of fiction. In short, music and dance are not treated as important elements of the American writer's craft, yet both were of utmost importance in the creation of *Moby-Dick* and in understanding *Benito Cereno.*

Emory Elliott provides a useful context: "Since the rise of the New Criticism in the 1950s, which focused attention of critics and readers upon the text itself—apart from history, biography, and society—there has emerged a wide variety of critical methods which have brought to literary works a rich diversity of perspectives: social, historical, political, psychological, economic, ideological, and philosophical." But growing insight into a writer such as Melville, who was preeminently concerned with ranging beyond known sources and means of craft to enrich the creative work, continued to be forestalled because music and dance have not been used to open up "possibilities for new readings and new meanings."[4]

It is not surprising, therefore, given Melville's interest in such arts, that so little has been written on how he, relating the one to the other, came to hone this major aspect of his art. An examination of slave music and dance in New York City and Albany during Melville's time tells us much about what he was exposed to artistically. Despite the fact that historians of slavery have been practically silent on this, we know, for example, that circular dance and juba beating, both widespread in slavery, were prevalent among blacks in New York and in other Northern states. But such silence, it will be demonstrated, has not carried over to students of dance and music who have studied antebellum America. Moreover, a means of mapping Melville's exploration of the music and dance that inform his work is to study the various addresses of the Melville family in New York City in relation to the parade routes of marching black bands.

Perhaps unsurpassed as an influence on Melville's art is Albany, New York, the Melville family's ancestral home. Dance and music concerts were unavoidable there in the summer months. Young Herman Melville visited Albany, one of the great centers of dance culture in America, in the summers, and he later lived there for nearly ten years. The Pinkster festival tradition was strong there; one of America's greatest dancers, King Charley, performed there. His style, almost certainly known to Melville, is said to have influenced that of John Diamond, the superb white dancer who challenged William Henry Lane, "Master Juba," the black dancer who is treated at length in the chapter on New York in Dickens's *American Notes.*

Melville's Albany experience, crucial to his vision of slave art in America, made him one of the few whites in the country with a sense of how the music and dance of the slave North at times dovetailed with that of the slave South, forming a sort of cultural bridge that helps explain the appearance of free black artists who preside over celebrations at sea in *Moby-Dick.* And it is to his credit that in time he was so serious a student of black culture that he made no more cultural distinction between Africans and descendants of Africans in America than between Southern and Northern blacks. This we see in *Moby-Dick:* Pip, for example, is at one time referred to as an Alabama boy, and at another as a native of Connecticut.

Because Melville was very young when he first visited Albany, what he experienced there became a part of his consciousness, from which he later drew for artistic purposes. Thus he was being prepared for mastery of black musical and dance forms from which he was later able to derive social meaning. Important aspects of *Moby-Dick,* in fact, are based on his intimate knowledge of descendants of Africans in America. Particularly stunning is his depiction of African-derived music and dance of American blacks, who provide the dominant musical and dance forms in *Moby-Dick.* His depiction of their music in that work reflects its continuing character deep into the twentieth century and establishes him as a preeminent student of the subject.

Slaves and ex-slaves were very much a part of Melville's life in both New York City and Albany. In both places, his family lived within reach of black artistic expression, from which Melville greatly benefited. He studied slave music and dance seriously, and his uses of the two, and of African music and dance, are not easily matched. As his handling of music shows in *Moby-Dick,* he became sufficiently skilled to commune at the highest level with Frederick Douglass, the greatest authority on black music.

Douglass directed Melville's attention to America's richest musical and dance tradition in which Melville works with great powers of imagination. Inspired by Douglass, Melville builds on a major premise of the black musical aesthetic set forth in *Narrative of the Life of Frederick Douglass,* which appeared in 1845, six years before the publication of *Moby-Dick.* Though blacks were not far away from Melville geographically, they were continents away from him socially, which is probably a factor in principal forms of slave art being as subtlety wrought in *Moby-Dick* as any feature of Melville's art. Before his reading of Douglass, Albany and New York City helped prepare him for this ambitious musical and writing effort in *Moby-Dick.*

In that work, some creative gifts of blacks are obvious with Melville calling attention to them, whereas others, though profoundly influential in the novel, are hidden from us. Particular influences of slave culture dominate portions of the work, providing its tragic musical theme, a theme that at once gives voice to and is indistinguishable from qualities of Melville's writing style. For a novel long regarded as deeply American to be inspired in this way by the music and dance of a despised segment of the population is a revolutionary move artistically. Beneath much of the splendid surface of *Moby-Dick,* slave music and dance are subterranean forces, heightening its complexity and quality overall. The last half of the novel, especially, is written with slave art functioning as a kind of spiritual compass for the *Pequod.* Melville's use of Douglass's *Narrative* makes slavery a theme of great importance in both *Moby-Dick* and *Benito Cereno.*

Douglass writes of music that is a deep force in Melville's imagination, causing him ultimately to make unique use of certain tools of his craft. As formulated by Douglass and reimagined by Melville, slave music allows Melville to use language in ways seldom if ever before employed. And like Douglass, a master writer in his own right, Melville uses music as an emblem or metaphor of social status of individuals and of groups—perhaps, in the end, of the American nation. In a long moment of revolutionary daring, through music he brings forth the travail of slavery as a subtheme on which *Moby-Dick* takes flight. But there is a problem: it is virtually impossible for the reader to discover that music, as much as the wind, propels the *Pequod.*

Douglass lays indispensable groundwork for an avant-garde experimentalism that has been missed in Melville's work, an experimentalism in which Melville demonstrates the uses to which music is put even when he is not referring to music. In the process he encompasses much more than music as he brings the blues to life in *Moby-Dick* without leaving overt clues. His strategy is as hidden as the varied materials on which he draws to give life to his art. Again the strategy is layered, interconnected. If uncommon subtlety and irony in the use of materials in radically new ways is to be valued in a writer, then Melville's art is greatly undervalued. This is more evident than ever as Douglass helps us see rich dimensions of another cultural and spiritual world opening before us in *Moby-Dick*.

In *Moby-Dick* we have the principal ritual of slave life in the American South, possibly the principal ritual of nineteenth-century America, for the major musical forms of the nation—the spirituals, the blues, and jazz—all benefited from association with the sacred Ring Shout dance.[5] Melville offers one of the earliest depictions of what the blues experience, in relation to the Ring Shout, began to mean not only to Americans, including Ahab, but to sailors from different points on the globe. Not only that, but jazz dance is called to mind in relation to the Ring Shout and the sound of the blues. In Melville's mind, the music of the blues is associated with various forms of suffering and not confined to blacks. Perhaps he was the first American to present the blues as the American national music.

Melville had to have known blacks in America extremely well to have written with such understanding. Learned critics must ponder his achievement and determine if there is anything quite like it among great writers born into and working in dominant cultural environments. Have any others crossed over into a submerged and reviled culture with comparable insight? A great truth of *Moby-Dick* is that the art of blacks is a chief means by which problems of the profoundest sort are acted out by people of many cultures, dramatically extending the reach of slave culture well before its music and dance received recognition in the coming century. As Fred Bernard called to our attention, slavery is an important though neglected theme in *Moby-Dick*.

Hegel is important to Melville, and Melville wisely invokes him in relation to slavery. Because Hegel's thought applies so certainly to the resistance of slaves in *Benito Cereno,* Melville was ahead of his time in deciding that Hegel might give his fictional account of the slave revolt added resonance and complexity. But oddly, the historical revolt was indistinguishable from art itself, capturing Melville's interest for that reason and, consequently, demonstrating the limits of Hegel's thought. In fact, Hegel's thought is seldom so limited as when applied to the souls of blacks, as the young W.E.B. Du Bois, writing with Hegel and Schopenhauer in mind, noted in 1888: "A quarter of a century ago, these people were slaves and truly learned philosophers cleverly declared they had no souls . . ."[6]

For African slaves, in *Benito Cereno,* to rise in revolt, demand to be taken back to West Africa by a slave trading captain, and demand that the whites on the slave ship act as though they are still in control when another captain boards raises all sorts of Hegelian issues, some beyond the scope of Hegel's thought. Not the least of the issues is that the consciousness of the supremely confident African leader, who is convinced that the visitor will not discover that the blacks are in control, was hardly as yoked to the will of his original captor as Hegel might posit. Elaborate artistry with illusion the face of reality is the principal weapon of African defense. This much Melville knew from reading Amasa Delano's *Narrative of Voyages and Travels in the Northern and Southern Hemispheres,* which is why he depicts Babo, the African leader in *Benito Cereno,* as all brain. This was no typical slave revolt that easily lends itself to Hegelian analysis, or to easy conclusions about African emphasis on inflicting punishment. Neither is *Moby-Dick,* in which African influences are carried over into the Americas, cut and dried with respect to Hegel, who did not focus on modern slavery.

Melville was probably exposed to the dialectic from reading Douglass some years before his extensive discussions of Hegel, in 1849, with German philologist George Adler. The dialectic appears to have come to Douglass on his own or from an undetermined source. In any event, he felt philosophy failed to provide sufficient insight into the anguish of soul, as expressed musically, of the African slave.[7] Neither Douglass nor Melville suffered Hegel's ignorance of slave spirituality, a spirituality from which the blues were born. Without Melville's awareness of that heritage, chapter 40 of *Moby-Dick* could not have taken the pivotal turn that it takes in determining the course of much that follows.

Thanks to Douglass, we know of Hegel's almost certain influence in *Moby-Dick;* otherwise the novel can be read, as it has been for generations, without the reader sensing a Hegelian presence. The dialectic helps explain Douglass on slave music, but so evident are artistic resonances between Douglass and Melville that we don't need a particular philosopher to detect Douglass's influence on Melville. This is the case mainly because no philosopher works with the dialectic of contrasting yet melded musical tones in a way, if at all, approaching Douglass. Consequently, Melville's creative response to Douglass, which amounts to some of the most experimental writing ever undertaken by a novelist. This is encouraged by Douglass having adorned the dialectic in the music of the blues. Although Melville uses the dialectic, it is Douglass's language that he uses in applying it to music, the form in which it finds its finest artistic expression. As philosophy is not generally expected to appear in American fiction, Melville's readers cannot as easily be faulted for not recognizing the dialectic, from whatever source, in *Moby-Dick.*

It would seem unwise, however, to rule out the possibility that Melville, like Douglass, was familiar with dialectical thought before reading a philosopher. Fine poets, in their command of irony, know something of dialectical thought and Melville's command of the dialectic, whether it was so designated in his circles, is likely. If the dialectic has been used more powerfully than by Melville in chapter 42, "The Whiteness of the Whale," then one would want to know where and by whom. This chapter assures us that Melville was ideally suited to take Douglass's dialectic, even in music, and to make it his own. Here is but one of several instances in that chapter in which he uses dialectical thought:

> With reference to the Polar bear, it may possibly be urged by him who would fain go still deeper into this matter, that it is not the whiteness, separately regarded, which heightens the intolerable hideousness of that brute; for, analyzed, that heightened hideousness, it might be said, only arises from the circumstances that the irresponsible ferociousness of the creature stands invested in the fleece of celestial innocence and love; and hence, by bringing together two such opposite emotions in our minds, the Polar bear frightens us with so unnatural a contrast. But even assuming all this to be true; yet, were it not for the whiteness, you would not have that intensified terror.

These are not concerns to Harold Bloom. There is no apprehension by Bloom of remote associations that yield spiritual/musical emphasis in Douglass's *Narrative,* of an artistic underground theme as powerful and pervasive as it is subtle. Bloom thinks of *Narrative* as principally concerned with brute force. Consequently, he is unaware that Douglass is explicit about the spiritual cost of slavery being inestimable. In that spirituality and art one finds Douglass's finest expression, his magnificent portrait of his grandmother, Betsey Bailey, perhaps at once the most moving—it has more than a touch of the blues about it—and gracefully expressed prose in the *Narrative.* But Bloom finds Douglass's "rhetoric, though a touch uncontrolled" having "just enough irony to qualify as authentic literary language . . ."[8] Actually, irony is the chief feature of Douglass's thought and prose, perhaps as much a part of his writing style as of any nineteenth-century writer, including Melville, who focuses on precisely that quality of style in *Narrative.*

Had Melville come to mind or, say, Plato or Aristotle, the dialectic in *Narrative* might have been identified by Bloom together with ironies related to the creative act that Douglass and Melville immortalize in these pages. With Bloom even comparing Douglass to James Baldwin, who clearly read Douglass, without recognizing this, it is small wonder that critics in his tradition have given little attention to music and dance in American literature.

Bloom contends that *Narrative* is "wildly uneven" but, not surprisingly, fails to show us where and how this is so.[9]

A problem of a different order occurs when Melville, in writing *Benito Cereno,* transforms accounts of events from numerous chapters of a book long associated with him, from chapters, however, that are unfamiliar to the reader. This has been a major obstacle to understanding because even most critics seem aware of only a single chapter from the book in question, Delano's *Voyages and Travels.* Consequently, the problem is compounded by Melville's multiple transformations of material from *Voyages.* First surprised to find additional material in *Voyages* that Melville had worked into the novella, some years later I realized that I might have begun with the assumption that Melville, finding chapter 18 of *Voyages* important, almost certainly read the book in its entirety. The problem is that so few Melville scholars have read beyond chapter 18 of *Voyages.*

In time, my students and I at Northwestern University in the late 1970s began reading the Delano volume, in history classes, a bit more systematically. Some of us also read *The Encantadas* together with the Galapagos chapter of *Voyages* and had stimulating discussions of *The Encantadas'* "Sketches," which were mainsprings to Melville's creative process in fashioning the African warriors, the hatchet-polishers, in *Benito Cereno.* Readings from *Voyages and Travels,* as the years went by, led to discoveries, such as chapter 16, central to how Melville created *Benito Cereno.*[10]

Given the genius of the leaders of the historical revolt, and the level of performance of those under their direction, is it any wonder that the distinguished Harrison Hayford writes that while creating *Benito Cereno,* Melville kept chapter 18 of Delano's *Voyages and Travels* before him? Certainly the historical event recounted by Delano was suggestive enough to stir Melville's imagination. But as true to the historical account as Melville is, and as surely as he discovered, in *Voyages and Travels,* revolution hidden in the folds of art, his inventions, based on reimaginings of chapters of *Voyages,* have been greatly underestimated.[11]

Without any mention of Ashantees among the Africans who revolt at sea, *Voyages and Travels* contains the clue to their cultural world, with which Melville is deeply concerned. In the attachments to chapter 18, Melville discovered the Ashantee influence that drove the revolt, and that led him, working with that influence in a boldly experimental way, to join *Moby-Dick* and *Benito Cereno.* At the same time, he places the Ashantee's cultural world below the horizon of the reader, thousands of miles away, one might say in darkness. Even so, that he refers specifically to Ashantees in the novella is the surest evidence that Melville wanted the critic one day to discover how so much of his art came to flower.

Although it may not be fashionable in some literary circles to pay much attention to the plot of *Benito Cereno,* such a position, with respect to the Ashantee example alone, is now in need of reexamination. For well over a century, readers simply accepted an Ashantee presence in the novella because Melville made that presence an accepted fact in the tale. Relatively little seemed needed to build on that knowledge, and nobody posed the problem: How do we know there is an Ashantee presence in *Benito Cereno?* But the plot containing the dance and singing of the Ashantee women points to that influence as they use art to inspire their men to deeds of warrior valor. It should be emphasized that it is Melville himself who identifies Ashantees in the historical revolt and places them on the *Pequod.* There is no mention of them in Delano's *Voyages and Travels.*

So from crossing conventional boundaries of literary scholarship to enter the realm of music and dance a new approach to Melville is fashioned, enabling us ultimately to consider cultural influences that mark the novella as a work as deeply African as any to come out of the Americas. The arts, then, provide the key that unlocks larger mysteries, a possible whole new world of cultural influence in the novella. To a much greater degree, music and dance figure in *Moby-Dick* but as a function of both the African and African American experience. The music of the novel, thanks to Melville's reimagining of some aspects of Douglass on slave music, is, at the same time, African and profoundly American. Moreover, the arts as much as any other quality of craft derived from them enable us to recognize, and to follow, the grand design of Melville's aesthetic—to follow the course of the *Pequod.*

Thanks to Mungo Park's *Travels into the Interior Districts of Africa,* the relationship between industry and pastime is evident in *Benito Cereno* and a first step in understanding how Melville created the African warriors on the *San Dominick* in *Benito Cereno.* In addition, examination of the Park volume not only reveals its subtle artistic influence on the novella but leads to the conclusion that the young Melville found Park's views on Africa in stark contrast to what Americans generally knew about that continent. Park's impact, then, on Melville's aesthetic, on how African culture is fused into the performance of the hatchet-polishers, should not be discounted.

But texts on Africa that are much more important than Park's enable Melville, with consummate skill, to use history to deepen and extend art in *Benito Cereno.* Ashantee values, in his hands, are indispensable to the grand design of the revolt. Owing to his rare insight into the creative process, the gap between history and fiction, if it exists at all, is extremely difficult to detect. Who, in equal measure, before or after Melville, accomplished this or even attempted it? Indeed, the culture of the Ashantees is so much a part of the behavior of the Africans in the novella that main ingredients of the union of illusion and reality in the novella are formed from it. The Park volume, on a far more limited scale than other sources on Africa, is used for such purposes.[12]

Frederick Austus Ramsayer and Johannes Kuhne's *Four Years in Ashantee,* though published after the appearance of *Benito Cereno,* helps one interpret the dance and behavior of the women in the novella. More precisely, it explores the relationship of dance to warfare in Ashantee culture, an aspect of the novella that might otherwise pass without particular notice unless more is known of Ashantee culture. This volume, published, as mentioned, after *Benito Cereno* appeared, was not available to Melville. Robert S. Rattray's *Religion and Art in Ashanti* was found to contain needed information about Ashantee burial rites of kings that helps us understand what was done to the body of the owner of the slaves, Alexandro Aranda, after he is slain by the Africans in *Benito Cereno.* But the Rattray study was also published after the appearance of the novella.[13]

Sources available during Melville's lifetime were needed. Actually, a number of sources were read by him, enabling him to probe in depth Ashantee burial and other practices. Accounts of Dutch and British travelers representing their governments in West Africa in areas where an imperial foothold was gained or sought were the ones on which Melville drew. The works referred to are Joseph Dupuis's *Journal of a Residence in Ashantee,* T. E. Bowdich's *Mission from Cape Coast Castle to Ashantee,* and Willem Bosman's *A New and Accurate Description of the Coast of Guinea*—all immensely important to Melville studies.[14] The Bowdich volume achieves what the Rattray volume does not in having appeared a few years after Melville's birth, providing still more evidence of how Ashantees reduced bodies to skeletons. As we know, some of Melville's finest writing projects the image of Aranda's skeleton on the *San Dominick* from beginning to end. The Bosman account of the Ashantee provides the evidence we were seeking for the *Follow Your Leader* legend that appears beneath Aranda's skeleton at the prow of the *San Dominick.*

Considering the place of Africa in the estimates of Americans and the reading habits of Americans, Melville was assured that few of his contemporaries knew of the Dupuis book. Well into the second century since the publication of *Moby-Dick* and *Benito Cereno, Journal of a Residence* is still not included in studies that list the books it is thought Melville read. The same applies, sadly, to the Bowdich and Bosman volumes. In this regard, one might turn, for example, to Mary K. Bercaw's *Melville's Sources,* published in 1987, which does not mention the volumes just discussed.[15]

Journal of a Residence is the common source from which Melville worked in linking *Moby-Dick* and *Benito Cereno* and is one of the most important books ever in influencing Melville's art. Without knowing that Melville re-worked passages from this book, the startling connection between the novella and *Moby-Dick* would be extremely difficult, if not impossible, to perceive. In other words, with there being no comparison of the *Journal* with what Mel-ville makes of it, the window onto the vital connection between the novella and *Moby-Dick* would not be available to us. The method of creation would simply be attributed, once more, to Melville's extraordinary imaginative gifts, which have a way of quieting questions about his process of creation. Ac-tually, numerous creative acts in the novella that resulted from Melville's reading of *Journal of a Residence* remain concealed until the *Pequod*, it might be said, sails beyond the horizon and West Africa comes into view. I intend to demonstrate that as complicated a process of symbolic interrelatedness as one is likely ever to encounter results from Melville's work with African sources. In the process, interlacing lines of creation are witnessed as he brings together his findings from Bowdich, Dupuis, and Bosman.

[II]

Convinced that Melville "wrote nothing of major significance in the forty years he lived after writing *Pierre*," R. P. Blackmur might be forgiven for not knowing that one possibly unique act of writing—on the grand scale—joins *Benito Cereno* and *Moby-Dick*. His by no means exclusive failure to under-stand that *Benito Cereno* is a great achievement on many levels is bad enough, but his consigning that work with others by Melville to the realm of non-fiction cannot be forgiven. He goes further, contending that Melville "left nothing to those who followed him except the occasional particular spur of an image or a rhythm. It is not that he is inimitable but that there was noth-ing formally organized enough in his work to imitate or modify or perfect." Blackmur himself points us to the chief weakness of his own criticism, con-tending that "Melville had never predominantly relied upon the means of the novelist, *had never attempted to use more than the overt form of the novel*, until he attempted *Pierre*."[16]

Further, oblivious to *Benito Cereno*, Blackmur argues that *Pierre* proved that "the material of illustration had been exhausted in 'Moby-Dick.'" Few critics today are likely to agree with that position but more agree that *Moby-Dick* lacks a center that "establishes direction."[17] Melville's work with Douglass goes a long way toward undercutting that last assumption. There is reason to believe that Douglass's concealed influence is largely respon-sible for so much that takes place in *Moby-Dick* being thought as elusive as Moby Dick himself, about which Melville writes, "For as the secrets of the currents in the seas have never yet been divulged, even to the most erudite research; so the hidden ways of the Sperm Whale when beneath the surface remain, in great part, unaccountable to his pursuers; and from time to time have originated the most curious and contradictory speculations regarding them, especially concerning the mystic modes whereby, after sounding to a great depth, he transports himself with such vast swiftness to the most widely distant points."[18]

Blackmur's concern with a particular kind of "dramatic form" prevents him from enlightening us on Melville and dramatic form, which is radically different from anything he imagined—form in view guided by form beneath surfaces, the language of music shaping character and dialogue and storyline even without mention of music. In *Moby-Dick,* language and music, one the flip side of the other, are major elements of form, showing how, in Blackmur's own words, "form is the way things go together."[19]

Newton Arvin speaks of Melville and exhaustion and makes the excellent point—according to the conventional wisdom—that his development as a writer, when it came, "came with a rush and a force that had the menace of quick exhaustion in it." He asks, "Could it possibly be maintained at that pitch over the span of a long career?" Even so, Arvin did not know how greatly Melville created in a short period of time, making the concern about Melville's longevity more questionable than previously thought. Also Arvin's position that Melville "came to the profession of letters as a kind of brilliant amateur," unable "to take on, whether for better or for worse, the mentality of the professional," contains a hint of truth but is open to question in light of all that Arvin missed in, among other works, *Benito Cereno.*[20] He comments on Atufal, the hatchet-polishers, and the scene in which Benito Cereno is shaved, subjects of particular concern in this volume. He questions Melville's imaginative ability, writing that "the hatchet-polishers on the poop are rather comic than genuinely sinister; the symbolism of the key hanging round Don Benito's neck is painfully crude; and it needed only a very commonplace and magazinish inventiveness to conceive the scene in which Benito is shaved by the wily Babo."[21]

Arvin finds "the rhythms of the prose" of *Benito Cereno* unsatisfying— "slow, torpid, and stiff-limbed; and they remain so, with a few moments of relief, throughout." I respond to this argument in the pages that follow, but I must say now that the prose used to describe the hatchet-polishers' rhythmic clash of hatchets calls to mind an accomplished black musical ensemble that is mainly driven by rhythm. Less subtle and much less impressive is Arvin's assertion about the "atmosphere" of *Benito Cereno*—a clear case of his failure to take the time to try to understand what Melville has to say about the atmosphere of the work, especially at the beginning of the novella. Arvin writes, "Nor is the famous 'atmosphere' of 'Benito' created swiftly, boldly, and hypnotically, as Melville at his highest pitch might have created it; on the contrary, it is 'built-up' tediously and wastefully through an accumulation of incident upon incident, detail upon detail, as if to overwhelm the dullest-witted and most resistant reader." Let's just say that Arvin was a resistant reader. The question of atmosphere is a principal question in this book.[22]

Whether it is for better or for worse that Melville is not a conventional man of letters is for the reader to decide. The decision, to be fair, must take into account what we haven't known about his strategy of craft together with the extent to which his breadth of vision ranges beyond other writers. A lack of knowledge leads Arvin to write that Delano is too simply conceived without telling us how Delano *is* conceived (Arvin 1950, 240). There is, in fact, nothing at all simple about how Delano is conceived. His conception results from Melville writing at his highest level of artistry and, consequently, can be missed even when the materials with which Melville is working are right before us.

F. O. Matthiessen's uncommon respect for *Benito Cereno*—"one of the most sensitively poised pieces of writing"—should be kept in mind as one ponders what follows from this distinguished scholar: "The half-decade of 1850–55 saw the appearance of *Representative Men* (1850), *The Scarlet Letter* (1850), *The House of the Seven Gables* (1851), *Moby-Dick* (1851), *Pierre* (1852), *Walden* (1854), and *Leaves of Grass* (1855). You might search all the rest of American Literature without being able to collect a group of books equal to these in imaginative vitality." These were produced, Matthiessen writes, "in one extraordinarily concentrated moment of expression."[23]

Lewis Mumford has commented on what Melville's art, in its greatness, portends. Stating that *Moby-Dick* "stands by itself as complete as the *Divine Comedy* or the *Odyssey*" and must be understood "in terms of its own purpose," Mumford thinks "the book itself is greater than the fable it embodies," that it also prefigures "more than it actually reflects." In his view, "as a work of art, *Moby-Dick* is part of a new integration of thought, a widening of the fringe of consciousness, a deepening of insight, through which the modern version of life will finally be embodied."[24] I believe it will be demonstrated that every line of that analysis is confirmed.

Benito Cereno and *Moby-Dick* are intimately connected and in some ways are deeper and more universal works of art than critics have suspected. Indeed, critics must now adjust their estimate higher for both works. But who can venture a thoughtful opinion on why Melville united them so invisibly that it would require well over a century before the bridge leading from one work to the other could be seen? What is now clear, however, is that, because of new revelations of its depth and range of riches, *Benito Cereno* deserves a place of its own on any list of great works of fiction. Its "imaginative vitality" requires that either the novella or the novel, as forms of fiction, be redefined. Given Melville's mode of working seemingly endless riches into these works, more findings that dazzle are undoubtedly in store.

That the worlds of *Benito Cereno* and *Moby-Dick* so largely turn on an African cultural axis raises new questions about the nature of American literature. Because of this, I argue, much that is vital in Melville's works has not been known, a problem compounded by the skill with which he handles the tools of his craft. Although time and again his very talent militates against the recognition he deserves, there is no way that he can be faulted for his skill—a conclusion that rests on the findings presented in this book, which the reader will of course judge. But before I demonstrate the claims of the introduction, some words about how I came to read and interpret Melville are in order.

[III]

I have never regarded myself as a student of the methods and materials of history alone, nor have I regarded the realm of the arts as foreign to me. Long before I was introduced to Herman Melville, I was being prepared for eventually working on artistic aspects of *Moby-Dick*. In fact, growing up in Memphis, Tennessee, I could hardly have been better exposed to African American culture, whose impact in *Moby-Dick* is undeniable. The bandmaster of the school I attended, Manassas, was once James "Jimmie" Lunceford, a great orchestra leader whose legacy lives today in histories of jazz. Lunceford and his drummer, Jimmy Crawford, were personal friends of my parents, and on a photograph of Crawford with an inscription to my mother, the poet Elma Stuckey, he calls her his "little Dixie pal."

The earliest distinct memory of my life takes me back to the "front room" of my grandparents' home when I was two or three. College students gathered around the piano and sang a Negro spiritual, R. Nathaniel Dett's "Listen to the Lambs." The music of the spiritual was created originally in the Ring Shout, or African Circle Dance, found in chapter 40 of *Moby-Dick* and an underground theme in *Narrative of the Life of Frederick Douglass*. One of my best friends in those days was Freeman Lester, whose skill as a tap dancer was lauded throughout a number of Memphis neighborhoods. Freeman was good enough to have danced in the Catharine Market that Melville visited in New York City, where dance competition between blacks from Long Island, New Jersey, and New York City was fierce, with "cutting sessions" that prefigured jazz music competition by nearly a century. Melville's visits to the Market no doubt prepared him for the highly improvisational dancer found in Dickens's *American Notes.*

Among the children in my North Memphis neighborhood, music and dance seemed as natural as the air we breathed. Music had a sacred aura that pulled me, years before my teens, to the edge of bandstands, ever at ease when jazz was being played. We were too young to appreciate the blues, which, related to jazz and the spirituals, had an even stronger base than the spirituals in Memphis. Still, the blues were in the air and I could not be completely unmindful of their presence even when very young. The blues were long sung to dance in a ring as well, but it took some time before I began appreciating that art form, which is a major force in the Douglass's text and in *Moby-Dick.* In my Memphis years, as a preteen, however, I had heard of neither Douglass nor Melville and knew nothing of the Ring Shout.

The music of the blues and spirituals wove through the poetry I began hearing as far back as I can recall. The melodies and rhythms of my mother's poems very early filled my consciousness, and irony, irrespective of the theme and style, crowned poem after poem. A poet of slavery and of other subjects, my mother read each new poem to my father, my sister, and me. A great many sing like the blues and spirituals, and not a few are poems of resistance reminiscent of Babo in *Benito Cereno.*[25] But my mother never read *Benito Cereno,* only *Bartleby.* In any case, slavery was not avoided in my immediate family, nor were the blues, despite their being thought of elsewhere, often wrongly, as merely profane.

Ironies abounded. I knew nothing of Africa's influence on black music and dance in my Memphis days, just as the nation knew nothing of jazz dance, the blues, and the prefiguring of jazz music in *Moby-Dick,* a work in which African influences are profound. Recognizing the blues when reading *Moby-Dick,* however, is not difficult for me, even though Melville made a particularly brilliant effort to hide the blues from us altogether. At times, as stated, he intimates the sounds of the blues while offering no recognizable clue that music is his subject.

Ex-slaves were living in my North Memphis neighborhood, practicing African customs that I later read about many years later while receiving graduate training in African history. Returning to Memphis from my home in Chicago, I noticed for the first time as many as sixteen or seventeen African "shotgun houses" lining both sides of the street in more than one North Memphis neighborhood. From reading art history, and from conversations with family members, I discerned a link between the Ring Shout and family burial sites decorated with cowrie shells, which mirror the orbit of the sun in the southern hemisphere and relate to the counterclockwise movement of the Ring Shout. So not only was there an African presence in music and dance, but an African material presence in Memphis and Arkansas.

Urging me to reintroduce a new edition of his volume of poems, *Southern Road,* poet and critic Sterling A. Brown, who had done some *Benito Cereno* criticism, also encouraged me to read *Benito Cereno* and *Moby-Dick.* He inscribed a copy of *Moby-Dick,* which he gave to me in 1967, as follows: "Isolatos too, I call such, not acknowledging the common continent of men, but each Isolato living on a separate continent of his own."[26] Although I had read neither *Benito Cereno* nor *Moby-Dick,* I had seen both listed among the Great Books championed by the University of Chicago when that institution was especially known for celebrating such works. Despite Sterling Brown's urging, I did not read either for a number of years; I began with and then taught *Benito Cereno.*

The background of experience from my Memphis years, to which I have alluded, was brought forth into graduate study and related to certain disciplines in cross-disciplinary inquiry that was anything but studied. Though there was otherwise no discussion of dance and music, what was background was at times, when relevant, as much a part of my consciousness as anything offered in assigned texts. There was, then, a feeling of natural kinship with *Benito Cereno* and *Moby-Dick* when reading Melville on music and dance, certainly no disciplinary barriers to understanding.

Only with *Benito Cereno* and *Moby-Dick* before us can still more light be cast on symbols, characterizations, and the theme of slavery, illumining them in their once dark, obscure forms of expression. And close attention to the plot in both works, once a breakthrough discovery is made, enables the critic, in very precise and subtle ways, to *show* how Melville's creative process works in relation to both the novella and *Moby-Dick.* Attention to the plot would seem imperative in working with a writer who so often withholds from view so much of the process by which he fashions main elements of his art.

In this journey, which began some twenty-eight years ago, I have traveled undreamed-of and at times intersecting paths through *Benito Cereno* and *Moby-Dick.* Those paths have led to deeper levels of Melville's creative process and have yielded the finding that *Benito Cereno* and *Moby-Dick* are joined organically, each sustained, in vital ways, by a common source of origin in African culture.

CHAPTER I

The Tambourine in Glory

*I pushed on my way, till I got to Chapel-street, which I crossed;
and then going under a cloister-like arch of stone . . . I emerged
into the fine quadrangle of the Merchants' Exchange.*
—Herman Melville, Redburn

*I walk a world that is mine; and enter many nations,
as Mungo Park rested in African cots.*
—Herman Melville, Mardi

Poor Alabama boy! On the grim Pequod's *forecastle, ye shall
ere long see him, beating his tambourine; prelusive of the
eternal time, when sent for, to the great quarter-deck
on high, he was bid strike in with angels, and beat
his tambourine in glory.*
—Herman Melville, Moby-Dick

In his first eleven years, Herman Melville lived in an environment in which slavery was being gradually legislated out of existence, its shadow receding across New York State. Despite the movement to abolish slavery, however, denials of freedom less severe but no less real were much in evidence. There was, for that matter, little indication that racial equality was being considered by Northern whites, most of whom did not oppose Southern slavery.

Melville was born in August 1819, a time when slave music and dance and tale enjoyed brilliantly ironic expression in public and private, North as well as South. In New York City and across the state, slaves were observed dancing and making music on street corners and in market places, as if preparing for the Pinkster Festival that once a year in May, for several days and at times in multiple locations, engaged the attention of white spectators. As in expressions of black culture in America generally, participants in festivals revealed but a portion of their art because it was dangerous to communicate clear signs of African spirituality.[1]

The appreciation of irony allowed slaves to conceal, beneath a protective covering of improvisation, things that were unpalatable to whites, thereby preserving what was proper to them by almost endlessly changing its face. In other words, harsh reality encouraged experimentation to alter cherished values in order to protect them at their core. Slaves, then, perceived reality as flux artistically, and therefore in a religious sense as well, for they did not often draw a distinction between the sacred and the secular—perhaps the least understood quality of their culture.[2]

Melville's family was well placed, residentially, to be exposed to black celebrations in nineteenth-century New York City, and Melville to scenes at sea into which he later incorporated African artistic expression. Number 6 Pearl Street, where he was born, faced Manhattan Island's tip on one side, and the shipping offices and wharves of the South Street waterfront on the other. His initial horizon was the ocean. Slaves were known to entertain whites along the wharves of New York and to reach their destinations in skiffs.[3] Only later would settings near the sea become important to Melville, but celebrations of blacks along Broadway were, from an early age, impossible for him to ignore. The music alone commanded attention, as did the rhythmic march/dance of people in processions.

The Melville family addresses were located in sections of the city either near or on Broadway; one at 55 Cortlandt was ideal for hearing or attending Broadway celebrations. From that address a procession celebrating the coming abolition of slavery in New York almost certainly was heard, for its path brought it within hearing distance in the southern Broadway area where the celebrants made music that to the young might seem as natural as the sound of rain or the play of sunlight. Melville's exposure to black music was unusually full in his youth: he was but six in 1825, when the "great procession of negroes, some of them well-dressed" paraded, "two by two, preceded by music and a flag . . . down Broadway." The parade held the attention of those witnessing it:

> An African club, called the Wilberforce Society, thus celebrated the . . . abolition of slavery in New York, and concluded the day by a dinner and ball. The colored people of New York, belonging to this society, have a fund, contained of their own, raised by weekly subscription, which is employed in assisting sick and unfortunate blacks. This fund, contained in a sky-blue box, was carried in the procession; the treasurer holding in his hand a large gilt key; the rest of the officers wore ribands of several colors, and badges like the officers of free masons; marshals with long staves walked outside the procession.

During a quarter of an hour, scarcely any but black faces were to be seen on Broadway.[4]

This was part of the cultural world of New Yorkers, who had little inclination to deny that the music of blacks was substantially different from that of white Americans. The Wilberforce Society was known to march with its own band, and its style of marching was not substantially different from what it was before or following the celebration of that year. In this regard, it is more than coincidence that many of its members, whether born in Africa or in America, referred to themselves as "Africans."[5]

The 55 Cortlandt address was but a ten-minute walk from City Hall and the Commons, the latter a staging area for parades and for celebrations like Pinkster. Moreover, the Negroes' Burial Ground, in which 20,000 African women, men, and children were buried, was part of the Commons, a sacred place revered by people of African descent that attracted African dancers, and musicians and storytellers throughout the year. Young Herman Melville, when no more than six or seven, surely would have been aware of Pinkster activity at the Commons, or at its burial ground, as both were in his own neighborhood.[6]

Reports of firearms and displays of firecrackers announced Fourth of July celebrations for whites in New York City and signaled for blacks their own day of celebration or regret to follow. In 1827, however, their celebration was special. On that July fifth, the New York Emancipation Day parade, beginning at City Hall near 55 Cortlandt and continuing down Broadway to the Battery, won the attention of most who glanced in its direction: the Grand Marshal for the day was Samuel Hardenburgh, "a splendid looking man, in cocked hat and drawn sword, mounted on a milk-white steed . . . his aides on horseback dashing up and down the line." For this sacred event and time of jubilee, the participants assembled just a block from the Negroes' Burial Ground, around which hundreds of Africans gathered while waiting for thousands more before following the line of march toward the southern terminus of Broadway.[7]

It does not greatly matter whether Melville observed this particular celebration of the abolition of slavery, for many white children did attend, and just as black youths remembered the event long after it occurred, it also remained a part of the consciousness of young whites who saw and heard the jubilant marchers. Melville might have been standing, chaperoned, among them on the Broadway sidewalk, hearing and observing resplendently dressed—"in scarfs of silk with gold-edgings"—members of black mutual aid societies "with colored bands of music and their banners appropriately lettered and painted: 'The New York African Society for Mutual Relief,' 'The Wilberforce Benevolent Society,' and 'The Clarkson Benevolent Society.'" Then followed "the people five or six abreast, from grown men to small boys." Also marching were members of the various African marine societies, who when not at home were at sea on ships out of New York port.[8]

News accounts preceding and following Emancipation Day appeared in various New York newspapers and were known to literate New Yorkers. The *New York Gazette and General Advertiser*, which had hoped the parade would not occur, reported approvingly before it took place: "We have much satisfaction in observing from . . . resolutions passed at a meeting of people of color, that the contemplated public rejoicing and procession by that part of the community are thus discountenanced."[9] An example of intercultural concern across the color line, the *Gazette* did not comment when the parade took place.

The *New York Statesman* reported that "a large body of coloured people from Brooklyn and other towns in this state" made their way "through the principal streets . . . under their respective banners."[10] They were heard for many blocks, east and west, north and south, especially because, in the heat of summer, windows were up as the joyous celebrants moved along their rather suburban route. A participant in the parade described the scene:

> The side-walks were crowded with the wives, daughters, sisters, and mothers of the celebrants, representing every State in the Union, and not a few with gay bandanna handkerchiefs, betraying their West Indian birth: neither was Africa itself unrepresented; hundreds who had survived the middle passage and a youth in slavery joined in the joyful procession. The people of those days rejoiced in their nationality and hesitated not to call each other "Africans," or "descendants of Africa" . . . It was a proud day for Samuel Hardenburgh, Grand Marshal, splendidly mounted, as he passed through the west gate of the Park, saluted the Mayor on the City Hall steps, and then took his way down Broadway to the Battery.[11]

Black schoolboys fell "into the ranks of the great celebration" of "between three and four thousand." Stating that "the concourse was very great," the *New York American* added: "The music was unusually good: there were four or five bands, comprising a great variety of instruments, played with much skill, as will be readily believed, from the acknowledged talent for music of the African race."[12]

Few families could ignore a celebration of such dramatic quality, described by one source as a "shouting for joy . . . with *feet jubilant* to songs of freedom," which suggests a procession of improvised dance movements characteristic of black marchers in Africa and America. Improvising dance while marching was the rule in the North as well as the South, and nowhere were the ingredients for such processions more pronounced than in Albany, whose slaves were second to none for improvisation in dance and music and known to parade on Pinkster Hill.[13]

One of the great festivals of New York, Pinkster was thought to be more robust in Melville's mother's hometown, Albany, than anywhere else in New York State.[14] Her mother's family knew the festival from the time Africans began dominating its cultural forms in the late colonial period. More especially, Maria Gansevoort's patrician family was connected to Pinkster as few others were. Though one cannot speak of the connection with great certitude, the most noted Pinkster drummer, Jackie Quackenboss, may well have been owned by the Quackenboss family that married into the Gansevoort family in the late eighteenth century, when "every family of wealth and distinction owned one or more slaves."[15] Jackie was such a dramatic figure in Albany's cultural history that family lore concerning him would have been relished by one of Melville's imagination, and there is no reason to suppose it would have been withheld. In allowing Jackie to drum at Pinkster, the Quackenboss family provided crucial support to the festival and must have been proud that he bore their name.

We have a description of his drumming and the play of rhythm in early Pinkster days, probably in the early 1770s, when the whole Albany community was said to have observed the celebration:

> The principal instrument selected to furnish this important portion of the ceremony was a symmetrically formed *eel-pot,* with a cleanly dressed sheep skin drawn tightly over its wide and open extremity . . . Astride this rude utensil sat Jackie Quackenboss, then in his prime of life and well known energy, beating lustily with his naked hands upon its loud sounding head, successively repeating the ever wild, though euphonic cry of *Hi-a bomba, bomba, bomba,* in full harmony with the thumping sounds. These vocal sounds were readily taken up and as oft repeated by the female portion of the spectators not otherwise engaged in the exercises of the scene, and accompanied by the beating of time with their ungloved hands, in strict accordance with the eel-pot melody.[16]

The dancers danced to such sounds, at times encircling Pinkster King Charley. He was from the Congo, where circularity was the principal symbol of a subtle Bakongo faith that affirmed the spirituality of dance rhythms not unlike those considered "secular" by Westerners. What was sacred for the African was regulated by such rhythms, which contributed to a form of spiritual recreation for the hundreds of slave participants in the festival. Drum rhythms and rhythmic cries from Jackie Quackenboss, joined by the chanting cries and hand clapping of African women, satisfied both sacred and "secular" needs of Africans. But most whites thought they were viewing the dance and music of heathens bereft of spirituality.[17]

In 1793, arson in Albany caused such devastation that "the heart of the city was enveloped in smoke and flames." Munsell reports that of Albany's 5,000 residents, "every man, woman, and child able to handle an empty leather fire bucket was pressed into service." Melville's mother's family contributed to the fire brigades: the fire flared first at the home of his great-uncle, Leonard Gansevoort, who was targeted by a suitor either forbidden to see one of his daughters or rejected by her. A slave named Pomp, said to have been offered a gold watch to put the Gansevoort residence to flames, allegedly enlisted the support of two slave women to that end. All three were executed on Pinkster Hill, first the women and later Pomp, and buried in its cemetery for blacks. The fire was a searing reminder to whites of their connection to the festival, to slaves at Pinkster of shadows in the light.[18]

Had Melville's mother, grandmother, and other relatives elected to discuss the conflagration with the youngster when he visited Albany in the 1820s, or when he later lived there, they would have had much to talk about. The number of slaves in the ward in which the family lived at the time—they made up close to 26 percent of the ward—meant that the Gansevoorts and other whites there shared living quarters with a higher percentage of slaves than usual. Still, the relative paucity of slaves in Albany County and New York State—5.41 and 7.64 percent in 1790, respectively—undercuts the assumption that slaves, in a given county or state, had to constitute the majority or at least a large minority of the population to have power in the cultural sphere.[19]

By the time Melville was eight, he was taking dancing lessons and becoming sensitive to forms of dance that might be seen near his New York City home. No less exciting was New York's Catharine Market, where challenging dance drew slave artists from Long Island, New Jersey, and, as the competition for honors became more intense, from the city itself. Given the rigor of the competition, dancers from New York could not afford to perform only in the market for a few days annually. Just as dancers from Long Island practiced year round "on the barn floor, or in a frolic," those from the city could not have excelled at Pinkster, as they did in time, without much practice before the market in the spring.[20]

Though Pinkster in Albany was said to have ended in 1811 (a matter that remains to be resolved), the more important point is that slave dance and music defined Pinkster rather than the reverse. Dance and music brought to Pinkster would have been practiced following Pinkster as before. The opposing argument is that Pinkster in Albany lasted beyond King Charley's death in 1824, after which it "was observed with less enthusiasm, and finally sank into such a low nuisance as to fall under the ban of the authorities." The memory of Pinkster lived in the springtime, perhaps into the mid-1830s, which was well after the Melvilles took up residence in Albany in 1830. But under no circumstances could Melville, in the 1820s, have missed black dance and music during summer visits to Albany, for Munsell writes that during that time "*every* corner was vocal with the concerts of whistling negroes."[21]

When living in Albany, Melville was enrolled in the Albany Academy, which his grandparents helped endow and establish in 1813 to educate all but those "in an absolute state of penury." Just "a few rods" from Pinkster Hill and its burial grounds, the Academy was in a large park surrounded by a picket fence.[22] Consequently, on his way to and from school, and while there, Melville saw Pinkster Hill and the grounds that spread out around it. Indeed, the Academy practically shared those grounds. Although he would not appreciate the significance of that location until later, his preparation for understanding had already begun with exposure to Pinkster music and dance on Albany corners in the previous decade.

Pinkster's special relationship to his family on his mother's side, together with his family's location in New York near Pinkster Commons and its burial ground, meant that it was virtually impossible for Melville to avoid, over nearly twenty years, contact with African culture—and issues—before leaving the United States. Moreover, he enriched his knowledge of black culture by reading African travel accounts, which gave him special insight into how blacks were affected by life in America and how their values affected others. His interest in foreign places, through travel no less than through reading, is convincing evidence that Melville was more prone than most Americans to immerse himself in different values: Newton Arvin writes that names of travelers such as Captain Cook, Krusenstern, Ledyard, Vancouver, and Mungo Park "scintillated before him like constellations during his whole boyhood, as the names of great soldiers do before other boys."[23]

Because black Americans around him in his youth held a certain fascination for Melville, particularly in the arts, in music and dance, it was natural that his interest in them would lead him to travel accounts on Africa. It is also probable that he read books on Africa in his youth, especially because we now know their influence on a number of his works, among them *Moby-Dick* and *Benito Cereno*. Given the prominence of Africans in Melville's greatest works, one would think that critics might have devoted more attention to uncovering what he read, except that Africans have been in such disrepute in this country. To be fair, works by Joseph Dupuis, T. E. Bowdich, and Willem Bosman are about as obscure today, except to specialists, as they were in Melville's youth.

Melville found in Park's *Travels into the Interior Districts of Africa* revelations of African humanity so at odds with conceptions of Africa held by whites and free blacks in America that a dramatic shift in his thinking about Africa was encouraged. However favorably disposed toward Africans he may have been before reading *Interior Districts,* what is revealed there concerning their work skills must have startled him, for the thought that Africans brought any skills into slavery clashed violently with the thesis of the day that, as a people, they were by nature ignorant, hopelessly inferior to whites.

Melville was made to confront, in a highly personal way, his relationship to African people, and through them to people of African descent in America. Contesting another youth for intellectual leadership of a youth organization in Albany, he was accused of being a "moral Ethiopian," a charge related to a companion reference to him as a "Ciceronian baboon." Both epithets sought to place him among the despised blacks of Africa and America. The injustice of the attacks made him feel something of what blacks in Albany and the nation routinely were made to feel.[24] But beyond all personal considerations, his grasp of the economic value of slavery to the nation, derived in part from travel accounts of Africa, was at least as certain as his awareness, derived from experience, that dance formed the radiating core of slave culture in America, a force of such power even in the North that it met needs of whites as well as blacks. His understanding was crystallizing in his Albany years as a teenager, and relatively early thereafter it took impressive form in *Moby-Dick.*

But first, Melville went to sea and reflected on certain creative problems from his floating university: "Beware of enlisting in your vigilant fisheries any lad with lean brow and hollow eye," he wrote, "who offers to ship with the *Phaedon* instead of Bowditch in his head."[25] Had there been no blacks on the *Saint Lawrence,* the ship on which he first sailed at nineteen, the fact that its cargo was cotton bound for Liverpool, once a major slave trading port, would have excited interest in slavery related to Bowdich's travels in Africa in one as sensitive and as bright as he. More precisely, movement of the principal product of antebellum slavery to a port from which ships once sailed to deliver Africans to the slave fields of the South was not lost on young Melville, whose father had also sailed to Liverpool and taken an interest in the city.

While he was there, Melville's imagination was seized by statuary honoring the memory of Lord Nelson, erected twenty-three years before his arrival on the *Saint Lawrence.* The figure of Nelson, triumphant though dying, looms above four suffering victims chained around the base. They reminded young Melville of slaves, his thought reverting "to Virginia and Carolina." During his initial stay in Liverpool, he returned to this sculpture many times to see the "woe-begone figures of captives . . . with swarthy limbs and manacles" prominently represented, and he later put it to use in both *Redburn* and *Benito Cereno.*[26]

Tracing the footsteps of his father through Liverpool, Redburn had come upon the statuary group. There is reason to believe that Redburn's father was drawn from Allan Melville, Herman Melville's own father, who had himself, like his fictional counterpart, befriended the distinguished abolitionist described in *Redburn:* "the good and great Roscoe, the intrepid enemy of the [slave] trade who in every way devoted his fine talents to its suppression," writing a poem about it—"The Wrongs of Africa" (*R,* 156). In search of the spirit of his father, Redburn identified that father, and hence Melville's father, with the values of a leading opponent of slavery and the slave trade.

Despite its moving treatment of poverty and slavery, *Redburn* has not been considered particularly important in Melville's corpus. The author himself asserted that it was written primarily because he needed money, that such a need defined its value.[27] But just as he accumulated material in youth from which he later fashioned a stunning dance scene in *Moby-Dick,* he drew from his Liverpool experience thoughts on how to fashion, in *Benito Cereno,* perhaps as complicated a symbol as has been discussed in literature. His Harvard, his Yale—his time at sea—gave him time to consider how he might transform what he was learning into art.

Melville's presence on the *Acushnet* afforded him a fine opportunity to explore cultural interaction between black and white sailors. The *Acushnet* had "the usual mixture of free Negroes, Portuguese, and strays from the north of Europe" together with a majority "with good New England names," which made for a cultural laboratory in which Melville might thrive as a student of that difference he increasingly came to value.[28] Being at sea tested, in a highly focused manner, his cultural perceptions. In this regard, one must not underestimate the degree to which African influences in music and dance remained with free Negroes, resulting in artistic and spiritual qualities that distinguished them from other sailors.

When in his mid-twenties with his years at sea behind him, Melville explored Pinkster and Catharine Market in New York City. In addition, he had the opportunity, through reading James Fenimore Cooper, to more than glimpse the festival historically. Cooper, one of Melville's favorite writers, having witnessed Pinkster growing up in New York, projected something of its spirit back into the colonial period in which he situates the festival in

Satanstoe. Melville must have had strange feelings about Cooper's description of thousands of blacks and whites on the Commons, just minutes from his old Cortlandt address, for Cooper refers to excitement that, from early morning, started white youths on long walks through New York to the Commons. Within a few hours,

> nine-tenths of the blacks of the city, and of the whole country within thirty or forty miles, were collected in thousands in the field, beating banjoes, singing African songs, drinking, and worst of all, laughing in a way that seemed to set their very hearts rattling within their ribs. Everything wore the aspect of good-humor in its broadest and coarsest forms. Every sort of common game was in requisition, while drinking was far from being neglected. Still, not a man was drunk. A drunken negro, indeed, is not a common thing . . . Hundreds of whites were walking through the fields, amused spectators. Among these last were a great many children of the better class, who had come to look at the enjoyment of those who attended them, in their ordinary amusements . . . A great many young ladies between the ages of fifteen and twenty were also in the field, either escorted by male companions, or, what was equally certain of producing deference, under the care of old female nurses, who belonged to the race that kept the festival.[29]

Around the time of the appearance of *Satanstoe,* Charles Dickens published his masterful description of dance in *American Notes.* Melville read about William Henry Lane, a free black from Rhode Island considered by Dickens, without qualification, "the greatest of all dancers." We learn that as he entered a dive in the Five Points district, Dickens and his party were asked by the proprietor, "What will we please to call for? A dance? It shall be done directly, sir: 'a regular break-down.'" Every effort was made to please the whites. Lane, according to Dickens, never ceased to make "queer faces . . . to the delight of all the rest, who grin from ear to ear incessantly." And, writes Dickens, "The fiddler grins, and goes at it tooth and nail; there is new energy in the tambourine; new laughter in the dancers; new smiles in the landlady; new confidence in the landlord; new brightness in the very candles." Then he immortalizes Lane: "Single shuffle, double shuffle, cut and cross-cut; snapping his fingers, rolling his eyes, turning in his knees, presenting the backs of his legs in front, spinning about on his toes and heels like nothing but the man's fingers on the tambourine; dancing with two left legs, two right legs, two wooden legs, two wire legs, two spring legs,—all sorts of legs and no legs—what is this to him." As applause "thundered about him,"

Lane "finished by leaping gloriously on the bar-counter, and calling for something to drink."[30]

Some dances seen in New York City probably were done even earlier in Albany. We know, for example, that Charley of Pinkster fame, one of the great dancers of the eighteenth century, influenced dancers in and out of Albany. He was a master of the extremely inventive breakdown—described by Dickens—and superior to his imitator, John Diamond, a superb white dancer at times seen in New York.[31] Simple logic holds that Albany slaves, after Charley began his decline as a dancer, extended dance that he helped fashion into the nineteenth century, for they were not less attentive to the master than Diamond and hardly less gifted. According to Munsell, "Charley generally led off the dance, when the Sambos and Philises, juvenile and antiquated, would put in a double-shuffle heel and toe breakdown, in a manner that would have put Master Diamond and other *cork*-onions somewhat in the *shade*."[32] Thus we have some indication of the superiority of the dancers close to Charley and active in the ring dance and double shuffle tradition that he helped pioneer.

Ring dance to juba rhythms—William Henry Lane was known as "Master Juba"—were performed in New York City, but with few students as sensitive as Melville observing them. Although there was probably juba circular dance at Catharine Market, a less often remarked dance attracted the attention of Thomas De Voe, who described the music to which it was done: "Their music or time was usually given by one of their own party, which was done by beating their hands on the sides of their legs and the noise of their heels" (*De Voe,* 344). He then refers to a popular form of dance to juba rhythms on "spring" boards held down at each end that narrow—yet heighten—possibilities for improvisation crowned by one astonishing display after another.

There is evidence that Melville made his way to Catharine Market before the appearance of *Moby-Dick.*[33] In fact, his sustained presentation of slave music and dance in *Moby-Dick* enables us to bring together much of the dance and music that we have been considering. We find confirmation that Melville was exposed to a great deal of African cultural practice. When reading the chapter "Midnight, Forecastle," for example, one thinks of his long proximity to black performance art and of what he read concerning it. We are reminded of his youth in New York City and Albany and are persuaded that he read *American Notes,* which is explored in greater detail in chapter 4.

In Melville's fiction, African culture reaches beyond the black community to dazzle even those not particularly friendly toward blacks. To be sure, there is a sense in which, in "Midnight, Forecastle," through sailors from numerous points on the globe, the universal appeal of African dance and music—of instrumentation through the tambourine—is suggested despite marked insularity: "They were nearly all Islanders in the Pequod, *Isolatoes* too, I call such," Melville writes, "not acknowledging the common continent of men, but each *Isolato* living on a separate continent of his own." The entire crew of the ship is aware of the music and dance, "federated along one keel" in that sense as well, alive to the fleeting if somewhat threatening possibility of a common, universal dance and musical culture—"belike the whole world's a ball, as you scholars have it; and so 'tis right to make one ball-room of it"—regulated by the rhythms of Pip's tambourine (*MD*, 121, 175; emphasis in original). As we shall see, African dance is not the only dance in this chapter; rather, it is the dance on which Melville mainly focuses.

When the Iceland Sailor, who finds the floor on which dance will take place "too *springy*" for his taste (*MD*, 171; emphasis added), the Azore sailor throws Pip's tambourine to him and, as half the sailors dance, urges him: "Go it Pip! Bang it . . . Rig it, dig it, stig it, quig it, bell-boy!" (*MD*, 174–5) The Azore sailor's voice is itself improvisational. Fast and percussive, it not only invites dance rhythms but prefigures the scat singing of jazz. The sophisticated West African conception—to *dig,* that is, to understand or like—acquaints one with what was, outside a certain segment of the slave community, highly esoteric knowledge.

And so, at midnight, when asked to expend much energy, to "make fire-flies," to "break the jinglers!" Pip is equal to the occasion: "Jinglers, you say?—there goes another, dropped off; I pound it so." As sparks from Pip's tambourine, riding jagged currents of sound, light the night, Melville has the Manx Sailor remark, "Dance on, lads, you're young; I was once"—very likely an utterance that resonated in Melville's consciousness not simply because he danced when young but because he took dancing lessons in his youth as well (*MD*, 175).

As the sailors dance, comical antics are expected of Pip, raising the specter of minstrelsy. Pip is urged, for example, to "wag thy ears" and to "rattle thy teeth," but nothing so perverse as mere minstrelsy is affirmed by Melville, for perceived insults are rejected a number of times in the chapter (*MD*, 174, 175).

Ring dance enters gracefully when the Maltese sailor introduces the reader to a diverse set of dance relationships: "It's the waves—the snow's caps turn to jig it now. They'll shake their tassels soon. Now would all the waves were women, then I'd go drown, and chassee with them evermore! There's naught so sweet on earth—heaven may not match it!—as those swift glances of warm, wild bosoms in the dance, when the over-arboring arms hide such ripe, bursting grapes" (*MD*, 176).

As we imagine the left foot followed in the same direction by the right and the right by the left on the ocean floor, Melville revisits, with remarkable subtlety in *Moby-Dick,* dance in *Omoo,* in which women, doing the "Lory-Lory," "fly round and round: bosoms heaving, hair streaming." Then later: "Presently, raising a strange chant, they softly sway themselves, gradually quickening the movement, until, at length, for a few passionate moments, with throbbing bosoms and glowing cheeks, they abandon themselves to all the spirit of the dance." Though a different dance, its circularity calls to mind ring dance at Pinkster, the principal form of dance there.[34]

Once more Melville relates dance in the Pacific Isles to African dance and slave culture when the China Sailor calls to Pip to "make a pagoda of thyself" (*MD,* 175), for in *Omoo* he writes of the clearing where the dance took place, "Near the trees, on one side of the clear space, was a ruinous pile of stones, many rods in extent, upon which had formerly stood a temple" (*O,* 240). Movement began slowly and then proceeded swiftly in the Ring Shout, the most influential slave dance in nineteenth-century America. That Melville has sailors attempting black dance steps, even improvising, to the rhythms of Pip's tambourine is a reflection of the power of black dance nationally.

In "Midnight, Forecastle" Melville translates some of his knowledge of black dance and music into literary art. Moreover, when reading *Moby-Dick,* we revisit with him scenes of his youth in Albany and in New York City and rediscover what scholars have largely failed to reflect on—the presence of black culture in the North and the African aesthetic that informs it. Although we encounter whites who are fascinated by the culture of people said to be their inferiors, it is now clear that Melville's depiction of African music and dance is a convincing representation—and here is the great irony—of American art in *Moby-Dick.*

But in *Benito Cereno* there are aspects of African culture, including music and dance, so elusive and abstruse that we may never know why Melville made them so. What we know is that Africans in that work do not believe that God is white, which helps explain the militance of their dance in a novella largely based on an 1801 slave revolt off the coast of South America that, for ironic subtlety, remains as brilliant as anything recorded in history.[35] In the novella, dance inspires those resisting oppression to acts of valor, a practice but dimly remembered by old Africans in America when Melville was writing *Benito Cereno.*

In fact, Melville bases his treatment of *dance purpose* in *Benito Cereno* on an African tradition seldom if ever drawn on in America. It is not likely, therefore, that when creating *Benito Cereno* he had before him examples of African dance, apart from their rhythms and the flow of form, still practiced in this country. His deep reading in Ashantee sources informs the dance scene in the novella, leading him to carry subtlety beyond the bounds familiar to his readership. He created the novella's governing symbol by fusing models from widely divergent cultural worlds before concealing them deep beneath surface appearances, calling to mind a cardinal principle of his aesthetic: "I love all men who *dive*. Any fish can swim near the surface." Melville was thinking "of the whole corps of thought-divers who have been diving and coming up again with bloodshot-eyes since the world began." In fact, in the novella's creation, like "the great whale," he goes "down stairs five miles or more" to defining depths to complicate what is read on the surface.[36] The very nature of dance in the work, then, barely suggests the complexity of its most important symbol, without understanding of which there is no knowing that African values, deep beneath appearances, are crucial to the formation of the novella's finest art.

The reader will remember that slaves, thought tractable by their owner Alexandro Aranda and allowed to sleep unchained on the deck of the *San Dominick,* suddenly revolt under their leader Babo's direction, tie up and throw overboard a number of Spaniards, stab others to death, and spare captain Don Benito Cereno's life in exchange for a promise to navigate them back to West Africa.[37] The danger, however, is that a ship might appear in the distance and its captain decide to make contact with the *San Dominick,* which would place in jeopardy the revolt and possible lasting freedom. The attempted return to Africa, therefore, could be as dangerous to the interests of the Africans as the Atlantic voyage that brought them into Latin American waters. Babo's plan anticipates the appearance of an unfriendly captain and crew who would not question the right of whites to reenslave blacks who had broken free. He decides that in such an eventuality the revolt should be disguised (*BC,* 108–9).

Melville's masterly creation is an expression of artistic irony of a type before unknown to the world of fiction. Such irony is possible because the impulse to art in the novella, as in the historical revolt, is indistinguishable from the impulse to be free, and both are sustained on nearly every page of the novella. From beginning to end, Babo directs each actor to determine his or her character in light of changing realities but consonant with the new power relations, as when Amasa Delano boards and whites and blacks "in one language, and as with one voice . . . all poured out a common tale of suffering"; as when immediately after Delano has a brush with death "the work of hoisting in the casks was resumed, whites and blacks singing at the tackle" (*BC,* 49, 79–80).

In the novella, martial intent is hidden behind the rhythmic play of hatchets, a regular reminder to the Spaniards that the hatchets are in hand for more than musical purposes. But the rhythmic play of Ashantees at times takes the complex form of eerie comment on vague suspicions. Even those comments should be considered together with more disturbing and decisive strains of improvised, martial rhythms—rhythms so orchestrated that at precisely the right time the hatchets were clashed side by side, which confirms Melville's more than passing knowledge of African rhythm in the Americas.

But the more complicated issue is how he came by his knowledge of African music. The evidence suggests that Melville's sense of African musical culture was cultivated in places no more exotic than New York City and Albany. In a word, Ashantee rhythms were not noticeably different, despite the ends to which they were directed, from those of Northern slaves and their descendants. Melville drew on travel accounts and his personal exposure to African performance style, mainly in America, in presenting the rhythms of the classic "hatchet polisher" scene. In a sense, however, that invention, clever as it is, is on the surface, above underlying Ashantee realities to be examined.

The degree of slaveholder dependence on the slave in the historical revolt recounted by Delano is related to master-class dependence on African work skills. In fact, Melville's knowledge of African work skills enabled him to sweep away spiritual and intellectual cobwebs that blinded other Americans. He knew that there was no greater myth, cherished in his day, than that Africans were unable to take care of themselves and, consequently, had to be taught how to labor in workshop and field in the plantation South. Mungo Park's *Interior Districts* offered an informed view of African labor in the economic history of America from the time of the American Revolution. From reading Park, one sees that thousands of Africans entered America with prior knowledge of tobacco cultivation, and in even larger numbers knowing how to cultivate cotton, major crops in the development of the American economy. But the list of skills does not stop there: the working of leather, iron, and gold were common, Park discloses, in many parts of black Africa affected by the slave trade.[38]

It was not lost on Melville that an African named Karfa, according to Park, on "observing the improved state of our manufactures, and our manifest superiority in the arts of civilized life, would sometimes appear pensive, and exclaim with an involuntary sigh, 'black men are nothing,'" as if he really meant it, thought Park.[39] So Park made no attempt to disabuse Karfa of that sentiment, though he owed his life to the humanity and work skills of African women, calling to mind Babo's response to a remark from Benito Cereno:

"But it is Babo here to whom, under God, I owe not only my own preservation, but likewise to him, chiefly, the merit is due, of pacifying his more ignorant brethren, when at intervals tempted to mur-murings."

"Ah, master," sighed the black, bowing his face, "don't speak of me; Babo is nothing . . ."

"Faithful fellow!" cried Captain Delano. "Don Benito, I envy you such a friend; slave I cannot call him." (*BC, 57*)

Melville offers numerous examples of Babo holding up the unstable Don Benito: Don Benito "fell heavily against his supporter"; "but the ser-vant was more alert, who, with one hand sustaining his master"; "his vital energy failed, so that to better support him, the servant, placing his master's hand on his naked shoulder, and gently holding it there, formed himself into a sort of crutch"; "His servant sustained him and drawing a cordial from his pocket placed it to his lips"; "As he mentioned this name, his air was heart-broken; his knees shook; his servant supported him"; "Presently master and man came forth; Don Benito leaning on his servant"; "And so, still presenting himself as a crutch, [Babo] walking between the two captains" (*BC,* 55, 60, 70, 80, 88, 97). But Benito Cereno's instability is suggested by the life of another American, to be taken up later, that argues an influence on Melville that affected the creation of the novella in truly astonishing ways.

A decade and a half ago, Joshua Leslie and I wrote, though it was Leslie's brilliant idea, that Melville was under Hegelian influence in one vital respect. He argues that the slave in *Benito Cereno* is the creative force, the master parasitic. We wrote, "We have been unable to find a specific reference to Hegel in Melville's work. However, the earliest reference to freedom as the recognition of necessity is from Hegel, and Melville, introducing *The Bell Tower* with lines of poetry 'from a private MS.,' tells us: 'Seeking to conquer a larger liberty, man but extends the empire of necessity.'" "The Hegelian echo," we concluded, "is deafening."[40] With the appearance of the Melville *Journals* in 1989, what we had argued was confirmed. The proof we were looking for, supplied by the scholarship of David Roediger, was recorded by Melville in 1849:

Monday Oct 22   Clear and cold; wind not favorable. I forgot to men-tion, that *last night* about 9:30 P.M. Adler and Taylor came into my room, and it was proposed to have whiskey punches, which we *did* have, accordingly . . . We had an extraordinary time and did not break up until after two in the morning. We talked metaphysics continually, and Hegel, Schlegel, Kant and others were discussed.[41]

One is reminded of Edward Margolies's observation that because "ambiguity sits at the center of Melville's metaphysics, would not this hold for his vision of a people whom he could not have known very well?" Hegel's philosophical consideration of the master-slave relationship is hardly ambiguous, and because Melville provides the finest expression in literature of this relationship, the first part of Margolies's argument is no more convincing than his assertion that Melville did not know blacks well.[42] On the contrary, because he knew them well, Hegel was very useful as Melville imagined Don Benito's dependence on Babo. In fact, it seems that Melville was almost waiting for Hegel to provide the philosophical terms for what he had long thought and espoused. Melville ties the slave trade to the wealth of England in *Redburn,* informing us that the wealth of Liverpool derived mainly from the slave trade, which underscores his command of the economics of master-slave relations (*R,* 170). Hence *Redburn's* connection to *Benito Cereno* on the deepest possible level. In fact, what appear to be relatively unimportant ties between *Redburn* and *Benito Cereno* merit serious attention. For example, Melville reveals a link between *Benito Cereno* and the *Highlander,* the ship in *Redburn,* writing that Jackson, in *Redburn,* "used to tell of the *middle passage,* where the slaves were stowed, heel and point, like logs, and the suffocated and dead were unmanacled, and weeded out from the living every morning" (*R,* 107). For those who doubt *Redburn's* connection to the novella, there is also a more elusive connection between the two works that is related to Scottish Highlanders. Melville's naming the ship in *Redburn* the *Highlander* suggests that, if not as early as *Redburn,* then perhaps not long thereafter, he was associating the carving of flesh from the backs and thighs of Africans, reported in Delano's *Voyages and Travels,* with the Highlanders' deadly use of sharp blades against the British at Preston Pans.[43]

Redburn is far more important to Melville's art than has long been assumed. There is, above all, the passage in which he describes the Nelson monument:

> The ornament in question is a group of statuary in bronze, elevated upon a marble pedestal and basement, representing Lord Nelson expiring in the arms of Victory. One foot rests on a rolling foe, and the other on a cannon. Victory is dropping a wreath on the dying Admiral's brow . . . At uniform intervals round the base of the pedestal, four naked figures in chains, somewhat larger than life, are seated in various attitudes of humiliation and despair . . . These woe-begone figures of captives are emblematic of Nelson's principal victories; but I could never look at their swarthy limbs and manacles, without being

involuntarily reminded of four African slaves in the market-place. And my thoughts would revert to Virginia and Carolina. (*R*, 170)

This treatment of the Nelson statuary is subtly tied to a description of the *San Dominick*'s appearance near the beginning of *Benito Cereno:*

> Whether the ship had a figure-head, or only a plain beak, was not quite certain, owing to the canvas wrapped around that part, either to protect it while undergoing a re-furbishing, or else decently to hide its decay. Rudely painted or chalked . . . along the forward side of a sort of pedestal below the canvas, was the sentence "*Sequid vuestro jefe,*" (follow your leader); while upon the tarnished head-boards, near by, appeared, in stately capitals, once gilt, the ship's name, "San Dominick," each letter streakingly corroded with tricklings of copper-spike rust; while, like mourning weeds, dark festoons of seagrass slim-ily swept to and fro over the name, with each hearse-like roll of the hull. (*BC*, 49)

The reference to the pedestal in the passage above and in the novella is not the only analogue to be found. Melville writes, in the same paragraph of *Redburn,* of one of the chained and swarthy figures, "his head buried in despondency," looking "mournfully out of his eyes," which brings to mind the "mourning weeds" reference in *Benito Cereno.* And Redburn notes that "Victory is dropping a wreath on the dying admiral's brow; while Death, under the similitude of *a hideous skeleton,* is insinuating his bony hand under the hero's robe, and groping after his heart" (*R*, 155; emphasis added). (It should be noted that the skeletal Death in the Nelson monument is actually emerging from under the canvas folds of a fallen sail.)

Melville uses Lord Nelson's skeleton as a model for Aranda's, and Lord Nelson for Delano as the masked figure on the stern-piece with his foot on another. He also depicts Babo, determined that Don Benito follow his leader, choosing a design no less striking than the one in the statuary by aiming a dagger at Don Benito's heart before being cast underfoot. So when Delano's mask is removed, we see that he represents himself as well as Nelson. Lord Nelson, then, is a model for both Delano and Alexandro Aranda, the owner of the slaves .

The sovereign and, conceptually related, most far-reaching symbol of *Benito Cereno,* Aranda's skeleton, hovers over the novella from the start. Most dramatically, just before the final battle, it is starkly cast—by moonlight—upon the water. (*BC*, 102). And yet Delano is as ignorant on leaving the *San Dominick* as when he boarded it. As he puts his oars into the sea, Don

Benito leaps screaming into the boat, followed by Babo, dagger in hand. Thus Melville makes a dramatic and major variation from the original plot, getting Babo off the ship by having him pursue Don Benito. He describes what happens thereafter: "Seeing the negro coming, Captain Delano had flung the Spaniard aside, almost in the act of clutching him . . . shifting his place, with arms thrown up, so promptly grappled the servant in his descent" (BC, 98).

At this juncture, the left hand of Captain Delano, on one side, again clutched the half-reclining Don Benito . . . while his right foot, on the other side, ground the prostrate negro" (BC, 98–99). It was then that he "saw the negroes, not as if frantically concerned for Don Benito, but with mask torn away, flourishing hatchets and knives, in ferocious piratical revolt." Meanwhile, like "delirious black dervishes," the six Ashantees "danced on the poop" (BC, 99). Their leaping, counterclockwise movement was not the only instance of dance being used to encourage resistance. The Ashantee women "sang songs and danced—not gaily, but solemnly; and before the engagement with the boats, as well as during the action, they sang melancholy songs to the negroes, and . . . this melancholy tone was more inflaming than a different one would have been, and was so intended; that all this is believed because the negroes have said it" (BC, 112).

Melville's recognition of abstruse aspects of Ashantee culture in Delano's account—the dance and music of the women—in which there is no mention of Ashantees, is the best indication of his knowledge of their culture.[44]

Although there is no doubt that, by the end of the novella, the masked satyr figure on the stern-piece, with his foot on another figure, represents Delano, until now it has not been argued that Melville modeled him after Lord Nelson, who on the Liverpool monument has, as shown, his foot on a foe (R, 155).[45] This argument is more persuasive in context, for not only did the chained figures at the base of the pedestal remind Melville of slaves, he knew that Delano, on reaching the Perseverance in the historical account, ordered "the ports run up and the guns [cannon] run out as soon as possible," which reminded him of Nelson, cannon at his side.[46]

In Benito Cereno, Melville has Delano hail the Bachelor's Delight and order the guns readied. But the San Dominick's cable had been cut, and the lashing out of the fag-end had "whipped away the canvas shroud about the beak, suddenly revealing, as the bleached hull swung round towards the open ocean, death for the figure-head, in a human skeleton; chalky comment on the chalked words below, Follow Your Leader." "At the sight," Benito Cereno, "covering his face, wailed out: 'Tis he, Aranda! My murdered, unburied friend!'" (BC, 99–100). If Delano noticed Aranda's skeleton, there is no mention of it in the novella.

A year after the appearance of *Benito Cereno,* Melville returned to Liverpool and wrote in his journal: "After dinner went to exchange. Looked at Nelson's statue, with peculiar emotion, mindful of twenty years ago."[47] Despite the lapse of time, he had used details of the statuary together with his knowledge of African culture, derived from Park and especially from Dupuis and Bowdich, to create some of the finest scenes in all of literature. We can be certain that, while standing there that day, he recalled how the statuary inspired the mythological figures on the stern-piece of the *San Dominick* and the scene, near the end of the novella, of Delano and Babo in the boat.

But we must look still closer at Melville's creative process, for there are subtleties within subtleties and relationships investigated above that, in some instances, require more attention. An especially pivotal relationship that requires close attention, one that reveals aspects of Melville's creative process that have not been remarked, is that between *Moby-Dick* and *Benito Cereno.* How they relate to each other is the primary concern of the next chapter, in which we discover how Melville created classic features of both works. Although our immediate purpose is to reveal how the novella and *Moby-Dick* feed into and enrich each other, links between them of a different order can also be established, as will be shown in later chapters.

But before investigating the relationship between *Benito Cereno* and *Moby-Dick*—in preparation for that investigation—we will demonstrate intertextuality between *The Encantadas* and *Benito Cereno* in which the atmosphere of the former is superimposed on the latter in yet another stunning instance of the indistinguishability of illusion and reality in the novella. Thus we begin with *The Encantadas* and *Benito Cereno* before moving on to how *Benito Cereno* and *Moby-Dick* are forever linked.

CHAPTER II

Benito Cereno and *Moby-Dick*

His way in Benito Cereno *is like that of an artist carving a three-dimensional scene in ivory and ebony, working subtle designs that are hidden away in the recesses. Still, the ideas in the tale are not meant to be hidden forever.*
—Joyce Adler, War in Melville's Imagination

In the harbor of Santa Maria, a desert island off the coast of Chile, Captain Amasa Delano, of Duxbury, Massachusetts, is resting in his berth on a gray morning when he is informed by his mate that a strange ship is sailing into the bay. Within minutes, Delano watches through his glass the seemingly irregular moves of the *San Dominick*. Wanting to help, he orders that his whale-boat be dropped. Immediately thereafter, he places a number of baskets of fish, as presents, into the boat and pulls away. As he rows toward the ship in the distance, the play of the wind among vapors makes it difficult for him to distinguish appearance from reality, and more than once he revises his opinion of what he is seeing. At first, the ship, raggedly furred with "shreds of fog," has the appearance of "a whitewashed monastery after a thunderstorm," but that appearance is "modified, and the true character of the vessel" is made plain—a Spanish merchantman of the first class, carrying negro slaves, amongst other valuable freight from one colonial port to another."[1]

But before the whale-boat of the *Bachelor's Delight* sets out to help, we learn from the deposition, the ship is itself being watched. With Delano two or three hours away, Babo, under whose direction explosive violence had twice occurred on the *San Dominick*, confers with Atufal, his chief aide, and asks if he thinks strangers should be allowed to board. Though Atufal advises against it, Babo concludes that there is nothing to fear. In the interval, he conceives a plan of deception and defense to clothe the actions of those on the *San Dominick*, as if in fog and vapors. He insists that the whites, on pain of death, must appear to rule, but not oppose, the blacks. For their part, the blacks should act like subjects, but without losing control. It is as though the atmosphere of Melville's Encantadas prevails: Delano is trying to make out what he is rowing toward, and on the *San Dominick* itself, according to Babo's plan, illusion and reality will be indistinguishable.[2]

With the whale-boat approaching, certain of the Encantadas' volcanic formations hold special meaning for what has occurred and will occur on the *San Dominick*: "There toil the demons of fire, who, at intervals, irradiate the nights with a strange spectral illumination," suddenly letting loose "terrific concussions, and the full drama of a volcanic eruption" (*EN*, 141). Meanwhile, an ominous sign of what that day might offer is brilliantly imagined by Melville: "Flights of troubled gray fowl, kith and kin with flights of troubled gray vapors among which they were mixed, skimmed low and fitfully over the waters, as swallows over meadows before storms. Shadows present, foreshadowing deeper shadows to come" (*BC*, 46).

When Delano boards the *San Dominick,* he is confronted by "a clamorous throng of whites and blacks" pouring out a tale of suffering. They exclaim in Spanish—which helps conceal the deeper reality—that the "scurvy, together with the fever, had swept off a great part of their number, more especially the Spaniards," that the *San Dominick* "had lain tranced without wind," the breeze having "suddenly deserted her, in unknown waters, to sultry calms." Indeed, Don Benito, at Babo's command, informs the stranger that the *San Dominick* had lost "whole families of the Africans, and yet a larger number, proportionately, of the Spaniards, including, by a luckless fatality, every remaining officer on board." In one voice, with lips apparently baked, the horror of the sultry calm is confirmed. Moreover, Don Benito added that the *San Dominick,* on more than one occasion "had doubled back upon her own track" (*BC*, 49, 56). Thus, in an unexpected leap of the imagination, Melville has Babo put to use, as a means of safeguarding the revolt, tragic experiences previously recounted by Melville in *The Encantadas.*

We discover that, along the coast of South America, at least one other ship had become "the vexed sport of malicious calms and currents" and was enveloped by "frequent fogs" and "vapors." When all on that ship "were joyously anticipating sight of their destination, lo! the vapors lifted and disclosed the mountains from which they had taken their departure. In the like deceptive vapors she at last struck upon a reef, whence ensued a long series of calamities too sad to detail" (*EN*, 139). Melville thereby reminds us that Delano, when first viewing the *San Dominick* through his glass, had noticed that it "was drawing too near the land; a sunken reef making out off her bow" (*BC*, 47). Despite the great distance between Santa Maria and the Encantadas, the seeming incongruity is accounted for when Delano concludes that the portion of the tale recounted for him that "most excited interest, as well as some surprise, considering the latitude in question, was the long calms spoken of, and more particularly the ship's so long drifting about." He concludes, however, that faulty navigation and clumsy seamanship might explain matters when the *San Dominick,* Melville seems to suggest at the start, was suffering from a more fundamental problem (*BC,* 58).

The Encantadas signal as much by being bound, in remarkable degree, to *Benito Cereno.* But such union of texts is more startlingly—and profoundly— represented by *Benito Cereno's* relationship to *Moby-Dick,* a principal concern of this chapter. Because symbolically and in characterization they enjoy a common ancestry that heretofore has not been remarked, the two works represent one of the most stunning examples of intertextuality known to literature. Indeed, the influence of African culture in the two great works is now so evident that our way of perceiving each has been transformed, radically altering our understanding of Melville's aesthetic.

[I]

As *Benito Cereno* unfolds, Delano seeks a clearer understanding of those who assail him with anguish, feigned and real. He approaches the *San Dominick's* captain, Don Benito Cereno, who speaks brokenly, yet "no landsman could have dreamed that in him was lodged a dictatorship beyond which, while at sea, there was no earthly appeal," Delano concludes (*BC,* 53). Delano's interest in having Don Benito favor him with the complete story of what occurred on the *San Dominick* sets the tone for much that follows. Attempting to recount developments, Don Benito is seized by "a sudden feinting attack of his cough, brought on, no doubt, by his mental distress." Babo, however, drew "a cordial from his pocket" and "placed it to his lips," a little reviving him, while eying Don Benito "as if to watch for the first sign of complete restoration, or relapse, as the event might prove" (*BC,* 55).

As in a dream, Don Benito proceeded: "Oh, my God! rather than pass through what I have, with joy I would have hailed the most terrible gales; but—." Coughing with greater violence, he then "fell heavily against his supporter," causing Babo, plaintively sighing, to exclaim, "His mind wanders. He was thinking of the plague that followed the gales . . . my poor, poor master!" Turning to Captain Delano, Babo urges patience, assuring him that Don Benito's fits were not long-lasting, that "master will soon be himself" (*BC,* 55–56). Resuming his lines while turning in Babo's arms, Don Benito remarks, "But throughout these calamities . . . I have to thank those negroes you see, who, though to your inexperienced eyes appearing unruly, have, indeed, conducted themselves with less of restlessness than even their owner could have thought possible under such circumstances" (*BC,* 56).

Captain Delano would have been horrified to know that violence had swept their former owner, Alexandro Aranda, into oblivion, his skeletal remains, after an African ritual performed below deck, riveted to the prow. When Don Benito was called to the deck some days after Aranda was killed, Babo had shown him the skeleton. He then asked Don Benito whose skeleton it was, "and whether, from its whiteness, he should not think it a white's." Don Benito later let it be known that, as long as he continued to believe in reason, he could not divulge how Aranda's body was reduced to a skeleton (*BC*, 107, 111–12).

When asked if Aranda died of fever, and perhaps thinking, erroneously, that Aranda had been cannibalized, Don Benito responds, "Died of the fever. Oh, could I but—" before quivering and pausing. When Delano remarks, "Were your friend's remains now on board this ship, Don Benito, not thus strangely would the mention of his name affect you," the Spaniard returns, "On board this ship?" before, with "horrified gestures," as though directed "against some spectre," he "fell into the ready arms of his attendant, who, with a silent rapt appeal toward Captain Delano, seemed beseeching him not again to broach a theme so unspeakably distressing to his master," whose knees shook even when thinking of Aranda's death (*BC*, 60–61).

As Delano tries to acquaint himself with the anguished Benito Cereno, the forecastle bell, "with a dreary grave-yard toll, betokening a flaw," is struck by a grizzled oakum-picker and "proclaimed ten o'clock, through the leaden calm." As the graveyard sound is heard, Captain Delano's attention is caught "by the moving figure of a gigantic black, emerging from the general crowd below, and slowly advancing towards the elevated poop." Delano notices "an iron collar" about the black's neck, "from which depended a chain, thrice wound round his body; the terminating links padlocked together at a broad band of iron, his girdle" (*BC*, 61).

On seeing Atufal approaching and hearing the bell toll, Don Benito starts, shaken, "his white lips glued together." Cast by Babo to delude Delano by confirming chief elements of Babo's strategy, Atufal is made to seem so subdued that Babo remarks, "How like a mute Atufal moves." A minute or so later, looking at Atufal's gigantic form, not without a degree of admiration, Delano thinks, "This is some mulish mutineer," in one of the few times that he was at least partially right in judging a black on the *San Dominick* (*BC*, 62). But apparently believing blacks incapable of resisting slavery, he thought of mutiny rather than slave resistance.

Sounded for Delano's benefit, the forecastle bell signals that it is time for Atufal to report to Don Benito to ask to be pardoned for some unspecified offense. Shortly thereafter, Atufal dutifully "mounted the steps of the poop, and, like a brave prisoner, brought up to receive sentence, stood in unquailing muteness before Don Benito, now recovered from his attack" (*BC*, 61). In this respect as in others, Babo's strategy seems to be working. He speaks to Don Benito, pressing him to ask the vital question, and Don Benito obliges:

"Atufal, will you ask my pardon, now?"

The black was silent.

"Again, master," murmured the servant, with bitter upbraiding eyeing his countryman, "Again, master; he will bend to master yet."

"Answer," said Don Benito, still averting his glance, "say but the one word, pardon, and your chains shall be off."

Upon this, the black, slowly raising both arms, let them lifelessly fall, his links clanking, his head bowed; as much as to say, "no, I am content."

"Go," said Don Benito, with inkept and unknown emotion.

Deliberately as he had come, the black obeyed. (*BC*, 62)

Surprised by the scene, Delano asks its meaning, to which Don Benito answers, "It means that that negro alone, of all the band, has given me peculiar cause of offense, I have put him in chains; I——." At this moment, Melville writes, "a swimming" in Don Benito's head causes him to raise his hand there before being urged on by Babo's "kindly glance," continuing, "I could not scourge such a form. But I told him he must ask my pardon. As yet he has not." Don Benito states that at his command every two hours Atufal is summoned before him. "And how long has this been?" asks Delano. "Some sixty days," answers Don Benito, which leads Delano to remark, "Upon my conscience, then . . . he has a royal spirit in him, this fellow." "He may have some right to it," replies Don Benito piercingly, "he says he was king in his own land." Babo then volunteers, "Yes . . . those slits in Atufal's ears once held wedges of gold; but poor Babo here, in his own land, was only a poor slave; a black man's slave was Babo, who now is the white's" (*BC*, 62).

Melville critics have assumed the soundness of Babo's claim that Atufal was a king in Africa, but I want to argue that Melville created Atufal mainly from a nameless Ashantee found in Joseph Dupuis's *Journal of a Residence in Ashantee*, long unknown to Melville critics, which appeared in 1824 and was probably first read by Melville as a teenager.[3] The critical passage in Dupuis reads as follows:

The torches threw a brilliant stream of light on all around, and increased the savage splendour of the scene . . . A number of warriors bedecked with argus plumes, gold ornaments and bells, preceded the canopy; performing certain evolutions representing the invocations and inspirations blended in the war dance; twirling also their gold-mounted guns, and screaming in terrific transports. A gigantic negro followed in the train, bearing the execution stool, encrusted with gore, and howling the song of death. The herald . . . followed next, announcing the monarch's high titles and deeds in arms.[4]

Melville reimagined the slave after whom Atufal is modeled as a king in the novella and thereby invested the African giant with a quality of nobility and subtle authority he otherwise would not have had. This is consonant with what we learn of Atufal's level of education in Amasa Delano's *Narrative of Voyages and Travels,* in which we are told that Atufal joined Babo in signing papers of agreement with Don Benito following Aranda's death. As Melville effects the inversion of the Dupuis figure, fine details are carried over into the novella, enhancing our understanding of Atufal's fearsome qualities and the sheer brilliance of his creation. In fact, in discovering how Melville put together the materials from which Atufal was created, we find that he did so by drawing on images from across texts, from different and complex realms of individual experience. The fusion of those sources accounts for Atufal's capacity for danger being so wonderfully yet disturbingly implied.

When Delano advises Don Benito that if Atufal's offense "was not something very serious," Don Benito should "take a fool's advice, and, in view of his general docility, as well as in some natural respect for his spirit, remit him his penalty," Babo assured Delano that "master never will do that," that "proud Atufal must first ask master's pardon. The slave there carries the padlock, but master here carries the key." His words have their intended effect: "His attention thus directed, Captain Delano now noticed for the first, that, suspended by a slender silken cord, from Don Benito's neck, hung a key. At once, from the servant's muttered syllables, divining the key's purpose, he smiled and said:—'So, Don Benito—padlock and key—significant symbols, truly'" (*BC,* 63).

We learn from Dupuis that from the "naked shoulder" of an Ashantee king "was suspended a thick silk plait or cord, to which were attached a string of amulets cased in gold, silver, and silk," a detail that matches the "silken cord" around Benito Cereno's neck. An object worn by the king was of particular interest to Melville, the "massive gold chain [that] encircled his waist, in the form of a zone, below the navel," to form an almost perfect analogue to the metal thrice wrapped round Atufal, the chain "bound together at the extremities by a twisted fastening of the same metal" into "a large clasp shaped into a tortoise." Melville substitutes the padlock here (Dupuis, 75, 175). As we know, the royal gold, in Melville's hands, became Atufal's iron. The "iron collar" about Atufal's neck was derived from Dupuis's reference to warriors "armed and equipped in their full military habits; some with iron chains suspended round the neck" (Dupuis, 77).

As we have seen, Don Benito told Delano that, over sixty days at two-hour intervals, Atufal was summoned before him to beg his pardon for some unknown offense. Reading such preposterous lines from Babo's script was, alone, enough to unsettle the Spaniard, yet Delano declined the opportunity to consider it clear evidence that Don Benito had no authority if a slave could refuse just once to beg his pardon. Moreover, Delano is asked to believe that a grizzled oakum-picker had come forth countless times to strike the dread forecastle bell that for two months had resounded in Don Benito's ear. Apparently Babo thought Don Benito's seeming genuineness on this point, on pain of death, would be convincing. But there are deeper resonances.

An identifying characteristic of Ashantee warriors is the principal source for the creation of the seldom-remarked forecastle bell. Involving a combination of African and Spanish influences, much like the flag of Spain draped around Benito Cereno as an apron in the shaving scene, to be taken up, the bell exerts an influence that is almost as consequential symbolically as Aranda's skeleton. And yet, in contrast to the other symbols, Melville appears to have made much less effort to draw the bell to our attention. Certainly it has received very little attention in the criticism.

How, then, did Melville create the forecastle bell? Like the shaving scene largely inspired by an Ashantee king's attire, Melville's forecastle bell derives largely from Ashantee inspiration. Dupuis writes that Ashantee military officers wore "a large gold, silver, or iron bell, suspended by a rope that girded the loins, and overhung the posteriors, causing at every movement a dull tinkling sound like the pasturing bells used in Spain" (Dupuis, 75). With Spain so unexpectedly brought to mind, Melville necessarily—no doubt with pleasure—recalling the flag in the shaving scene, is able to bring together Europe and Africa in creating the symbol of the bell whose dull, unringing sound is its flaw. But these sources are hidden from us.

Though Melville writes that the bell's toll gave it the sound of death, more is to be taken into account in determining his inspiration for the sound and the association of Atufal with it. Indeed, the bell's use in summoning Atufal only reinforces its meaning once we recall both the song of death and the execution stool. Beyond that, the loss of life on the *San Dominick,* the watery graves into which Spaniards are thrown or leap, come to mind as well. It appears that Melville had in mind the Liberty Bell, for there is no precise mention of the Ashantee bell being flawed, but its dull sound enables Melville to suggest that the forecastle bell, like the Liberty Bell, might portend the death knell of the Union.[5] The forecastle bell and more bring to mind *Moby-Dick's* Daggoo, who bears such resemblance to Atufal that the conclusion appears inescapable that his creation was also inspired by the Ashantee who sang the song of death. One of Melville's finest characterizations, Daggoo is said to have maintained "all his barbaric virtues, and erect as a giraffe moved about the decks in all the pomp of his six feet five in his socks." But this as well from Melville: "There was a corporeal humility in looking up at him; and a white man standing before him seemed a white flag come to beg truce of a fortress."[6]

Is not Melville's reference to Daggoo's "hearse-plumed head" as suggestive of death as the warrior "howling the song of death," as the "grave-yard toll"? Atufal and Daggoo are similar in other precise ways. Indeed, there are grounds for concluding that Atufal is in part modeled after Daggoo, as Melville uses similar language in describing them—Atufal: "a gigantic black," "colossal form"; Daggoo: "a gigantic, coal-black negro," "colossal limbs" (BC, 61, 62; MD, 120, 152). Daggoo's "hearse-plumed head" and Atufal's death song, however, appear to seal the argument. If Melville was not thinking ahead to Benito Cereno when writing Moby-Dick, we may be certain that he thought back to Moby-Dick, and thought deeply, when writing Benito Cereno.

Because Atufal's alleged royalty in Africa is directly related to Babo's claim to have been a slave there, we must raise anew the issue of Babo's status in Africa, and his consequent effectiveness as a leader of the revolt. The thought that he had been a slave made him appear more tractable when strangers boarded the San Dominick. Deflecting attention from the possibility that he is highborn and accustomed to assertiveness is a particularly clever and ironic tactic for Melville to have Babo employ. It might have been called into question had Delano known of his ability to write in his own language, but Delano knew nothing of Babo's writing ability.[7]

There is a side to Atufal about which more needs to be said, one that was referred to earlier: his having acted as Babo's right-hand man before Delano boarded the San Dominick. Considering what we know of Babo's fierce intelligence and brilliant imagination, that he chose Atufal, who could read and write in his own language, as his confidant marks Atufal as no ordinary man intellectually. In this regard, we should remember that Atufal had advised Babo to sail away rather than to allow strangers to board. As the Ashantee after whom Melville modeled Atufal was hardly extraordinary apart from his awesome stature and demeanor, Melville's granting Atufal strong intellectual qualities—he could not otherwise have been Babo's closest aide—deepens his complexity for Don Benito, heightening the Spaniard's fear.

Though Atufal's strength and ferocity are but suggested, there is enough uncertainty about him for Delano to feel unease in his presence. Through such understatement, Atufal is rescued from Dupuis's "savage" and racist depiction of the Ashantees. On the other hand, because Don Benito, with each sound of the forecastle bell, has to face Atufal, so much of whose real character is known to him, the wear on the Spaniard's nerves is frightful. In a sense, then, Atufal represents polar extremes: an immensely powerful figure and a man of intellect trusted by Babo.[8] And yet his immense size and seemingly defiant spirit strike Delano much of the time with a degree of apprehension. More threatening to the American, however, is Benito Cereno. Indeed, his suspicions of Don Benito, eventually paranoid, build with the thought, at the start, that Don Benito might be guilty of harboring a "secret vindictiveness" toward him, a possibility Babo counted on before Delano boarded (*BC*, 63).

The Atufal-Daggoo link does not exhaust the links between *Moby-Dick* and *Benito Cereno*. There are others of striking quality that require attention. Let us first focus on a feature of Ashantee culture that casts new light on Aranda's skeleton riveted to the ship as its figurehead, which opens the way to new interpretations of both *Moby-Dick* and *Benito Cereno*. This, too, we deduce from reading Dupuis, who writes of a victorious Ashantee warrior proudly displaying "a very large necklace of human teeth" and "a human jawbone." Dupuis asked the warrior "how he became possessed of these trophies," to which he obtained no satisfactory answer (Dupuis, 5). There is a later reference to "ostentatious trophies of negro splendour" "emblazoned to view": "Drums of every size, from five to six inches in length to the dimensions of as many feet, occasionally decorated with human relics, abounded in all directions; and in some (although few instances) the s[k]ulls of vanquished foemen [*sic*], and strings of human teeth were glaringly exposed on the persons of the youthful captains" (Dupuis, 71). The following passage from *Moby-Dick* provides the solution we are seeking:

> [B]ut take my word for it, you never saw such a rare old craft as this same rare old Pequod. She was a ship of the old school . . . Long seasoned and weather-stained in the typhoons and calms of all four oceans . . . She was a thing of trophies. A cannibal of a craft, tricking herself forth in the chased bones of her enemies. All round, her unpanelled, open bulwarks were garnished like one continuous jaw, with the long sharp teeth of the sperm whale . . . Scorning a turnstile wheel at her reverend helm, she sported a tiller; and that tiller was in one mass, curiously carved from the long narrow jaw of her hereditary foe . . . A noble craft, but somehow a most melancholy! All noble things are touched with that. (*MD*, 69, 70)

That passage is from "The Ship," a chapter of *Moby-Dick* in which major Ashantee influence in Melville's conception of the *Pequod* is revealed.

Moreover, there is little doubt, as we see from the passage, that *Benito Cereno* and *Moby Dick* are profoundly related, with the same African influence central to each. For who would doubt that, just as Babo has Aranda's skeleton displayed as the trophy-figurehead of the *San Dominick,* Ahab, "the supreme lord and dictator" of the *Pequod,* desired a place on its body for the remains of his great enemy, Moby Dick?

With his lower jaw, Moby Dick had "reaped away Ahab's leg," leaving him to fashion a leg "from the polished bone of the Sperm Whale's jaw," which was at once a constant reminder of the tragedy Ahab had experienced and a constant spur to his seeking Moby Dick's jaw as a trophy. Owing to Moby Dick's hue and his "unexampled, intelligent malignity," Ahab piled upon him "the sum of all general rage and hate felt by his whole race from Adam on down" (*MD,* 184). Consequently, as the novel unfolds and Ahab's intensity fails to abate, Moby Dick is pursued as the supreme trophy.[9]

In chapter 41, Melville again raises the image of the trophy, indirectly but certainly, in relation to Moby Dick, referring to the sailors encountering "whatever is astonishingly appalling in the sea; face to face they not only eye its greatest marvels, but hand to jaw, give battle to them." It is hard to miss the less subtle meaning conveyed in his assertion, almost immediately, that "few of those hunters were willing to encounter the perils of his jaw" (*MD,* 180, 181). Indeed, the focus on Moby Dick's jaw is heightened with references to "his deformed lower jaw, that so much invested the whale with natural terror," and to "his sickle-shaped lower jaw beneath him" (*MD,* 183, 184). Further, we learn that a "joyousness—a mighty mildness of repose in swiftness, invested the gliding whale," at least when not angered. But when he was angered, the terrors of his otherwise submerged trunk were revealed—above all, "the wrenched hideousness of his jaw" (*MD,* 548).

Much later, we hear Tashtego call out, "The birds!—the birds!" when "in long, Indian file the white birds flew toward Ahab's boat; and when within a few yards began fluttering over the water there, wheeling round and round, with joyous, expectant cries" and with vision sharper than man's. At first not seeing anything as "he peered into the sea beneath the wheeling birds," Ahab suddenly "peered down and down into its depths . . . saw a white, living spot no bigger than a white weasel with wonderful celerity uprising, and magnifying as it rose, till it turned, and then there were plainly revealed two long crooked rows of white glistening teeth, floating up from the undiscoverable bottom." These sentences call perfectly to mind the theme of death in *Benito Cereno:* "It was Moby Dick's open mouth and scrolled jaw; his vast, shadowed bulk still blending with the blue of the sea. The glittering mouth yawned beneath the boat like an open-doored marble tomb" (*MD,* 549).

The relentless pursuit and decoration of prey that caused Melville to describe the *Pequod* as a "tomb" was for him the same as calling it a hearse: "The ship! The hearse!" (*MD*, 571). The *San Dominick*'s life-destroying business led him, as we shall see, to provide, in this respect, perfect symmetry between the two works by describing the *San Dominick* as both a hearse and a tomb. These are easily among the more powerful images conveyed in the two works.[10]

The reference to the *Pequod* as a "cannibal of a craft" enables us to hold *Moby-Dick* and *Benito Cereno* in focus as the death image of the bone of a skeleton is invoked. To explain this particular resonance, we must go to "The Try-Works," chapter 96 of *Moby-Dick,* in which Melville states that "the harpooners wildly gesticulated with their huge pronged forks and dippers; as the wind howled on, and the sea leaped, and the ship groaned and dived, and yet steadfastly shot her red hell further into the blackness of the sea and the night, and scornfully champed the white bone in her mouth" (*MD*, 423). An analogue is created when Melville, aware that the historical Delano was the subconscious victim of a crime committed by an uncle, has the fictional Delano vaguely harbor that disturbing thought as he awaits the return of *Rover,* his whale-boat. Aware that the uncle helped cannibalize an Indian child, he gazes into the distance attempting to make out objects on the surface of the ocean, and remembers having heard that "long calms" can result in morbid thoughts. Soon thereafter, as he glances toward his boat, he thinks to himself: "Ha! . . . there's Rover; good dog; a white bone in her mouth. A pretty big bone though, it seems to me.—What? Yes, she has fallen afoul of the bubbling tide-rip there" (*BC*, 77).[11]

[II]

An especially subtle intimation of death is directed at Delano, an ocean breeze, but he does not take notice as "the ghostly cat's paw came fanning his cheek." Instead, his glance immediately

> fell upon the row of small, round dead-lights—all closed like coppered eyes of the coffined—and the state-cabin door, once connecting with the gallery, even as the dead-lights had once looked out upon it, but now calked fast like a sarcophagus lid . . . and he bethought him of the time, when that state-cabin and this state-balcony had heard the voices of the Spanish king's officers, and the forms of the Lima viceroy's daughters had perhaps leaned where he stood—as these and other images flitted through his mind, as the cat's paw through the cabin,

gradually he felt rising a dreamy inquietude, like that of one who alone on the prairie feels unrest from the repose of the noon. (*BC,* 74)

Thus Melville suggests that the ghostly breeze that fanned Delano's cheek is as much a sign of the ship's horrid business as the proclamations of the bell. Significantly, there is one more mention, as we shall see, of the breeze as a symbol of death, and once more he would not comprehend. In fact, he but vaguely takes in the ship's dire condition even as portions of it fall apart, threatening personal injury. Indeed, he leans against a balustrade that, partly covered with moss and partly stained with pitch, "seemed the charred ruin of some summer-house in a grand garden long running to waste." As he searches the waters for his boat and bends forward to gain a better view, the balustrade, like charcoal, gives way before him. Had he "not clutched an out-reaching rope he would have fallen into the sea." There followed the "crash, though feeble, and the fall, though hollow, of the rotten fragments" into the water (*BC,* 74, 75).

There is no indication that Delano regards one sign of decay as more disturbing than another, and thus "the principal relic of faded grandeur—the ample oval of the shield-like stern-piece," which immortalizes him in literary history, would not likely, even had he seen it, have meant much to him (*BC,* 49). And despite evidence of "corroded main-chains" that were "messy and rusty in link, shackle and bolt," that "seemed even more fit for the ship's present business than the one for which she had been built," he cannot put it all together (*BC,* 74). It never really hits home that slavery is leading both the ship and Don Benito to ruin. The American's failure to understand what is transpiring plunges him into a dangerous conviction that Don Benito is plotting against him, which leads to a murderous, though not altogether constant, form of paranoia.

In this regard, we are reminded of the atmosphere described at the outset of the novella when the horrors of the voyage were recounted for Delano's benefit. He had then recalled that the Spaniard's manner had about it a "gloomy hesitancy and subterfuge" that seemed brought on by evil. But as the recounting continued, Don Benito's story "corroborated not only the wailing ejaculations of the indiscriminate multitude, white and black, but likewise . . . the very expression and play of every human feature, which Captain Delano saw." For the moment, Delano thought, "If Don Benito's story was, throughout, an invention, then every soul on board, down to the youngest negress, was his carefully drilled recruit in the plot: an incredible inference" (*BC,* 68–69).

Certainly conspiracy had seemed real enough when Babo and Don Benito somewhat "discourteously crossed over" from Delano to linger "round the corner of the elevated skylight" and "began whispering together in low voices" (*BC*, 63). Such whisperings reach their most dangerous form when Babo proposes that the Spaniard "gain from Amasa Delano full particulars about his ship, and crew, and arms," but Don Benito reacts by refusing to ask the desired questions, which leads Babo to show him "the point of his dagger" and, after the answers are secured, to inform Don Benito that he will be, that very night, the captain of two ships (*BC*, 110).

Amid the whispers, Delano misses the opportunity to understand such a strange phenomenon, placing more emphasis on the lack of etiquette of the host and servant than on the temerity of a black whispering, under any circumstances, to his master. All Delano makes of his secretiveness is that Don Benito has lost a certain "stateliness" and that the familiarity of the servant has "lost its original charm of simple-hearted attachment" (*BC*, 63–64). Thus, he concludes, Don Benito's swings in behavior were accountable on "one or two suppositions—innocent lunacy, or wicked imposture." Delano chose the latter: "The man was an imposter. Some low-born adventurer, masquerading as an oceanic grandee; yet so ignorant of the first requisites of mere gentlemanhood as to be betrayed into the present remarkable indecorum." Even so, he concludes brutally and with mounting alarm, "under the aspect of infantile weakness, the most savage energies might be couched—those velvets of the Spaniard but the silky paw to his fangs" (*BC*, 64, 65).

The despotism of Don Benito's authority, however, is an estimate that Delano finds difficult to sustain, and more than once he chastises himself for thinking the Spaniard means him harm. Seeing Don Benito propped up by Babo is not incidental to his concluding, if only momentarily, that he has misjudged him. Indeed, as he notices Don Benito's "meagre form in the act of recovering itself from reclining in the servant's arms," into which he had fallen, "he could not but marvel at the panic by which [he] had been surprised, on the darting suspicion that such a commander," bereft of all self-command, was "going to bring about his murder" (*BC*, 80).

As Delano awaits the return of his whale-boat with supplies for the distraught crew, his attention is drawn to an unsettling event: "two blacks, to all appearances accidentally incommoded by one of the sailors, flew out against him with horrible curses, which the sailor somewhat resenting, the two blacks dashed him to the deck and jumped upon him, despite the earnest cries of the oakum-pickers." "'Don Benito,' asked Captain Delano, 'do you see what is going on there? Look!'" At that point, Don Benito, seized by a cough, staggers and begins to fall before Babo rescues him, applying the cordial (*BC*, 70). Any concern that Delano had about Don Benito's reaction to such a violent scene quickly evaporates, trumped by Babo's having so quickly met his master's needs, and so, smiling, he asks, "'Tell me, Don Benito . . . I should like to have your man here, myself—what will you take for him? Would fifty doubloons be any object?'" "'Master wouldn't part with Babo for a thousand doubloons,' murmured the black, overhearing the offer, and taking it in earnest, and, with the strange vanity of a faithful slave, appreciated by his master, scorning to hear so paltry a valuation put upon him by a stranger" (*BC,* 70–71).

In this regard, the Delano of *Voyages* could not put a meaningful valuation on Africans any more than he could measure the character of New Guinea blacks. Again and again, he engages in almost casual discussion of slavery, which helps explain the fictional Delano's desire to purchase Babo. Based on a reading of *Voyages* and the novella, the two Delanos are of one mind on the question of slavery. It does not occur to either to question its legitimacy or to consider slaves a part of the human family. Moreover, Delano in *Voyages* is a champion of European supremacy in general. Concerning New Guinea blacks, he reports that when Europeans first visited New Guinea, "the natives manifested no spirit of enmity" until whites began seizing them "for the most selfish and inhuman purposes." Actually, it was common for whites "to hook the yard tackles of a ship to a canoe, hoist her on deck with all the crew in her, transport them, and sell them as slaves" (Delano, 81 and 82). So there was much hatred of whites and a desire for revenge.

Here follows what Melville read in the New Guinea chapter of *Voyages* that helps inform *Benito Cereno*'s magnificently crafted shaving scene:

> We had now found how dangerous a duty this is at New Guinea. . . . I confess, that I felt myself relieved when the command of this excursion was given to another. I felt that I should never see old White again. We kept hostages however on board from among the savages to secure his safe return. When he was out of sight, he says, that the chief pulled a knife out of his basket, drew the edge of it across his own throat, counted his fingers, and pointed to his neck, to show how many heads he had cut off with his knife, and then would rub it across White's throat to prove how convenient the instrument was for the purpose of beheading a man . . . White, after all this variety of intercourse with the chief and the natives, returned to us as pale as a sheet. (Delano, 97)[12]

That development, acted out symbolically, was related to how the natives were rewarded for fighting whites. A black might be made a chief for bringing in a white man's head. "If he will bring three, they will make him a chief of the first rank. The causes of this hatred are, in great measure, traceable to our own misconduct toward them" (Delano, 80). The quick irrelevance of that misconduct for Delano in *Voyages* is fundamental to Melville's construction of his character in the novella. Moreover, when whites, wanting to enter an area of New Guinea occupied by Malays, were advised not to because of the many disputes that had arisen over white behaviour toward Malay women, Delano joined those trying to dissuade the Malay people from relying on past experience with whites. "We pledged," he writes, "that no improprieties of this nature, or of any other, should be committed by us, and satisfied them that our objects were those only of gaining information and gratifying a laudable curiosity." When whites were seen heading toward the shore where Malays lived, Malay women immediately left their homes with their children and ran into the woods (Delano, 84). This undoubtedly was agreed upon in advance by Malay men and women. The Delano of *Voyages* is no more concerned about Malay slaves than the Delano of *Benito Cereno* is about enslaved blacks on the *San Dominick*. If the offer to buy Babo had grated on Don Benito's nerves, Delano, as he neared Don Benito's cabin, was unaware that this had been the case. Nor were downcast thoughts of Babo being a slave on his mind. As he reached Don Benito's cabin door, he was prepared, as ever, to continue supporting slavery.

[III]

Delano's spirits are buoyed when he enters Don Benito's cabin and "through the cabin windows a slight rippling of the sea was discerned; and from the desired direction." "'There,' he said, 'I told you so, Don Benito, look!'" (*BC*, 91). At that time, the dreary sound of the forecastle bell resounds in Don Benito's ear, and a ghostly cat's paw, like the one that fanned Delano's cheek, fanned the Spaniard's cheek. Despite the fluttering curtain "against his pale cheek," Don Benito "seemed to have even less welcome for the breeze than the calm" (*BC*, 91). Still unaware that the *San Dominick* is a death ship, Delano has no inkling that the slave-trading Spaniard's relationship to death, and to internal decay, is intensely personal. With no understanding of the captain's plight, he leaves Don Benito's cabin.

Delano gains the deck to find Atufal "monumentally fixed at the threshold, like one of those sculptured porters of black marble guarding the porches of Egyptian tombs" (*BC*, 92).[13] Less than previously, he fails to appreciate why Atufal, this last time, has been summoned, no doubt because he thinks the whites are in control. Moreover, Atufal's refusals to ask for forgiveness further blind him to realities beneath the pose. And we are reminded, once more, of "subtle designs that are hidden away in the recesses," this time of a design that is associated less with Africa than with Europe.

This is so because Atufal has opportunities to seek a pardon just as an unrepentant Spanish woman, at the close of the eighteenth century, had similar opportunities. In developing the refusal of Atufal to ask for forgiveness, a re-solve underscored by his intimidating size, Melville worked splendidly from a passage in *Voyages and Travels* that reveals the source of the pardon idea in the novella, and the source of a hitherto unexamined feature of Babo's relationship to Spanish religious and political authority:

> They paid her a visit expecting that they should be able to convince her of her error . . . but they found themselves very much mistaken. She told them that the clergy were impostors; that they were oppress-ing the people . . . On which they took her into the court- house, or prison of the inquisition, and held an ecclesiastical court to try her for heresy. She was found guilty, and sentenced to be placed astride on [sic] an ass . . . and conveyed in that situation across the bridge to the common place of execution . . . and there to be beheaded, and her body burned; with the proviso, that if she would repent before crossing the bridge, and make a humble confession of her fault, and ask forgiveness, she should be pardoned. (Delano, 496)

The woman was frequently asked if she wanted to be pardoned "but all was to no purpose," Delano reports.[14]

Delano is initially startled on seeing Atufal at the threshold, but his alarm passes as he observes him "singularly attesting docility even in sullenness." The spectacle reminds him that as lax as Don Benito's authority might some-times be, "whenever he chose to exert it, no man so savage or colossal but must, more or less, bow" (*BC*, 92). Confidently grasping a trumpet hanging from the bulwarks and stepping forth freely, Delano begins to give orders, in the best Spanish that he can muster, and the Negroes and sailors, all pleased, begin heading the ship toward the harbor, the blacks apparently singing in Spanish as they work. Ominously, but not to his reckoning, Delano hears Babo's voice "faithfully repeating his orders" in Spanish, "and no brace or halyard was pulled," he feels, "but to the blithe songs of the inspired negroes." Evidently he is not surprised that, having been greeted by their chorus of woe on boarding, the blacks and whites are now happy to be returning to shore. "Good fellows," he thought, "a little training would make fine sailors of them. Why see, the very women pull and sing too. These must be some of those Ashantee negresses that make such capital soldiers, I've heard" (*BC*, 92).

Checking who is at the helm, he finds one whose hopefulness and con-fidence, in contrast to an earlier "shame-faced" air, are buoyed by the breeze, and exclaims, "Ah, it is you, my man . . . Good hand, I trust? And want to get into the harbor, don't you?" With inward delight and firmly grasping the tiller-head, Delano does not notice that the man is being eyed intently by a black on either side of each pulley end. After seeing how things are at the forecastle and giving last orders to the sailors, he decides to report developments to Benito Cereno. This is a good time to do so, he thinks, because Babo is engaged on deck, which would allow him finally to have an undisturbed conversation with the Spaniard (*BC*, 92, 93).

As he considers the most expeditious way of returning to Don Benito's cabin, he not only remains unaware of the violence that has occurred below deck but has forgotten what was once his major concern. Even when thinking of yet another trip below, at no time does he remember that he had once worried that his destruction was being plotted there by men acting in collusion with Don Benito: "And might not that same undiminished Spanish crew, alleged to have perished off to a remnant," he had thought, be "lurking in the hold?" That thought had led him even to imagine "fiends in human form," to conjure up Malay pirates, known to clear their decks "beneath which prowled a hundred spears with yellow arms ready to upthrust through the mats" (*BC*, 68).

Horrific things, of which Delano is totally unaware, had indeed taken place below deck, including bloodletting resulting from hatchet-polishers using hatchets to gash and mangle Alexandro Aranda, the rich owner of the ship and all the slaves. Aranda's failure to understand had set the stage for the first terrible explosion of violence that placed the blacks in charge of the *San Dominick*. Some weeks later, when Ashantees entered his berth with hatchets and raised them against him, that earlier miscalculation was tantamount to having ordered his own death. Then, too, a Spaniard in a nearby berth, awakened by Aranda's crying aloud and seeing the bloody hatchets, leaped through darkness to his death in the sea. Aranda's abrupt, agonized cries, moreover, alarmed Spaniards below, who, cowering, wondered if their deaths were imminent. But that was not all. An Ashantee performed funereal rites on Aranda's body and yet another Spaniard was "made away with" below deck (*BC*, 106–7; 111–13).

Melville suggests, therefore, that Delano is descending into a possible death trap, a theme he develops still more by equating slavery with entombment as Atufal, resembling the Egyptian porter, reminds us. Babo, however, prefers that no harm should come to the American unless the liberty of the blacks is put in jeopardy. Without the slightest understanding of what the future might hold, Delano considers how best to go below to Don Benito's cabin: "From opposite sides, there were, beneath the poop, two approaches to the cabin; one further forward than the other, and consequently communicating with a longer passage. Marking the servant still above, Captain Delano, taking the nighest entrance—the one last named, and at whose porch Atufal still stood—hurried on his way, till, arrived at the cabin threshold, he paused an instant, a little to recover from his eagerness. Then, with the words of his intended business upon his lips, he entered" (*BC,* 93).

And yet he hears "another footstep keeping time with his. From the opposite door, a salver in hand, the servant was likewise advancing." "Confound the faithful fellow," thinks Delano, but his vexation is countered in some degree by a breeze that he thinks would hold and increase. Still, "he felt a slight twinge, from a sudden indefinite association in his mind of Babo with Atufal." "By the way," he says to Don Benito, "your tall man and time-piece, Atufal, stands without. By your order, of course?" The remark is made in a way, we are told, that offered no handle for a response, and Don Benito recoils, saying nothing until Babo, adjusting a cushion for him, somehow reminds him that a response is needed. He responds, saying, "You are right. The slave appears where you saw him, according to my command; which is, that if at the given hour I am below, he must take his stand and abide my coming." "Ah, now, pardon me," returns Delano, "but that is treating the poor fellow like an ex-king indeed. Ah, Don Benito . . . for all the license you permit in some things, I fear lest, at bottom, you are a bitter hard master" (*BC,* 93, 94). Don Benito shrinks, Delano thinks, as if stung by a twinge of conscience. As Delano directs his attention to the movement of the keel cleaving the sea, the wind steadily rises and the ship is borne swiftly on toward the harbor.

When it rounds a point of land and Delano's *Bachelor's Delight* comes into view, Delano again repairs to the deck, where he remains for awhile before returning below to cheer up Don Benito. "Better and better," he blithely cries as he enters to forecast an end to Don Benito's cares, at least for a while, explaining, "For when, after a long, sad voyage, you know, the anchor drops in the haven, all its vast weight seems lifted from the captain's heart. We are getting on famously, Don Benito. My ship is within sight" (*BC,* 94).

In a buoyant mood, Delano urges Don Benito to look through a side-light and see "all a-taunt-o! The *Bachelor's Delight,*" before issuing an invitation to the Spaniard: "Come, you must take a cup of coffee with me this evening. My old steward will give you as fine a cup as ever any sultan tasted. What say you, Don Benito, will you?" (*BC,* 94). Almost instinctively the Spaniard casts a look of longing toward Delano's ship as Babo gazes into his face, which causes Don Benito to assume an air of coldness before dropping back into his cushioned seat, silent. The American presses the invitation, "You do not answer. Come, all day you have been my host; would you have hospitality all on one side?" "I cannot go," retorts Don Benito. At that Delano seeks to ease things for him, stating that the ships would be so close together that Don Benito would be able to step "from deck to deck, which is but as from room to room. Come, come, you must not refuse me." Babo's gaze into his master's face, however, has its intended effect, for Don Benito, biting his nails and glaring at Delano with "cadaverous sullenness," answers that he cannot go (*BC,* 94). Again the American returns to the deck and finds the *San Dominick* only two miles from the sealer, with his small boat "darting over the interval." Before long, the two ships lie "anchored together." Delano decides to report to Don Benito, and to say goodbye (*BC,* 95).

But Don Benito is even less forthcoming, and Delano withdraws from the cabin. As he faces the dark corridor, he has a premonition that trouble awaits him. In fact, he is scarcely halfway "in the narrow corridor, dim as a tunnel, leading from the cabin to the stairs, when a sound, as of the tolling for execution in some jail-yard, fell on his ears," a thought inspired in part by the "execution stool" carried by the slave in *Journal of a Residence in Ashantee.*[15] When the ship's flawed bell tolls for execution, its echo "drearily reverberated" below, in what is, according to Melville, a "subterranean vault," causing Delano, vaguely sensing that he is indeed caught in a death trap, to pause, his consciousness swarming "with superstitious suspicions." "In images far swifter than these sentences," Melville writes, "the minutest details of all his former distrusts swept through him" (*BC,* 95–96). Still in the corridor, he recalls Benito Cereno's equivocal behavior, how he "had risen to his feet . . . motioned toward his hat; then, in an instant, all was eclipsed in sinister muteness and gloom. Did this imply one brief, repentant relenting at the final moment, from some iniquitous plot, followed by remorseless return to it? His last glance seemed to express a calamitous, yet acquiescent farewell to Captain Delano forever. Why decline the invitation to visit the sealer that evening? Or was the Spaniard less hardened than the Jew, who refrained not from supping at the board of him whom the same night he meant to betray?" (*BC,* 96).

It appears Atufal foreshadowed deeper shadows. Delano wonders if Atufal, alerted by the bell, would stand between him and the deck, "Atufal, the pretended rebel, but punctual shadow." He considers the possibility that Atufal, "a sentry, and more," not a mere captive, might be lurking "by the threshold without." "Who, by his own confession, had stationed him there? Was the negro now lying in wait?" Delano seemed trapped. "The Spaniard behind—his creature before: to rush from darkness to light was the involuntary choice" open to him. Melville indicates the real nature of the danger Delano faces as he has him just as involuntarily—"with clenched jaw and hand"—pass Atufal before standing "unharmed in the light." He is not yet safe, however, for Babo has assigned "the six Ashantees, without anyone else" to take the ship because most of Delano's crew, after his return, would be away fishing. But thinking Atufal is chained, and observing "nature taking

her innocent repose in the evening," "the screened sun in . . . the west shin-
ing out like the mild light from Abraham's tent," Delano's "jaw and hand
relaxed" (*BC,* 96–97, 110). By writing that Delano, tense from possible danger, relaxed his jaw and hand, Melville invoked, for the final time in *Benito
Cereno,* the Ashantee trophy principle, but with such subtlety that he seems
actually to be encouraging the thought that there is nothing unusual about
Delano's behavior.

Shortly thereafter, Delano leaves the *San Dominick* and, after subduing
Babo, quickly makes his way to the *Bachelor's Delight.* Upon arrival, he ex-
horts his men to pursue and overpower the black revolutionaries or never
to show their faces again. And as his men pursue the *San Dominick,* it seems
to them that some of the Spaniards, thanks to the pressures of the masquerade, are collaborating with the blacks. One supposed collaborator is killed
because the sailors, thinking him in some way favoring the blacks, fire two
balls at him, "so that he fell wounded from the rigging, and was drowned in
the sea." As a final emblem of Babo's brilliant masquerade, a Spaniard with
his hatchet tied upright in his hand and facing out toward the attackers, is
"shot for a renegade seaman." With a certain confusion, then, the sailors attacked as they approached the *San Dominick,* earlier described by Melville as
a "slumbering volcano" (*BC,* 113, 68).

At this point, Melville restates a central theme of this chapter and, in so
doing, reminds us of Ashantee influences as the battle intensifies:

> With creaking masts, she came heavily round to the wind; the prow
> slowly swinging into view of the boats, its skeleton gleaming in the
> horizontal moonlight, and casting a gigantic ribbed shadow upon the
> water. One extended arm of the ghost seemed beckoning the whites
> to avenge it.
> "Follow your leader!" cried the mate; and one on each bow, the
> boats boarded. Sealing-spears and cutlasses crossed hatchets and hand-
> spikes. Huddled upon the long-boat amidships, the negresses raised a
> wailing chant, whose chorus was the clash of steel. (*BC,* 102)

And so the Ashantee womens' songs charge the blacks with renewed energy
for a while. But the whites, armed with muskets, sabers, and pikes, irresist-
ibly drive the Negroes toward the stern. Still, the blacks, emboldened by the
melancholy music and dance, fight heroically (*BC,* 102, 103).

A disturbing image of them, however, seems to call into question the very
purpose of their revolt: "Exhausted, the blacks now fought in despair. Their
red tongues lolled, wolf-like, from their black mouths" (*BC,* 102). Such a
description is unsettling, unless one probes beneath surfaces, and "Sketch

Fourth" of *The Encantadas* allows us once again to do so. A passage from "Sketch Fourth" provides an elegant solution to the problem before us, for in it Melville writes, "Cut a channel in the above letter joint, and the middle transverse limb is Narborough, and all the rest is Albermarle. Volcanic Narborough lies in the black jaws of Albermarle like a wolf's red tongue in his open mouth" (*EN,* 14).[16] The revolutionary release of energy on the *San Dominick* was as natural a reaction as a volcanic eruption.

Perhaps in the end, in some degree, Benito Cereno, knowing what suffering slave trading has brought him, understands that he captained a death ship, which Delano never understood, arguing, "See, yon bright sun has forgotten it all, and the blue sea, and the blue sky; these have turned over new leaves" (*BC,* 116). But Don Benito responds, "Because they have no memory; because they are not human," which enables Delano to reveal a complete and final lack of understanding of what had transpired that day: "But these mild trades that now fan your cheek, do they not come with a human-like healing to you? Warm friends, steadfast friends are the trades." "With their steadfastness they but waft me to my tomb, Señor," is Don Benito's response. "You are saved," cries Captain Delano, more and more astonished and pained; "you are saved: what has cast such a shadow upon you?" "The negro," Melville has Don Benito reply, and adds, "There was silence, while the moody man sat, slowly and unconsciously gathering his mantle about him, as if it were a pall" (*BC,* 116).

Though Babo's lieutenant in all, Atufal, loses his life as the sailors attempt to board, Babo survives the battle to face court proceedings. On the first day of those proceedings, Benito Cereno is ordered to appear in court, "which he did in his litter, attended by the monk Infelez; of whom he received the oath, which he took by God, our Lord, and a sign of the Cross." The court decrees that Babo be dragged across the Rimac Bridge and beheaded, his body burned, like the Spanish woman who defied Church/State authority and was dragged across that bridge to the place of execution. Hence Melville's model for Babo suffered a similar fate (*BC,* 103–104, 116–17). Like her, he acted in defiance of the Church of powerful, reactionary Spanish Americans.

The sad truth is that Melville, when thinking of *Moby-Dick*'s relationship to *Benito Cereno,* and at times of the works individually, of necessity communed alone, with little expectation that circumstances would change in his lifetime. No doubt he kept similar counsel when thinking of the uses to which he put *The Encantadas* and *Voyages and Travels* in creating *Benito Cereno.* But he must have experienced lasting unhappiness in knowing that African cultural influences that join the two great works were not only invisible to critics but foreign to what they considered worthy of attention.

It would hardly have been less disturbing to him that resonances between *Benito Cereno* and *Moby-Dick*, noted in this chapter, would not be recognized for more than 150 years after their publication.

We now turn to Melville's characterizations of the hatchet-polishers, Amasa Delano and Benito Cereno, and find these dimensions of his creative process no less far reaching than the discoveries we have just made. And, once again, at critical points, the organic relationship between *The Encantadas* and *Benito Cereno,* and *Moby-Dick* and *Benito Cereno,* will be taken into account.

CHAPTER III

The Hatchet-Polishers,
Benito Cereno, and Amasa Delano

Narborough, the loftiest land of the cluster; no soil whatever; one
seamed clinker from top to bottom; abounding in black caves like
smithies; its metallic shore ringing under foot like plates of iron; its
central volcanoes standing grouped like a gigantic chimney-stack.
—*Herman Melville, "Sketch Fourth," The Encantadas*

In the ballet of the hatchets of Benito Cereno, we are
dramatically made aware again of the unparalleled breadth
of vision of Herman Melville.
—*Samuel W. Allen*

"Sketch Fourth" of Melville's *The Encantadas* offers astonishing insight, conveyed in a handful of words, into how Melville created the hatchet-polishers. That insight is in many ways analogous to the rich store of information in Joseph Dupuis's *Journal of a Residence in Ashantee,* on which Melville drew heavily in their creation. Though relatively little attention is devoted to "Sketch Fourth," it is decisive in helping us solve the problem of how the hatchet-polishers were brought into being, which has heretofore scarcely been touched on. Perhaps the very mystery and brilliance of their depiction in *Benito Cereno* contributed to the belief that there was little left to probe, a consideration doubtless reinforced by the foreignness of Ashantees to Americans. A great work such as *Benito Cereno* was thus read for generations without our understanding the degree of artistry that went into the making of some important characters.[1]

Atufal, as we have seen, suffered similar neglect over a similar period of time, and so the complexity of Melville's creative process, especially in *Benito Cereno,* has at best been but partially perceived. More will be added in this chapter concerning the relative neglect of other notable additions to the list of characters in the novella and in world literature. I refer especially to Amasa Delano, whose literary origins have been more assumed than demonstrated, and to Benito Cereno, who has, in that regard, largely been ignored. As the hatchet-polishers and Delano head the list of virtually unexamined characters and Benito Cereno is in need of further exploration, what Melville has concealed from us about their creation offers fertile ground for discussion.

Although "Sketch Fourth" of *The Encantadas* provides an indispensable component of the characterization of the hatchet-polishers, the context of their creation—and more besides—is derived from Melville's reading of Joseph Dupuis's *Journal*. "Sketch Fourth" and the *Journal* complement each other almost perfectly to help us see how Melville created the black warriors on the *San Dominick*. We will take up the *Journal* first, because it provides the wider context of their creation and, hence, how they relate to the novella as a whole.

For the chief traits of the hatchet-polishers against which the findings in this chapter may be measured, we begin with the "finished phase" of their characterization, their first depiction in *Benito Cereno*. It comes after we are introduced to the oakum-pickers, with whom they work in concert on board the *San Dominick*. An unusual sight under any circumstances, to come upon the oakum-pickers and hatchet-polishers from the blank ocean heightens the aura of mystery about them.

The oakum-pickers are elevated conspicuously on the poop. They are four in number, elderly and grizzled, "their heads like black, doddered willow tops, who in venerable contrast to the tumult below them, were couched sphinx-like, one on the starboard cat-head, another on the larboard, and the remaining pair face to face on the opposite bulwarks above the main chains." These elders are positioned to see all that is happening on the ship. They can drop down to move among others below or call forth from their perch to prevent the revolt from being unmasked by strangers boarding the ship. As they pick small, unstranded old junk into oakum, they accompany their task "with a continuous, low, monotonous chant; droning and drooling like so many gray-headed bag-pipers playing a funeral march."[2]

Sitting cross-legged on the poop, eight feet above the throng below, six hatchet-polishers form a row, separated at regular intervals, with rusty hatchets in their hands. With "a bit of brick and a rag," each is "engaged like a scullion in scouring; while between each two" is a "stack of hatchets, their rusted edges turned forward awaiting a like operation." Melville writes that all six, unlike the blacks generally, have "the raw aspect of unsophisticated Africans" (*BC,* 50). Moreover, "Though occasionally the four oakum-pickers would briefly address some person or persons in the crowd below, yet the six hatchet-polishers neither spoke to others, nor breathed a whisper among themselves, but sat intent upon their task, except at intervals, when, with the peculiar love in Negroes of uniting industry with pastime, two-

and-two they sideways clashed their hatchets together, like cymbals, with a barbarous din" (*BC, 50*).

We have in effect read the sections on the hatchet-polishers, as we once did those on Atufal, without probing to see how they were brought into being. But Melville's creative process in fashioning the hatchet-polishers, we have discovered, enhances our understanding of how much else was created even when not seeking more than one solution. In other words, while searching for solutions to a particular problem, we have discovered "solutions" to "problems"—the creation of Atufal, Aranda's skeleton, and more—that were not even conceived previously.

The vast landscape of Melville's creative imagination enables him—and ultimately the reader—to see in his creative process particular creations in relation to each other.

[I]

Though we will never know the precise order in which Melville read—and reread—"Sketch Fourth" and Dupuis's *Journal of a Residence in Ashantee* as he created the hatchet-polishers, knowing the sequence is less important than knowing the relevant materials that went into their making. What does appear certain, however, is that he thought about the hatchet-polishers over some time and was reminded of their origin in materials from which characters and scenes in *Moby-Dick* were also created.

As we read Dupuis, we get a relatively clear sense of how Melville developed aspects of the hatchet-polishers apart from the hatchets. Suddenly, most of the necessary choices are identified and brought together to take on the qualities of character of those whom we know as the hatchet-polishers. Almost at the beginning of his *Journal,* Dupuis writes, "The distant tinkling of an iron castanet now attracted our notice, as it announced the approach of strangers; another instant presented to our view a party of five Ashantees" (Dupuis, 5).[3] Though the discovery of Ashantees with musical instruments is promising, the number is not the number we seek. So, too, is the use of the castanet promising, because in the novella, the hatchet-polishers use their hatchets musically and as weapons.

The conjunction of five Ashantees with mention that one of them is decorated with a trophy and is "fastening a human jawbone to . . . a little ivory blowing horn" is related to big issues in chapter 2 and provides some sense of the cultural framework in which the hatchet-polishers may be placed. Their warrior character is underlined when Dupuis, asking the

Ashantee how the trophies were come by, cannot get a satisfactory answer, but is convinced that "the question was of a gratifying nature, in as much as it was interpreted into a compliment of [Ashantee] military prowess" (Dupuis, 5). Even so, of course, six Ashantees are needed to match the number of hatchet-polishers in *Benito Cereno*.

Matters are further illuminated rather quickly, enabling us to see how Melville, in *Benito Cereno*, went about creating a group of Ashantees working side by side, combining martial prowess with music making. "On leaving the swamp, we caught the distant tinkling of the castanet, and at the turning of an angle fell in with six Ashantees" (Dupuis, 21). Here we have Melville's source for the six Ashantees in *Benito Cereno*, who are paired into three groups, an extraordinary revelation. As we follow Dupuis's journey, we begin to understand how Melville came to fashion particular character traits for the hatchet-polishers and to decide on some vital aspects of *Benito Cereno*'s plot. And we come to understand Dupuis's self-satisfaction as he moves among blacks on the African continent. At one point a "concourse of spectators" collects to show respect for "white men," which fills Dupuis with pride, as every face is "stamped with those genuine feelings of respectful admiration" (Dupuis, 42).

Melville read that Dupuis thinks Africans are ever pleased to have whites among them, and that they have good reason to feel that way. He also saw that Dupuis has virtually nothing good to say about blacks that is not watered down to an insult. Dupuis's lack of respect for blacks takes on a particularly perverse quality in relation to African women and children, and we are reminded of Delano, on the *San Dominick*, whose attention was "drawn to a slumbering Negress, partly disclosed through the lace-work of some rigging, lying, with youthful limbs carelessly disposed, under the lee of the bulwarks, like a doe in the shade of a woodland rock" (*BC*, 73). The comparison is apt, for Dupuis speaks of one Ashantee location in which he sees, as he crosses a rivulet, "a party of women and young girls, skipping over the rocks, and laving their limbs in the current." Continuing, he speaks of "the nymphs of the African wilderness" not "wanting in the decorum of the sex, for they modestly screened their persons amidst the foliage" (Dupuis, 52).

The analogue is strengthened. As the young woman in the novella sleeps, Delano reports, "her fawn" is "stark naked, its little body half lifted from the deck . . . ; its hands, like two paws, clambering upon her; its mouth and nose ineffectually rooting to get at the mark; and meantime giving a vexatious grunt, blending in with the composed snore of the Negress" (*BC*, 73). Dupuis follows with an extended statement revealing the Englishman's sexual longings that could well explain why Melville depicts Ashantee women with unalloyed hatred of white men in the novella:

I was next honoured with a visit by a female member of the royal family, a daughter of the king, whose age was probably about ten years . .
. A sugar offering to the princess, with the addition of a little rum to
the attendants, introduced us to a familiar acquaintance at sight. The
matrons endeavored to win my notice to their ward, by intimating that
she was very fond of white men's caresses; but her timidity gave a flat
contradiction to the assertion. I endeavored to soothe her therefore, in
language somewhat adapted to the female ear, but the compliments I
paid were unaccountably appropriated by my auditresses to their own
youth and beauty, or to other inclinations; for they assured me by way
of reply, that although the princess was young, yet in a very few moons
she would be ready to take to wife; and if I admired her, they had no
doubt that the king would give her to me. (Dupuis, 62)

Though that child was not given to him, Dupuis says an invitation was offered him "to select a favorite *without scruple,* and keep her as long as [he]
thought fit" (Dupuis, 62, italics mine). He does not say whether he did or
did not.

Though a mounting, full-throated blare of music announces that he is
to be received by an important Ashantee chief, Dupuis thinks the sound is
nothing more than music. He clings to that interpretation even though, as
a stranger, he is often approached in a disrespectful way. On one occasion,
Ashantees shout out "strong names" in his presence—the names of those
who have performed heroic deeds—and brandish weapons. At one such
moment, an avenue is prepared through a mass of Ashantee males along
which Dupuis, touching the hands of numerous chiefs, advances in single
file to meet a more esteemed chief. As he does, a number of boys wave weapons over his head (Dupuis, 42).

He is hardly a favorite of the blacks, as another round of music indicates,
but he seems wholly unaware of the possibility that he was being viewed
without admiration, especially because the very sight of one instrument was
as suggestive of possible danger as its sound. Made from the horn "of an
enormous buffalo, which was decorated with a profusion of human jaw-
bones," it emits "abrupt, incessant blasts of the most dismal howling." As a
chief moves forward to take Dupuis's hand, a number of the chief's under-
ling soldiers repeat "strong names" with what even Dupuis describes as "of-
fensive intrusion." Still, he adds concerning the chief, "On a sudden he burst
from the crowd, and as he took me by the hand, perfect order and silence
ensued" (Dupuis, 43).

Even as trophy-bearing horns sound with mounting intensity, Dupuis
is befuddled by the horns, never reasoning that they might be blaring with

such disturbing effect because of his presence. A curious misadventure takes place when he arrives with his party in Coomassy, the Ashantee capitol, and a procession leads down an avenue to the Palace-gate. According to Dupuis, "The clamorous songs of my people, as the procession moved on, joined to the novel sound of the bugle, appeared to animate every countenance with tumultuous joy, which was momentarily subdued only as a royal *blunderbuss salutation* burst full, as it may be expressed, in my face" (Dupuis, 70).

Concerning Ashantee music, we read this important sentence from Dupuis: "Ivory horns, similarly ornamented, reed flutes, calabash rattles, and clanking bits of flat iron, composed the bands" (Dupuis, 71). We know that Melville focused on that sentence because he has Atufal, when facing Don Benito and refusing to utter the "one word, *pardon,*" slowly raise his arms and "let them lifelessly fall, his links clanking" (*BC*, 62). More fundamentally, flat iron can be imagined as the flat sides of hatchets being clashed together, which places us on the threshold of the solution to the problem.

In seeking it in precise terms, we turn to "Sketch Fourth" of *The Encantadas.* Melville might have derived the *idea* of hatchets from Narborough Isle, the sound of plates ringing there suggesting the flat sides of hatchets might work well in the novella with Ashantees clashing them together, but he might easily have associated such weapons with the warriors encountered in the Dupuis volume. He understood, in any event, that although not many weapons could be clashed together for musical purposes, hatchets could. Castanets were, therefore, ruled out, but not entirely, for they provided the ring of iron musically, and, in Dupuis, are associated with martial interests, but hardly as certainly as hatchets might be. In sum, two sources inspired Melville to treat the flat surface of iron: Dupuis's *Journal* and "Sketch Fourth," the latter especially. In that work, we recall a reference to metal "ringing under foot like plates of iron," language that examined more closely yields a definition of plate as "a flat, polished piece of metal" that can be "used in making armour," from which Melville, almost magically, created the "hatchet-polishers."[4]

With the flat sides of hatchets clashed together musically, the necessary military and artistic requirements are met for protecting the revolt on the *San Dominick.* The *movement* of the hatchets as described by Melville is derived from Dupuis's mention of young boys standing before Ashantee war captains, "waving short scimitars and knives, which they flourished in threatening attitudes," of other boys "waving scimitars and swords over [Dupuis's] head" while yelling out the name and "heroic achievements" of their patron, and of slaves advancing, "flourishing their scimitars over [Dupuis's] head with menacing violence." Such movement of weapons led Melville to have the hatchet-polishers clash their hatchets overhead "like cymbals with a barbarous din," bringing to mind certain phrases from Dupuis: "barbaric clamour," "tumultuous din," and "incessant din" (Dupuis, 42, 72, 76).

So disturbed is Dupuis that he cannot hide his "sincere contempt—disgust I may say, for the music of the Ashantee." On one such occasion, the king of Banna, a tributary, read the Englishman's mind and, with the wave of a hand, "silenced his band" (Dupuis, 78, 79). Dupuis describes what happened next, saying that the king, face to face with him, "snatched a scimitar from a youth in attendance, while his people formed a silent and distant circle." The king's harangue becomes more and more furious, "associated with rapid and vehement gestures, and flourishings of his weapon," in Dupuis's words, "within two or three paces of my feet" (Dupuis, 79).

Dupuis writes that one evening, after darkness descends and people begin wandering away from a gathering, he beholds "a novel scene of regal splendour" as blazing torches are seen some distance away and the approach of the king is announced with "a burst from the king's band." An extraordinary development follows:

By the time the foremost torches had advanced within fifty paces of the spot where I was seated, a most harsh discordance of yells, shouts, and howls, assailed the ears in a sudden peal, heightened by a re-animated burst of instruments . . . Thus ended a moment's reflection; for on a sudden my guards were forced by a rush of the king's guards . . . A rally was then made round my chair, to screen my person from the rude buffets of the warlike mob, but all efforts proved ineffectual, and another rush knocked over my seat, and almost threw me upon the earth. . . . The king's guards were now in the midst of our party, some with large ivory horns and wooden drums, chiming together the most *excruciating* harmony I ever heard in my life; others with burning vegetable torches and crooked sabres, which they flourished in attitudes of defiance and threat; yet it was evident they wielded their weapons with caution. My soldiers at last rallied again, and by dint of main strength forced a passage through the crowd and gained for me a more secure station behind a tree where I met Messrs. Collins and Salmon, who had been swept away in the boisterous eddy, and had suffered as much jostling as myself. (Dupuis, 81–82)[5]

Melville uses that incident from Dupuis to create an unforgettable scene of vigilance when Delano's boat, *Rover,* returns to the *San Dominick* with fresh supplies and the oakum-pickers attempt to restrain the blacks, who, seeing casks of water and pumpkins in the bow, "hung over the bulwarks in disorderly raptures." As the casks are hoisted to the *San Dominick,* "when

some of the Negroes accidentally jostled Captain Delano," Delano "with
good-natured authority bade the blacks stand back," and did so with a half-
menacing, half-mirthful gesture, which drew a response from the blacks that
was proportionate to the perceived danger: "Instantly the blacks paused, just
where they were, each Negro and Negress suspended in his or her posture,
exactly as the word had found them—for a few seconds continuing so—
while, as between the responsive posts of a telegraph, an unknown syllable
ran from man to man among the perched oakum-pickers. While Captain
Delano's attention was fixed by this scene, suddenly the hatchet-polishers
half-rose, and a rapid cry came from Don Benito" (BC, 79).

To Delano, Don Benito's cry is a signal for him to be massacred.
He "would have sprung for his boat" had the oakum-pickers not dropped
"down into the crowd with earnest exclamations and forced every white and
every Negro back, at the same moment, with gestures friendly and familiar,
almost jocose, bidding him, in substance, not be a fool" (BC, 79). As they
did, "the hatchet-polishers resumed their seats, quietly as so many tailors, and
at once, as if nothing had happened, the work of hoisting in the casks was
resumed, whites and blacks singing at the tackle" (BC, 79–80).

The behavior of the oakum-pickers, cutting both ways, has somewhat
assuaged Delano's fear while strangely contributing to it. The association
of these old men with death is reinforced each time one of them rises from
his sphinx-like position to strike the forecastle bell. Though the bell had not
been rung when Don Benito cried aloud, he understands, subconsciously,
and perhaps for that reason more disturbingly, the oakum-pickers' special
relationship to death, which is somehow, in a flash, called to consciousness
when the hatchet-polishers rise with murderous designs.

The foundation of this scene takes us back to our first view of the
hatchet-polishers, then forward to the jostling scene in the novella. Delano
asserts, in "Coast of Chili," chapter 16 of Voyages, regarding a sitting room,
"This elevated place was the usual seat of the ladies. Their mode of sitting
is cross-legged, in the Turkish fashion, or like a tailor on his shop board, and
near together" (Delano, 117). Melville makes fascinating use of each element of that description in depicting the hatchet-polishers. Not only are
they seated cross-legged on the elevated poop, but they are close enough together, as the initial portrait of them shows, to clash their hatchets overhead.
And after they half-rise, they resume "their seats, quietly as so many tailors"
(BC, 79). Although the foundation of each scene, one might say, is similar,
in the end Melville fashions a portrait of the six Ashantees that, as a work of
art, stands forever on it own. So we have a South American influence to be
added to our earlier discussion of how Melville characterized the hatchet-
polishers.

[II]

With Babo directing matters, the relationship between Delano and Don Benito is severely complicated. Delano has no way to know that the Spaniard will be killed if he does not navigate the ship back to Africa. Nor does he know that the hatchets being scoured by the hatchet-polishers had been used to shed blood in killings in which the victims were left gashed and mangled. The reason for terrible things such as the Spaniard's skeletal appearance and broken speech is not known to Delano.[6]

Don Benito's awareness that he is skin and bones is deepened when Babo shows him Aranda's skeleton, about which, to be sure, Delano knows nothing. The fact that Don Benito has asked where Aranda's remains are and pleads that they be "preserved for interment ashore," only to be ignored, makes him more susceptible to being shocked when later taken by Babo to the prow to see what is left of his friend. He sees the stark whiteness of Aranda's skeleton, and his trauma is in no way lessened when Babo asks whose it is, which causes him to cover his face. Babo responds by "coming close" and saying, "Keep faith with the blacks from here to Senegal, or you shall in spirit, as now in body, follow your leader," pointing to the skeleton. Summoning each Spaniard forward to see Aranda's skeleton, Babo asks if it is not the skeleton of a white man (BC, 107).[7] Small wonder that when Delano, with the arrival of his boat, makes half-menacing gestures, a cry of alarm comes from Benito Cereno.

The arcane rite leading to the preparation of Aranda's skeleton and the meaning of the "Follow Your Leader" legend beneath it can be explained, enabling us to link Aranda and the legend to Ashantee kings. English traveler T. E. Bowdich, who visited the Ashantees before Dupuis, writes that "The Kings, and kings only, are buried in the cemetery at Batama, and the sacred gold with them," and that "their bones are afterwards deposited in a building there." In this regard, it should be noted that in the last paragraph of Benito Cereno, Melville refers to "St. Bartholomew's church, in whose vaults slept then, as now, the recovered bones of Aranda" (BC, 117). Bowdich contends that others must die when the Ashantee king dies, "to water the graves of kings." Willem Bosman, who also spent time among the Ashantees, and who wrote over a century before Bowdich and Dupuis, sheds more light on the meaning of the "Follow Your Leader" legend, commenting, "Slaves of the Deceased are killed and sacrificed on [the king's] account in order to serve him in the other world."[8] That someone must follow the king is assured in Ashantee culture, giving Babo a theme on which to build the torment that culminates in the shaving scene.

When a white messenger boy carries forward to the forecastle the intelligence that it is time for the large bell to be struck, time for Don Benito to be shaved, Babo's command of Don Benito's fate is borne in upon the Spaniard as never before. The deathly sound of the bell is then more dreadful than ever to Don Benito, who knows he will see—and feel—a razor in Babo's hand. The stage is thereby set for perhaps Benito Cereno's lone act of courage while Delano is on the *San Dominick,* an act the more courageous, or foolish, because Babo holds the razor so near and ascribes to Don Benito himself the desire to be shaved. Tension for Don Benito is unmistakably at a high point, intensifying the Spaniard's fear. Babo remarks, as Delano listens, that Don Benito has instructed him to remind him precisely when he is to be shaved and informs Don Benito that "Miguel has gone to strike the half-hour afternoon. It is *now,* master. Will master go into the cuddy?" (*BC,* 82).

Hearing Don Benito promise to resume conversing with Delano, Babo explains that if Don Benito wishes to talk to Don Amasa, "why not let Don Amasa sit by master in the cuddy, and master can talk, and Don Amasa can listen, while Babo here lathers and strops" (*BC,* 82). There is a risk that a resumption of mention of calms might cause Delano, who knows something of navigation along the South American coast, to become more alert intellectually, but Babo, following them into the cuddy, is willing to take it. Babo, "napkin on arm," makes "a motion as if waiting his master's good pleasure." Don Benito gives his consent, and it is then that Babo throws back the Spaniard's collar and loosens his cravat (*BC,* 83).

As Babo searches for the sharpest razor, Delano ruminates about black inferiority, not knowing that the Spaniard has been reading mainly from Babo's script; not knowing that Don Benito is wondering how he, Delano, could possibly believe that navigational problems of a particularly protracted period had afflicted the *San Dominick.* But as Babo strops a razor, Melville, in this scene, finds a particularly impressive way to remind the reader of the danger facing Delano, who muses, "Most negroes are natural valets and hairdressers; taking to the comb and brush congenially as to the castinets [*sic*], and flourishing them apparently with almost equal satisfaction" (*BC,* 83). Without going outside the novella to Dupuis's *Journal of a Residence,* there is simply no way to appreciate the significance of that seemingly innocuous remark.[9]

But Don Benito is thinking about navigational matters being fundamental. Atmosphere, then, though overlooked in criticism, is foundational in the shaving scene. We see this when Don Benito, thinking Babo will not understand, gambles his life in attempting to nudge Delano toward awareness of what is happening. It is not an altogether unreasonable gamble to take, considering the long coast of South America from the equator down to the

Cape. How, after all, is Babo to know, Don Benito must have reasoned, that winds farther north once wafted ships out into seemingly unending waters, where they were becalmed for months, the unhappy experience he claims for the *San Dominick?* Long periods of being becalmed, however, were far more characteristic of ships in the equatorial waters of the enchanted isles, about which Melville writes in "Sketch Fourth" of *The Encantadas,* than when sailing far down the coast between St. Maria and the Cape, which Don Benito claims the *San Dominick* had rounded.

Delano lets it be known, however, that it is not so much the rounding of the Cape that troubles him, remarking, "Ah, yes, these gales . . . but the more I think of your voyage, Don Benito, the more I wonder, not at gales, terrible as they must have been, but at the disastrous interval following them" (*BC,* 85). Disturbingly, he pursues this line of thought: "For here, by your account have you been these two months and more getting from Cape Horn to St. Maria, a distance which I myself, with a good wind, have sailed in a few days. True, you had calms and long ones, but to be becalmed for two months, that is, at least, unusual. Why, Don Benito, had almost any other gentleman told me such a story, I should have been half-disposed to a little incredulity" (*BC,* 85–86).

Hearing this, writes Melville, "an involuntary expression came over the Spaniard," and whether it was his starting, or "a sudden gawky roll of the hull in the calm, or a momentary unsteadiness of the servant's hand; however it was, the razor drew blood," staining the lather under his throat. With his face to Don Benito and his back to Delano, Babo keeps his professional attitude. His comment, while he holds up the razor, expresses "half humorous sorrow: 'See, master,—you shook so—here's Babo's first blood'" (*BC,* 86). Don Benito's terrified appearance causes Delano to scold himself for having thought the Spaniard wanted to spill his blood: "Tell it not when you get home, sappy Amasa. Well, well, he looks like a murderer, doesn't he? More like as if himself were to be done for. Well, well, this day's experience shall be a good lesson" (*BC,* 86).

After shaving Don Benito, Babo pours a few drops of scented water on Don Benito's head, rubbing them in with such vehemence that the muscles of the Spaniard's face twitch strangely. Delano closely observes as Babo wraps up his work with scissors, comb, and brush, smooths "a curl here" and gives "a graceful sweep to the temple-lock, with other impromptu touches evincing the hand of a master." According to Melville, Don Benito sits "so pale and rigid now, that the Negro seemed a Nubian sculptor finishing off a white statue-head" (*BC,* 87). With that remark the New Guinea scene in chapter 2 comes to mind as integral to the shaving scene.

Yet why would Melville, in that scene, have Babo use a flag as an apron as Don Benito is shaved? The answer to that question yields still more features of the shaving scene's creation, as we see from the Ashantee king's appearance in the Bowdich volume. When Melville read the following passage, his eyes fell upon this account of a procession that is the source of the apron in the novella:

> The King sent a handsome procession of flags, guns, and music to conduct us to the palace on the occasion; and meeting us in the outer square, preceded us to the inmost, where about 300 females were seated, in all the magnificence which a profusion of gold and silk could furnish. The splendor of this coup d'oeil made our surprise almost equal to theirs. We were seated with the King and the deputies, under large umbrellas in the centre, and I was desired to declare the objects of the embassy and the Treaty, to an old linguist, peculiar to the women. The King displayed the presents to them; the flags were all sewn together, and wrapped around him as a cloth. (Bowdich, 124)

The source of the "harlequin ensign" reference in the novella, which is drawn from the Ashantee king combining in his dress European and African influences, is also in that passage from Bowdich (*BC,* 87). With European flags sewn together and wrapped about him, the Ashantee king's outfit is a caricature, a model for a clown.[10] In addition, however, in the procession he is dressed in a "brown velveteen," "richly embroidered" costume with "an English epaulette sewn on each shoulder" and "a small dirk around his waist." The dirk was a possible inspiration for Don Benito's scabbard, one suspects, an inspiration, very likely, for the dagger that Babo uses when pursuing Don Benito into Delano's boat. In addition, the king possesses the gift of "a long silver headed cane" to be used as a walking staff (Bowdich, 122).

This last object figures in Melville's establishment of yet another link between the king and Benito Cereno. He places the king's walking staff in the shaving scene environment without really doing so: the ship's "absence of fine furniture and picturesque disarray of odd appurtenances, somewhat answering to the wide, cluttered hall of some eccentric bachelor-squire in the country who hangs his shooting-jacket and tobacco-pouch on deer antlers, and keeps his fishing-rod, tongs, and walking-stick in the same corner" (*BC,* 82).

Another piece of the puzzle, one of a series of shavings that take place on the *San Dominick,* must also be taken into account. Melville suggests as much in his description of the cuddy. Speaking of one of its extremities and of "ring bolts," he refers to "those shaven ones of the English at Preston Pans, made by the poled scythes of the Highlanders" (*BC,* 102). This image derives from his reading and recasting of Delano's account in *Voyages and*

Travels of his men butchering the defeated former slaves: "They had got all the men who were living made fast, hands and feet, to the ring bolts in the deck; some of them had part of their bowels hanging out, and some with half their backs and thighs shaved off" (Delano, 328).

A crucial yet indispensable element in understanding Melville's crafting of some of *Benito Cereno*'s richest art results from an overlooked section of *Voyages and Travels*—in chapter 16—that will be examined in greater detail later, but for now let us look at a portion of that finding: Benito Cereno's offer to Delano to breathe a bit of fresh air. Don Benito extends an invitation to his guest, for that purpose, to accompany him to the poop. But Babo whispers, "This excitement is bad for master," then draws him aside with "soothing words." But the words hurt, and the Spaniard takes on a "cadaverous aspect": "Ere long, with a joyless mien, looking up towards the poop," writes Melville, "the host invited his guest to accompany him there, for the benefit of what little breath of wind might be stirring" (*BC, 58*).

Don Benito insisted "upon his guest's preceding him up the ladder leading to the elevation; where, one on each side of the last step, sat for armorial supporters and sentries two of the ominous file." As Delano steps cautiously between the hatchet-polishers and leaves "them behind, like one running the gauntlet, he felt an apprehensive twitch in the calves of his legs" (*BC, 59*). The pathway along which he moves reminds us of Dupuis's negotiation of an avenue "in the order of single file" while young boys waved scimitars and swords over his head (*Dupuis, 42*). Rather like Dupuis, who was largely convinced no harm was intended toward him, Delano "saw the whole file, like so many organ-grinders, still stupidly intent on their work, unmindful of everything beside" and "could not but smile at his late fidgety panic" (*BC, 59*). The airing that Don Benito offers Delano is particularly ironic because it is an indication, from Don Benito himself, of how Melville created his character in the novella. Mention of airing will in due course be placed in context with other clues from chapter 16 of *Voyages* that Melville used to create Benito Cereno.

[III]

But before addressing the characterization of Don Benito, it should be mentioned that elsewhere in chapter 16, Melville must have been surprised, even stunned, to find an account of another eruption of violence and reversal of rule in South American waters with the life of the navigator being spared. Amazingly, a member of the historical Delano's crew was involved in this incident as well, adding to Melville's interest. Not surprisingly, he considered how the account might be used in furthering the creation of the novella. We have seen how he perfected a hatchet-polisher scene by applying findings from chapter 16 of *Voyages,* but reading that chapter captured his attention in numerous ways. What he found enabled him to write a novella that, without a consciousness of chapter 16, would read very differently. This we will get to, but let us first turn to the instance of a second navigator agreeing, in exchange for his life, to navigate the ship in the interest of his captors.

The incident involves Spanish and English ships, of equal force, fighting at sea. Though the English won the initial battle, the conquered Spanish rose one night "when part of the crew were asleep, and killed as many as they could before the rest awoke; and then despatched the others as soon as they came on deck; having first determined to save Halsey alive, as he understood navigation." The Spaniards then went below deck—as the Ashantees, in *Benito Cereno,* went below deck—"to the cabin," writes Delano, "in which my unfortunate gunner lay, and told him to get out of his birth," before striking him "with a carpenter's axe" that "nearly cut him in two with the first stroke" (Delano, 119). The gunner, one Charles Spence, had fought to put down the revolt on Aranda's ship before his own horrible death, which helps to confirm the importance of this incident to the tale Melville created.

When the two Spaniards, lured aloft to look out for land, return to deck, the first is "killed, and the other, wounded . . . jumped overboard, swam to the rings of the rudder, and held fast" until an Englishman breaks his hold by stabbing him with a ramrod—the model for Babo, weapon in hand, pursuing Benito Cereno into the fictional Delano's boat just as Don Benito, abandoning his ship, jumped overboard (Delano, 119). Captain Delano's *Voyages* provides a clear model for Babo's behavior after Don Benito leaps into his boat as he places the oars into the sea. Thus developments involving the English-Spanish battle kindled Melville's imagination for the final, great scene of the novella when Babo, taken alive from the *San Dominick,* is tried, executed, and his head placed on a pole in the Plaza in Lima.

In the historical incident, covered in the attachments to chapter 18, Babo is killed struggling to prevent Delano's crew from putting down the revolt. But the incident above provided Melville with the preferred strategy of the novella. Melville thereby lays additional groundwork, in tandem with the Nelson statuary, for the solution to the satyr figure problem. Moreover, the way is open for the hauntingly encouraging scene in the Plaza in Lima in which Babo's head, described as a "hive of subtlety," meets "unabashed the gaze of the whites" (*BC* 116).

As important to Melville's art as those developments from chapter 16 are, another development from that chapter is of such importance that it is difficult even to measure; it bears on the New Guinea material, and therefore on the shaving scene, and a great deal more. In fact, major dimensions of the novella result from Melville's transmutation into art of a passage from the chapter concerning a friend of Delano, one George Howe of Connecticut. Visiting Howe in Valparaiso, Delano describes him in a way that merits our fullest attention. According to Delano, Howe

> was lying on a miserable bed, or couch, in a very languishing state; his flesh was wasted, till he was almost a skeleton; and no one near to afford him assistance, or friend to offer him a word of comfort . . . My feelings on the occasion can be better imagined than described. We had spent many happy hours together; and I could not help contrasting those times with what I now saw. I endeavored to raise his spirits, and told him that I would take him aboard my ship, and bring him home. I procured a barber and had him shaved, his clothes shifted, and dressed him in a decent manner, putting on his handsome Spanish cloak, and led him into the parlour, with an intention of giving an airing; but the poor man was so reduced, that he fainted and was obliged to be placed on a sofa, and soon after carried back to his room, from which he never again was removed till a corpse. (Delano, 113)

This astounding passage from chapter 16 enables us, above all, to know how imaginatively Melville built from what little was known of the historical Benito Cereno, and to focus on a more familiar means of shaving to which others might be related.

The Howe discovery helps us discern more about Melville's method in fashioning one of his greatest scenes: *I procured a barber and had him shaved.* With that, Melville had his shaving scene, a variegated theme that resonates with Ashantee practices, with Scottish Highlander practice at Preston Pans, with Admiral Nelson's skeleton, and much more. The barber chair scene, moreover, in all its layered complexity, is a supreme achievement artistically. The architecture of its creation is more fully understood when we are reminded that there is no mention of anyone being shaved by a barber in chapter 18 of *Voyages*.

Without the example of Howe, we have no reason to suspect that Melville would have had Babo, in the role of barber, shave Don Benito. To state the matter differently, the scene is the pivot around which the various forms of shaving that have been detailed can ultimately be grouped as incidents that carry their own individual meanings while forming a far-ranging whole. With Babo dressing Don Benito in a harlequin ensign in this context, the tension for Don Benito is so taut at times it snaps. Babo, calibrating it precisely, is there to support Don Benito in a union of opposites that is a heretofore unrecognized, and constantly forming, symbol in the novella.

Major elements of Don Benito's characterization, it is now clear, resulted from Howe's plight. Melville's remark in the novella that he "seemed never to have been robust . . . was almost worn to a skeleton" almost certainly stems from Delano's finding Howe lying on a wretched bed, "his flesh wasted, till he was almost a skeleton." As Howe's spirits were low when Delano endeavored to raise them, Melville noticed, remarkably coincidentally, that the historical Don Benito was "frightened at his own shadow . . . effectually conquered and his spirits broken" (BC, 52). It is likely that because Howe looked like a skeleton Melville decided to depict the fictional Don Benito that way. But that, however, is not the whole story.

Another characteristic of Howe, his fainting, is given to Benito Cereno to brilliant effect throughout the novella. Benito Cereno's fainting, therefore, attains symbolic significance as the perfect metaphor for slave master's dependency on the slave.[11] The depiction of Don Benito as a parasite is wonderfully demonstrated artistically. In fact, there is nothing comparable to in fiction, but there is no avoiding the conclusion that Melville often thought of Hegel when depicting the Spaniard fainting. This element of Benito Cereno's character, a weakened state that causes him continually to rely on Babo, enabled Melville to create a rich relationship between the two. Don Benito's fainting, and Babo's propping him up, is a master stroke that becomes symbolic of the Spaniard's condition, of the master's dependence on the slave. By having Don Benito so frequently lose consciousness, Melville made that aspect of his character, and Babo's response to it, perhaps the single most memorable feature of the novella, especially now that we know George Howe is Melville's model for so rare an occurrence as fainting.

Laying out the dress for Don Benito is one of Babo's most brilliant stratagems, and his own dress, superbly conceived, suggests, by contrast, a destitute, supplicatory status that makes Delano's acceptance of the Spaniard's attire more certain. Because Babo exhibited an eye for fashion, his outfitting of Don Benito, suggested to Melville by Howe being dressed by Delano, requires attention here. Don Benito is wearing "a loose Chili jacket of dark velvet; white small-clothes and stockings, with silver buckles at the knee and instep; a high-crowned sombrero, of fine grass; a slender sword, silver-mounted, hung from a knot in his sash—the last being an almost invariable adjunct, more for utility than ornament, of a South American gentleman's dress to this hour. Excepting when his occasional nervous contortions brought about disarray, there was a certain precision in his attire, curiously at variance with the unsightly disorder around; especially in the belittered Ghetto, forward of the main-mast, wholly occupied by the blacks" (*BC,* 57).

Unaware that Babo has chosen Don Benito's outfit, which is a source of humiliation to the Spaniard's crew and a constant, visible reminder to them that they must either play their roles or die, Delano gave the briefest concern to Don Benito's outfit. Thanks to Babo's ease with fashion—he is himself wearing "wide trousers, apparently, from their coarseness and patches, made out of some old topsail" that are "confined at the waist by a bit of unstranded rope" (*BC,* 57)—the illusion of white control is underscored. Attire, then, is a major feature of the interplay of illusion and reality, as Melville suggests near the beginning: "The ship seems unreal; these strange costumes" (*BC,* 50).

With indispensable features of *Benito Cereno* formed in relation to Howe, Melville has made him as much American as the forecastle bell in the tale. Not only that, we now see the relationship between Delano and Benito Cereno in a new light—to some extent as fellow Americans. And just as the fictional Benito Cereno is fused with Howe, the fictional Delano is a combination of the historical Delano and, especially, Joseph Dupuis. In this connection, Atufal, we recall, is substantially based on Daggoo and, in his refusal to ask pardon, on the Spanish heretic. All are manifestations of Melville's remarkable ability to create characters—who show every sign of standing on their own—from multiple human experiences across cultural and geographical boundaries.[12]

The Historical Delano was mainly used by Melville, we long thought, to characterize Delano in the novella. However, far more intriguing influences in the fictional Delano's characterization are taken from the life of Dupuis, adding an unsuspected dimension to the novella. In fact, Dupuis's failure to understand what is happening around him offers a Delano second self that flows almost imperceptibly from *Journal of a Residence in Ashantee* into the novella. It is especially valuable because Melville found an alter ego to the historical Delano moving among Ashantee just as the fictional Delano moves, without knowing it, among Ashantee in the novella. The more intriguing point artistically is that Melville makes Dupuis, from the time he enters the novella, indistinguishable from the fictional Delano.

Music provides a running commentary on Dupuis's movements through Ashantee, much as the hatchets are a commentary on Delano's presence in the novella. But the character of the musical instruments in Dupuis's journal—their appearance as much as their sounds—leaves no doubt that his presence among blacks is cause for concern. The music of *Journal of a Residence in Ashantee,* however, is toned down, fostering a degree of ambiguity in the interest of art, which heightens and sustains suspense. Once Dupuis's link to the fictional Delano is known to us, however, the perception that Delano is endangered without knowing it is unavoidably reinforced. It is possible that the brilliance of Dupuis's disguised entry in *Benito Cereno* is unique in the craft of writing.

There are more reasons to marvel, not because Melville is introducing us to cultures thousands of miles away, but because his art is unexpectedly refracted through the experience of slaves in the United States. That one of his talent should depend as much as he does on any writer, however great, should to some extent surprise us, but that he depends, in *Moby-Dick,* as much as he does on the work of Frederick Douglass will perhaps be shocking to some, especially to those who acknowledge Melville's debt to Shakespeare. Whether what he works into *Moby-Dick* from Douglass is as important and enduring as inspiration received from Shakespeare is, of course, for others to determine. Despite the fact that *Benito Cereno* is not mentioned in the chapter that follows, its theme of slavery is of deep concern to Melville in *Moby-Dick.*

CHAPTER IV

Cheer and Gloom

Frederick Douglass and Herman Melville on Slave Music and Dance

> *From my earliest recollection, I date the entertainment of a deep conviction that slavery would not hold me in its foul embrace; and in the darkest hours of my career in slavery, this living word of faith and spirit of hope departed not from me, but remained like ministering angels to cheer me through the gloom.*
> —Frederick Douglass, Narrative of the Life of Frederick Douglass

> *So, be cheery, my lads! May your hearts never fail!*
> *While the bold harpooneer is striking the whale!*
> —From "Midnight, Forecastle" of Moby-Dick

Melville's use of music—within the context of dance—in *Moby-Dick* is one of his most remarkable literary achievements. Inspired by *Narrative of the Life of Frederick Douglass,* he creates characterizations, dialogue, and storylines that are shaped in part by the music of the *Narrative,* and more generally by his understanding of the importance of music and dance to black culture. As remarkable, then, as the high literary achievement is the fact that his innovations are inspired by the music of the despised slave. In an astonishing display of literary skill, and with rare subtlety even for him, Melville demonstrates that uncommon techniques of craft, long overlooked, went into the making of *Moby-Dick.* The writing in *Moby-Dick* is a rare demonstration of how music can meet needs of craft of a great writer.

The representation of music in the *Narrative* and *Moby-Dick* helps to illumine the previously obscure issue of how the spirituals and blues, as musical forms, relate to each other, a neglected problem in the history of American music.[1] Scholars and music critics generally argue that the spirituals were created in slavery and the blues scores of years later, at the close of the nineteenth and the opening of the twentieth century, though each began evolving around the same time, possibly from a common spiritual and musical source. Basing his commentary on slave music of the 1820s and 1830s, Douglass leads us to that conclusion, and Melville builds on it.[2]

Douglass's rendering of slave music offers enormous advantages for re-visiting this largely unexamined problem in black music criticism, for he takes us back to that sacred moment when the spirituals and the blues appear to have been one, to that moment, however, when the blues is actually the foundational form. That is, qualities of the spirituals inhered in blues song as early as Douglass's time but lacked the consolations of faith that later distinguish the spirituals. Such qualities came later, or were heard apart from the singing of the field hand, whose song was more gloomy and widespread, its musical shadows not frequently relieved by the light of hope, which even then, like joy, deepened the sense of gloom or sadness.

The notion that the blues are meant for solo singing, as Eileen Southern suggests, and are structured with "a repetitious leading line (sometimes with slight variation), and generally a third, rhyming line" as literary and music critic Sterling A. Brown asserts, is in need of reexamination. The music Douglass describes is a deep form of the blues without being rendered in solo form, without the structured leading and rhyming lines, and without necessarily conveying a sense of rootlessness. Douglass works largely without referring to lyrics that were difficult to grasp—perhaps owing to improvised, African-inflected song intensified by the sheer agony of the slavery he experienced—indicating that the music he heard on Colonel Lloyd's Maryland plantation predated conventional spirituals. Slave song, in Douglass's words, was sung "as a chorus, to words which to many would seem unmeaning jargon, but which, nevertheless, were full of meaning to themselves. I have sometimes thought that the mere hearing of those songs would do more to impress some minds with the horrible character of slavery than the reading of whole volumes of philosophy on the subject could do" (N, 24). Despite appeals to God, this music was of this world and, on balance, hardly other-worldly.[3]

Both the *Narrative* and *Moby-Dick* give us reason to question the thesis that the spirituals preceded the blues. But much more than the question of sequence is at stake. We have come to understand that the soul of the nation is tied to that of black Africa, from which the nation has tried so desperately to distance itself. Both authors grapple with that issue. It will not be easy for us to read one without thinking of the other when either *Moby-Dick* or the *Narrative* is the text. Indeed, Melville's use of the music described by Douglass is so faithful to its tragic joy-sorrow quality that blues form and feeling suffuse his writing style at critical junctures in the novel.

Dance and music propel each other in slave art, in which the creation of musical forms is attended by dance, but in Douglass's writings the emphasis is on music (though we should keep dance in mind). The absence of a specific mention of dance, in this case the sacred Ring Shout, does not mean it is any less important to music, driving its rhythms. This works well for Melville because slave song lends itself more readily to forms of literary invention as the novel unfolds.

Owing to the importance of the Ring Shout in *Narrative of the Life of Frederick Douglass* and in *Moby-Dick,* Charles Dickens's *American Notes for General Circulation* takes on even greater relevance in this chapter. In fact, one of Melville's most brilliant strokes is in linking the dance style of William Henry Lane to the Ring Shout, in which a great deal of slave song was rooted.

[I]

Douglass's interpretation of slave song owes much to what he and other children experienced in slavery almost from the time they first walked. When he treats slave song and dance, he sets them against a backdrop that is a near constant in slave life, the tragedy of the slave experience for young and old alike. In some ways his most tragic reference to dance and song takes in generations of slave children viewed in relation to his great-grandmother Betsey Bailey, before whose hearth he once danced. She had seen "her children, her grandchildren, and her great-grandchildren, divided like so many sheep, without being gratified with the small privilege of a single word, as to their or her own destiny" (*N,* 47). With the grave at her door, she is consigned to live alone: "The hearth is desolate. The children, the unconscious children, who once sang and danced in her presence, are gone. She gropes her way, in the darkness of age, for a drink of water. Instead of the voices of her children, she hears by day the moans of the dove, and by night the screams of the hideous owl. All is gloom" (*N,* 48–49).

Douglass's childhood slave experience is shot through with acute personal sorrow and awareness of the everyday wretchedness of life. In his *Life and Times,* he is reduced to singing for bread when "very severely pinched with hunger." That bittersweet experience is later reinforced when he sings hymns with a white man who flogs him. Because we can conclude from reading Douglass that song for the slave is a means of reflecting on and feeling the life he is leading, it is impossible for him to view the music as whites might (*N,* 57; *L,* 519). Like his fellow slave, whether near field hands as they sing during breaks or listening to them sing on their way to secure provisions, Douglass experiences slave song from the inside. The conclusion is inescapable that the music that overwhelms him, that precedes the spirituals and the blues as we know them, is the creation of field hands. His youthful understanding is the foundation for his later mastery, due to years of reflection after slavery, of slave song.

That slaves sing to *make* themselves happy is the source in slave song of the fusion of sorrow and joy, of seeming opposites, that is at the heart of the singing that Douglass immortalizes for us (*N*, 24). There was for Douglass, therefore, no greater mistake than to think slaves sang because they were happy. In fact, he was "utterly astonished to find persons who could speak of the singing among slaves, as evidence of their contentment and happiness." Rather, the pain of the slave experience is eased by song "as an aching heart is relieved by its tears" (*N*, 24–25).

He writes that while watching ships on Chesapeake Bay, "robed in purest white," make their way to the ocean, he "traced with saddened heart and tearful eye, the countless number of sails" and poured out his "soul's complaint": "You are loosed from your moorings, and are free; I am fast in my chains, and am a slave! You move merrily before the gentle gale, and I sadly before the bloody whip! You are freedom's swift-winged angels, that fly round the world; I am confined in bands of iron! O that I were free! O, that I were on one of your gallant decks, and under your protecting wing! . . . O that I could also go! Could I but swim! If I could fly! O, why was I born a man, of whom to make a brute! The glad ship is gone; she hides in the dim distance. I am left in the hottest hell of unending slavery. O God, save me! God, deliver me! Let me be free! Is there any God?" (*N*, 59). As they distanced themselves from him, entering the mighty Atlantic Ocean, the ships took on the guise of "so many shrouded ghosts," terrifying and tormenting him as he recalled the complaint of his soul (*N*, 59).

In *Life and Times*, decades after the printing of the *Narrative*, Douglass writes, "I used to contrast my condition with that of the blackbirds, in whose wild and sweet songs I fancied them so happy. Their apparent joy only deepened the shades of my sorrow" (*L*, 72). Stating the principle somewhat differently, while reflecting on his youth in slavery, he writes in *My Bondage*, "The smiles of my mistress could not remove the deep sorrow that dwelled in my young bosom. Indeed, these came, in time, but to deepen the sorrow" (*B*, 209). The manner in which he relates seeming opposites captures the spirit of the blues without specific mention of slave song, which prefigures Melville.

We can, therefore, better understand why in the *Narrative* joy and sadness find simultaneous expression in musical tones that work in relation to each other as cheer and gloom do in the epigraph. Melville takes particular notice of this, using "gloomy," and "jolly" as Douglass uses "sadness" and "joy," to describe both music and the social condition that it reflects on the *Pequod*. In other words, for Douglass the cardinal feature of the slave musical aesthetic is that joy and sadness are continually fused. Their ironic coupling is the core element of slave song and the foundation on which the best black music criticism rests. Moreover, the joining of sadness and joy by slaves singing as a group, not as solo performers, is not the least remarkable of Douglass's findings and an indication, in fact, of *blues performance* that he invites us to consider. In one of the most important statements ever regarding music in America, he writes the following:

> The slaves selected to go to the Great House Farm, for the monthly allowance for themselves and their fellow-slaves, were peculiarly enthusiastic. While on their way, they would make the dense old woods, for miles around, reverberate with their wild songs, revealing *at once* the highest joy and the deepest sadness. They would compose and sing as they went along, consulting neither time nor tune. The thought that came up, came out—if not in the word, in the sound;—and as frequently in the one as in the other. They would sometimes sing the most pathetic sentiment in the most rapturous tone, and the most rapturous sentiment in the most pathetic tone. (*N,* 23)

Douglass writes that the notion of the master class taking care of slaves, as a matter of reciprocal rights, is so absurd that "nature laughs it to scorn." While slaves, to avoid the monotony of steady, grueling labor, know joy from going to the Great House Farm, the source of joy in their singing is counterbalanced by the tragedy of their experience and the cruelty of the master. They are acutely aware of violations of their humanity, Douglass notes in *Life and Times,* as they make their way to the farm for pork that was "often tainted," for fish "of the poorest quality," for meal 15 percent of which "was more fit for pigs than for men" (*L,* 503). The trip to the Great House Farm, therefore, was a mixed blessing that, although relieving them of labor, reminded them of the rank callousness of the slave holder (*N,* 24–25). Hence, the bold irony of

> I am going to the great house farm,
> O yea! O yea! O yea!
> My old master is a good old master,
> O yea! O yea! O yea! (*L,* 502)

Slave songs "were not always merry because they were wild. On the contrary, they were mostly of a plaintive cast, and told a tale of grief and sorrow," thereby indicating once more that sorrow and joy informed slave song. Somewhat varying his approach, as Melville does in *Moby-Dick,* Douglass would have us understand that "in the most boisterous outbursts of rapturous sentiment, there was ever a tinge of deep melancholy" (*B,* 184). We are reminded of James Baldwin writing on the blues.[4]

Much of slave song, and of his own experience, convinces Douglass that the soul is the final theater of resistance to slavery, the last shield of the slave's humanity. Slavery threatens to destroy that humanity and causes self-doubt that the spirit, time and again, struggles against. Douglass's struggle is between self-doubt and resistance to slavery, between freedom and slavery. The battle with the slave breaker, Covey, "revived within me," he writes, "the few expiring embers of freedom, and revived within me a sense of my own manhood. It recalled the departed self-confidence, and inspired me again with a determination to be free" (N, 65). On occasion his spiritual resistance sprang from a challenge to his soul: "At times I would rise up, a flash of energetic freedom would dart through my soul, accompanied with a faint beam of hope, that flickered for a moment, and then vanished. I sank down again, mourning over my wretched condition." At another time, he was frightened and feeling cowardly, his "long-crushed spirit rose, cowardice departed," and "bold defiance took its place" (N, 58, 65).

In truth, Douglass argues, the greatest threat to the slave regime is absolute suppression of the slave, from which, if there is not some release, a "spirit will go forth, in their midst, more to be dreaded than the most appalling earthquake" (B, 291). It is hard for the slave to articulate this, even hard for Douglass, one of the great masters of the English language, for resistance to slavery takes place as much in the realm of the individual spirit or soul as anywhere else. Hence Douglass opens up a new realm of analysis in considering the nature of oppression and the uses of art, at the level of the blues, to reevaluate the slave condition and the claims of the master class and its defenders.

The music that makes Douglass blue from childhood until late in life is sacred, a fierce, interior musicality, the very language of which helps to disguise the slave's bitter complaint. Still, Douglass writes, "the mere hearing of these songs would do more to impress truly spiritual-minded men and women with the soul-crushing and death-dealing character of slavery, than the reading of whole volumes of philosophy on the subject could do" (N, 24). His enslavement under such a condition was a source of special torment: "By the combined physical force of the community, I am . . . a slave for life," he writes, adding, "With thoughts like these, I was perplexed and chafed; they rendered me gloomy and disconsolate" (B, 304).

Douglass writes of music that breathes "the prayer and complaint of souls boiling over with the bitterest anguish," which gives us insight into his own condition, for he writes that the "anguish" of his mind "may not be written" (N, 24; B, 304). He amplifies this observation, stating that his soul is at times, in fact, stung to "unutterable anguish," beneath which he writhes. Moreover, his soul gives tongue to thoughts that flash through his mind but "die away for want of utterance" (*N*, 42). Again we see that the music of the slave is more about the state of the slave's soul, about the slave's conception of his humanity, about the competing claims, within the soul, of self-confidence and self-abnegation, than about physical cruelties. Its every tone is "a prayer to God for deliverance from chains" (*N*, 24). One's ascent will be from "the dark and pestiferous tomb of slavery, to the heaven of comparative freedom," which suggests that critic Michel Imbert is right in contending that although there is hope, there is little prospect of actual freedom for slaves described in Douglass's *Narrative*. A blues undercurrent moves the text.[5]

There were slaves on the Lloyd plantation "direct from Guinea" and "many who could say that their fathers and mothers were stolen from Africa—forced from their homes, and compelled to serve as slaves" (*B*, 179). This knowledge fills Douglass with a searing hatred of slavery, increases his suffering, but leaves him with no means of breaking away from bondage. He writes that slave language is strongly influenced by African speech, which, under the stress of oppression, gives way in song, we can infer, to tortured moans heightened by the rhythms of dance that, when the slaves are alone, can lead to spiritual possession. Our focus here is on African-inflected slave song rendered in a classic form of Negro dialect, of which Douglass writes, "There is not, probably in the whole South, a plantation where the English language is more imperfectly spoken than on Colonel Lloyd's"; he describes it as

> a mixture of Guinea and everything else you please. At the time of which I am now writing, there were slaves there who had been brought over from the coast of Africa . . . I could scarcely understand them when I first went among them, so broken was their speech; and I am persuaded that I could not have been dropped anywhere on the globe, where I could reap less, in the way of knowledge, from my immediate associates, than on this plantation. Even Mas' Daniel, by his association with his father's slaves, had measurably adopted their dialect and their ideas, so far as they had ideas to be adopted." (*B*, 168–69)

Small wonder that Douglass, who speaks of a dialect as strongly African as that found anywhere in the Deep South, had trouble understanding slave song. But added to that, implicitly, is the religion of the field hand. Both are conveyed in these revealing lines: "I did not, when a slave, understand the deep meaning of those rude and apparently incoherent songs. I was myself within the circle, so that I neither saw nor heard as those without might see and hear" (*N*, 37). But he leaves no doubt that the language or dialect spoken by Colonel Lloyd's field hands was perfectly suited for its artistic and spiritual function. To be sure, he realizes that in slave dialect the simultaneous union of joy and sorrow is magnificently captured along with the human condition that it reflects. He explains that "the constitution of the human mind" is such "that, when pressed to extremes, it often avails itself of the most opposite methods. Extremes meet in mind as in matter" (*B*, 185).[6] Perhaps few conditions in history have pressed the human mind to such extremes as slavery, of which tragedy Douglass provides abundant and searing evidence. He allows us to enter the souls of the bards who created the blues.

The very language of slave song causes Douglass to remark, "To those songs I trace my first glimmering conception of the dehumanizing character of slavery. I can never get rid of that conception."[7] Indeed, slave song's fusion of joy and sorrow gives fresh artistic meaning to Hegel's dialecic, dressing it in an art form previously unknown to the world. And yet some descendants of slaves with a little bit of education malign the language in which the blues, the slave spirituals, and slave tales were created. In truth, Douglass's reflections overall are set down in some of the finest prose of the nineteenth century by a thinker vastly superior to those who make a fetish, as does Ralph Ellison, of judging the dialect of their slave ancestors mainly through the prism of minstrelsy.[8]

Although implying much but saying little about slave dance, Douglass places himself in a peculiar position because he, above all others, knows that almost always slave dance, in some form, attends slave music. He has a compelling reason for his silence on the subject: he does not wish to reveal first-hand knowledge of it. On the other hand, he offers such subtle but suggestive clues to the presence of dance that one should avoid, as Melville avoids, the conclusion that dance is not on Douglass's mind when he discusses slave music. More than once, for example, Douglass refers to circularity when discussing slave song. In fact, he mentions being *in* the circle as a young slave, unable at that time to understand "the deep meanings of those rude, and apparently incoherent songs." He writes that he, while in the circle, "neither saw nor heard as those who were without might see and hear," but this alone is perhaps not enough to go on to conclude that he has the Ring Shout in mind (*N*, 24). When we add his comment about hearing field hands sing during a work lull, however, it is difficult to conclude that they are not dancing in a ring: "The few minutes allowed them at dinner time, after partaking of their coarse repast, are variously spent. Some lie down . . . and go to sleep; others draw together, and talk; and others are at work with needle and thread, mending their tattered garments. Sometimes you may hear a wild, hoarse laugh arise from a circle, and often a song. Soon, however, the overseer comes dashing through the field. 'Tumble up! Tumble, and to work, work,' is the cry; and now, from twelve o'clock (mid-day) till dark, the human cattle are in motion, wielding their clumsy hoes; hurried on with no hope of reward, no sense of gratitude" (B, 188–89). This reference to circularity and song comes shortly after mention of slave song and the Great House Farm, which favors the conclusion that some of the same slaves sang on both occasions.

Not until after the Civil War and Reconstruction, while visiting Egypt, does Douglass offer straightforward evidence that he knew the Shout in his youth. His very description of what he heard and saw, however, explains why he could not comprehend what was taking place in the circle during his youth, and why he would not have explained it had he comprehended it. He writes in The Life and Times: "If Rome has its unwashed monks, Cairo has its howling and dancing dervishes, and both seem deaf to the dictates of reason. The dancing and howling dervishes often spin around in their religious transports till their heads lose control and they fall to the floor sighing, groaning . . . reminding one of scenes that sometimes occur at our own camp-meetings" (L, 1013).[9]

Given his responsibilities as an abolitionist, evidently Douglass thinks it not in the interest of the cause to more than hint at such a dance. But how indeed could he have understood the deeper meaning of song in the context of counterclockwise dance and spirit possession? Small wonder that he writes of slave song, in his youth, as beyond his "feeble comprehension" (N, 24).

[II]

With awareness of Douglass's treatment of slave music and dance, new complexities and subtleties enter one's consciousness when reading Melville. The sentiment with which "Midnight, Forecastle" begins—the counsel of cheer when confronting the whale—establishes the fundamental Douglass connection that Melville wastes no time in making. Almost as quickly, he moves to a performance of the Ring Shout. The presence of the Ring Shout is no less remarkable than its context, reminiscent of Douglass, of cheer and gloom. Cheer and gloom represent social conditions pregnant with musical overtones.

Although music is explicit and dance implicit in Narrative of the Life, dance is explicit and music implicit in "Midnight, Forecastle." In the novel, Douglass's music and his interpretation of it establish the context in which action takes place and actors are characterized. Overtones or suggestions of the blues, not the music itself, provide the basis for new and daring writing by Melville as a serious division in the ranks of the Pequod becomes apparent. By using "gloom" and "jolly" (cheer), Melville elucidates the divide with the majority of crewmen on one side and a minority on the other, as the minority is cruelly reminded. Those vilifying the sacred Ring Shout are joyous, "jollies" (*MD*, 174); those urged to join in the desecration are sullen, "sulkies"(*MD*, 178).

Long after "Midnight, Forecastle," Melville reveals the long-term strategy that is concealed in this chapter. With an understanding of this aspect of his aesthetic code, *Moby-Dick* is suddenly illumined, allowing us to follow its direction to the end of the *Pequod*'s voyage and burial at sea. Meanwhile, a perversion of the sacred occurs as valued principles of the Ring Shout and slave performance style are appropriated and held up to ridicule. This development, worked out in some detail by Melville, helps explain Douglass's reluctance to use his enormous skill at writing to re-create the Ring Shout—in which he personally participated—in undisguised form.

Enacted at wildly popular minstrel performances at which blacks were unceasingly mocked, mimicking of the Ring Shout symbolized the difficulty of blacks and whites living in accord. But, we must conclude, there is even less hope of racial harmony as the *Pequod*, conveying hate in an atmosphere of minstrelsy, sails toward a storm. To be sure, the features and color of blacks are attacked with virtually no thought given to the purpose of the voyage, a sad fact of which Pip takes notice. Acutely conscious of the price the *Pequod* is paying for racial hate, Pip is the keeper of humane values of the crew at this point in the novel and will pay a price as much for the horror of the experience he undergoes in "Midnight, Forecastle" as for later being a castaway.

Melville introduces the Ring Shout as the French Sailor calls out, "Stand by all legs!" and "Pip! little Pip! Hurrah with your tambourine!" We are then taken back to Charles Dickens with "Form, now, Indian-file, and gallop into the double-shuffle? Throw yourselves! Legs! Legs!" (*MD*, 174). It is important to know that white missionaries in America also applied "Indian-file" to the Ring Shout.[10] But flagrant disrespect for the Ring Shout in "Midnight, Forrecastle"is apparent, especially when we contrast the Shout on the *Pequod* with a South Carolina Ring Shout that is characterized by dance remarkably similar to the virtuoso dance described by Dickens.

The minstrel atmosphere found in Dickens's chapter on New York helps explain why Douglass, sensitive to the prejudices of white readers, writes about the Ring Shout with such economy and subtlety of expression. The superimposition of the atmosphere of the Five Points dive onto the *Pequod* is part of a complicated strategy in which "Midnight, Forecastle" becomes the pivot for what follows in the novel. Recall that Lane, smiling the while, danced "with two left legs, two right legs, two wooden legs, two *wire* legs."

His dexterity, as the sailor calls out for "Legs! Legs!" is our index to Dickens. The exhortation that immediately follows, for the crew to dance Indian-file, refers us back to Douglass.

How Lane's "break-down" relates to the Shout is demonstrated in the South Carolina Ring Shout, a Shout that has about it the measured quality of blues: the repetitious second line of the song stands out, not the first. The song, however, is quite unmistakably a spiritual. Is Melville suggesting that the break-down evolved out of the Shout? The South Carolina Shout helps us, at least tentatively, answer that question:

My sister, don't you want religion?
Go down in the lonesome valley,
Go down in the lonesome valley,
Go down in the lonesome valley, my lord,
To meet my Jesus there.

As the singing gets louder and stronger, enthusiasm rises and the chorus rolls on. There is an uncanny resemblance in this Ring Shout to Lane's dance movements in *American Notes:*

William cannot sit still. He rises, begins a shuffle with his feet, jerking his arms. Ann, a short, thick-set, pure-blooded black woman, wearing a checked gingham dress, and an apron which was once a window curtain, can no longer keep her seat. Catherine and Sancho catch the inspiration. They go round in a circle, singing, shuffling, jerking, shouting louder and louder. Those upon the seats respond more vigorously, keeping time with feet and hands.

William seems in a trance; his eyes are fixed, *yet he goes into a double shuffle. Every joint in his body seems to be hung on wires. Feet, hands, arms, legs, body, jerk like a dandy jack.* Sancho enters into the praise with his whole heart, clasping his hands, looking upward upon the crowd as if they were his children, and he a patriarch. His countenance beams with joy. He is all but carried away with the excitement of the moment. So it goes until nature is exhausted.[11]

With the basic elements of a more African Ring Shout before us—Lane's emphasis on legs to the exclusion of arms was an influence of the Irish jig—we are in a position to see how Melville, with particular attention to the double shuffle, to juba beating with hands, and to the overall irreverence of the crew, treats the Ring Shout on the *Pequod*.[12] He has the French Sailor raise irreverence to a high pitch by calling for the Ring Shout and urging Pip, who says he cannot find his tambourine, to beat "thy belly, then, and wag thy ears." It is an exhortation to Pip to personally mock both the Ring Shout and black "jubilee beating," a means by which time is kept in the absence of the violin or drum. In other word, sailors on the *Pequod* would have those of color, especially Pip, beat their hands on their bodies as whites in black face might.[13] The call to "Jig it, men, I say, merry's the word; hurrah!" is a call for clearly secular dance in addition to the Ring Shout to be engaged in, as blacks would seldom do (*MD*, 174).

Meanwhile, Melville uses Dickens for additional purposes. After asking, "where's your girls?" the Maltese Sailor asks an additional question: "Who but a fool would take his left hand, and say to himself, how d'ye do? Partners! I must have partners!" (*MD*, 174). In *American Notes*, "Five or six couples come upon the floor. Among the dancers are two young mulatto girls, with large, black, drooping eyes . . . who are as shy, or feign to be, as though they never danced before, and so look down before the visitors, that their partners can see nothing but the long fringed lashes" (*AN*, 138).

One must ask if *American Notes*, because of the tambourine and the galvanizing talent of Lane, contributed to the depiction of Pip in *Moby-Dick*. Pip's unhappiness, in any case, is added reason to conclude that Lane, rolling his eyes, is wearing a mask simply to please. Pip would know, as Melville did, that Shouters were known to barely lift their feet from the floor as they circled counterclockwise, but the French Sailor calls for sailors on the *Pequod* to "gallop into the double shuffle" (*MD*, 174). When the Long Island Sailor threatens, "Well, well, ye sulkies, there's plenty more of us . . . Ah! Here comes the music for it!" (*MD*, 174) the abuse is rubbed in. The possibility of violence comes, one notices, as the threatened Pip is expected to entertain his abusers, the "jollies." The sense of awareness of the sailors is little better than that of slave masters listening to slaves sing or observing them dance the Ring Shout as the nation entered the critical decade of the 1850s.

It is in this atmosphere of bullying and race hate that Daggoo and Tashtego angrily reject claims to inferiority and refuse to embrace white standards of racial culture. Daggoo rejects the aesthetics that lightning they see was him "showing his teeth" and that fear of blackness is more warranted than fear of whiteness. In Daggoo's exchange with the Spanish Sailor, tension nearly flares into violence as the ominous elements in the sky worsen and waves crash against the *Pequod*. The Spaniard, holding a knife and moving toward Daggoo, is heedless that the flashes of lightning portend white squalls, the "crowning attribute of the terrible" (*MD*, 174, 177, 191).

When the sailors cry out, "The squall! The squall! Jump, my jollies!" the lines are drawn along those of color, and once again the sense of balance of the sailors is little better than that of the slave masters. The comparison is apt, for Melville writes, "The Nantucketer, he alone resides and riots on the sea;

he alone, in Bible language, goes down to it in ships; to and fro ploughing it as his own special plantation" (*MD*, 64).

Hence Pip's "Jollies? Lord help such jollies! Crish, crash! There goes the jib-stay! Blang-whang! God! Duck lower, Pip, here comes the royal yard! . . . Hold on hard! Jimmini, what a squall." Pip adds, "but those chaps there are worse yet—they are your white squalls, they." He proceeds to bring two dangers together: "White squalls, white whale, shirr! Shirr!—Here have I heard all their chat just now, and the white whale—shirr! shirr!—but spoken of once! And only this evening—it makes me jingle all over like my tambourine" (*MD*, 178).

Melville has worked Douglass's conception of contrasting tones into characterizations without revealing their relevance to music. But this does not become clear until deep into the novel, and in a seemingly inconsequential way—by using a punctuation mark, the hyphen, in "The Castaway," chapter 93, signaling that a rendering of music will soon begin: "Poor Pip, ye have heard of him before; ye must remember his tambourine on that dramatic midnight, so gloomy-jolly." Evidently Pip carried the burden of the blues with his tambourine, and maintained it, in life as in music, sadly "jingling all over" like the tambourine. The punctuation mark reveals new ways of appreciating Melville's aesthetic, of interpreting major aspects of *Moby-Dick*. Thus the hyphen comes into its own.

Not long thereafter, Melville depicts opposites in nature somehow meeting, and we are in the presence of the dialectic, as Douglass suggests in his account of slave song. One thinks of the dialectic as contrasting tones come into view and Melville shows how they can be brought together: "In outer aspect, Pip and Dough-Boy together made a match, like a black pony and a white one, of equal developments, though of dissimilar color, driven in one eccentric span." No less certainly, we think of Douglass's statement that extremes meet in matter, when Melville notes that "even blackness has its brilliancy," as seen in "lustrous ebony," and again as Ishmael moves the narration toward the music of the blues, setting the stage for Pip the castaway:

But Pip loved life, and all life's peaceable securities; so that the panic-striking business in which he had somehow unaccountably become entrapped, had most sadly blurred his brightness; though, as ere long will be seen, what was thus temporarily subdued in him, in the end was destined to be luridly illumined by strange wild fires, that fictitiously showed him off to ten times the natural lustre with which in his native Tolland County in Connecticut he had once enlivened many a fiddler's frolic on the green; and at melodious even-tide, with his gay ha-ha! had turned the round horizon into one star-belled tambourine.

So, though in the clear air of day, suspended against the blue-veined neck, the pure-watered diamond drop will healthful glow; yet, when the cunning jeweler would show you the diamond in its most impressive lustre, he lays it against a gloomy ground. (*MD*, 411–12)

Melville's evocation of music is at times so hidden that much in *Moby-Dick* is difficult to understand. But seventy-five chapters after "Midnight, Forecastle," we will recall Douglass's *Narrative* and recognize the music and the implied dance of the funeral procession. Melville's deep personal knowledge of black culture made this connection possible, for there is no mention at all of funeral processions in the *Narrative*. Douglass's work allows a creative leap by Melville. Working from the ex-slave's foundation of sadness and joy, the novelist introduces the procession at sea and the music's comment on the fate of the *Pequod*. The music of the funeral march flows from intimations of musical tones in "Midnight, Forecastle" as the Ring Shout is launched. One cannot help wondering why Melville was willing to risk his reader's failure to understand, well into the future, so important a theme in *Moby-Dick*.

[III]

As hidden thus far as any aspect of Melville's art is the movement of ships in the funeral procession. Still, mention of funerals is not foreign to *Moby-Dick;* references range from Ishmael, in the opening paragraph of the novel, finding himself "bringing up the rear of every funeral" to Pip's offer to beat Queequeg's "dying march" (*MD*, 3, 479). There are, moreover, cemeteries far down in the ocean that Melville relates to processions and to the Ring Shout. This leads us back to the Manx Sailor, who, as dance begins in "Midnight, Forecastle," draws our attention to cemeteries: "I wonder whether those jolly lads bethink them of what they are dancing over. I'll dance over your grave, I will. . . . "O Christ! To think of the green navies and the green-skulled crews!" Melville tells us that the limitless ocean holds possibilities for funeral processions analogous to those on earth. If dance can be imagined in the ocean, as has been illustrated, ships can be imagined in processions with cemeteries beneath them on the ocean floor (*MD*, 175).

References to processions to and from the cemetery resonate with musicologist Samuel Floyd's Jr.'s explanation of why the circularity of the Ring Shout gives way to linear movement on land, the procession from the church following the body to the cemetery before returning in procession to the community. We enter Melville's realm again: Pip's percussive beating of the tambourine is a part of African tradition in America, about which Floyd writes, "This mythic call to Dance, Drum, and Song in the form of parades goes back to the African processions . . . and back to the burial rites of Africans and African American slaves . . . From these ceremonies, because of the necessity of the participants to move to a remote destination, the ring straightened" to become the sad walk to the cemetery followed by the joyful return, which, Floyd notes, "remarkably mimics the walk-to-shout of the ring shout."[14]

Sailing the ocean in almost any direction, one is on the way to or from a cemetery, and a mournful procession to it, or a joyful return from it, might be imagined, as Melville would have us do. Moreover, there is a long tradition in the United States of processions to and from the cemetery. Indeed in the port city of Norfolk, Virginia, in 1820, a year after Melville's birth, there were gloomy-jolly processions. In that year in Norfolk, a procession of "25 or 30 black men and women" followed a horse-drawn hearse to a cemetery. Six blacks in front of the hearse sang, while walking, a "Hymn the lines of which were read line by line, in a loud sonorous voice, by the book-man: All was solemn," reports William Dunlap. Having arrived at the burial ground, Dunlap followed a procession of Baptists who were leaving and, a half-mile from the cemetery, singing in "full chorus." He caught up with three of the marchers who had fallen behind those singing and found them "vociferously merry." Slowing his pace "to learn the subject of their mirth," he discovered "it was Death and Immortality." One of the men "with loud laughter assured his two companions that he was certain of immortal happiness in Heaven, and the three with peals of laughter continued to treat this subject in a way contrasting strongly with the earnestness of the preacher at the grave."[15]

Deep into *Moby-Dick*, in "The Pequod Meets the Bachelor," Melville opens with, "And jolly enough were the sights and sounds that came bearing down before the wind, some few weeks after Ahab's harpoon had been welded"(*MD*, 493). The *Bachelor*'s joy, in contrast to the *Pequod*'s gloom, is similar to that of blacks returning from a cemetery in a partying spirit. Heading home after a successful voyage, the *Bachelor* is in "holiday apparel," with the lower jaw of a slain whale hanging from its bowsprit, a sign of a triumphant voyage. The ship "was joyously, though somewhat vaingloriously, sailing round among the widely-separated ships on the ground, previous to pointing her prow for home"; at her mast-head were three men wearing "long streamers of narrow red bunting at their hats"(*MD*, 493).

Reminding us of Douglass's "the glad ship is gone," Melville writes that as "this glad ship bore down upon the moody *Pequod*," the "barbarian sound of enormous drums"—the mythic call to drums?—rumbles forth. The crewmen are beating, hands clenched, on "huge try-pots, which, cov-

ered with the parchment-like *poke* or stomach skin of the black fish," produce
"a loud roar to every stroke" (*MD*, 494). As the drumming continues and the
drummers draw nearer, one can see the harpooners and mates "dancing with
the olive-hued girls who had eloped with them from the Polynesian Isles;
while suspended in an ornamented boat, firmly secured aloft between the
fore-mast and main-mast, three Long Island negroes, with glittering fiddle-
bows of whale ivory [are] presiding over the hilarious jig" (*MD*, 494).

The ships now side by side, the sailors of one observe the behavior of
those on the other. The joy on the *Bachelor* deepens the gloom on the *Pequod*,
intensifying the blues mood. Just as Pip is the principal musician on the *Pequod*, the principal musicians on the *Bachelor* are the drummers and the Long
Island Negroes (*MD*, 494). And it is evident, for Melville tells us as much,
that those on the *Bachelor* have "met with the most surprising success; all the
more wonderful," given the contrast, "that while cruising in the same sea
numerous other vessels had gone entire months without securing as single
fish" (*MD*, 493–94).

Of the captain of the *Bachelor*, Melville writes, "Lord and master over all
this scene, the captain stood erect on the ship's elevated quarter-deck, so that
the whole rejoicing drama was full before him, and seemed merely contrived
for his own diversion" (*MD*, 494). Contrasting emotions are fully drawn:

> And Ahab, he too was standing on his quarter-deck, shaggy and black,
> with a stubborn gloom; and as the two ships crossed each other's
> wakes—one all jubilation for things passed, the other all forebodings
> as to things to come—their two captains in themselves impersonated
> the whole striking contrast of the scene.
>   "Come aboard, come aboard!" cried the gay *Bachelor*'s com-
> mander, lifting a glass and a bottle in the air.
>   "Hast thou seen the White Whale?" gritted Ahab in reply.
>   "No; only heard of him; but don't believe in him at all," said the
> other good-humoredly.
>   "Come aboard!"

But Ahab replies, "Thou art too jolly. Sail on. Hast lost any men?"

> "Not enough to speak of—two islanders, that's all:—but come
> aboard, old hearty, come along. I'll soon take that black from your
> brow. Come along, will ye (merry's the play); a full ship and home-
> ward-bound."
>   "How wondrous familiar is a fool!" muttered Ahab; then aloud:
> "Thou art a full ship and homeward bound, thou sayst; well, then, call

me an empty ship, and outward-bound. So go thy ways, and I will mine. Forward there! Set all sails, and keep her to the wind!" (*MD,* 494–95)

Remote moods are joined as the ships part company:

And thus, while the one ship went before the breeze, the other stubbornly fought against it, and so the two vessels parted; the crew of the *Pequod* looking with grave, lingering glances toward the receding *Bachelor;* but the *Bachelor's* men never heeding their gaze for the lively revelry they were in. And as Ahab, leaning over the taffrail, eyed the home-ward bound craft, he took from his pocket a small vial of sand, and then looking from the ship to the vial, seemed thereby bringing two remote associations together, for that vial was filled with Nantucket soundings. (*MD,* 495)

The blues in "The Pequod Meets the Bachelor" informs dialogue and storyline and, again, characterization—all three in language in which Melville writes and thinks in *Moby-Dick*. Melville has us understand that the *Bachelor* and the *Pequod* combine contrasting moods before leaving each other, one proceeding sadly toward its own burial at sea, the other cheerily continuing its voyage; one representing the mournful march to the cemetery, the other the joyful return home. Working from Douglass's classic thesis regarding ironic core elements of slave music, Melville enables us, with the benefit of hindsight, to follow such processions deep into the twentieth century, into Norfolk, Mobile, Baltimore, Charleston, and New Orleans—all port cities.[16]

Melville's appropriation of the blues made possible sacred inventions at sea that the nation continues to witness on land. More than that, the blues aesthetic that informs *Narrative of the Life of Frederick Douglass* and *Moby-Dick* is at once as eternal and as modern as any known to human experience. That aesthetic just as certainly, as James Baldwin writes, informs jazz today and achieves universal reach in *Moby-Dick*. Musical currents in the novel reflect profound problems confronting the variegated crew of the *Pequod* as well as the larger cultural truth: that the very music of *Moby-Dick*—despite and because of the attitudes of the crew—reveals the paramount importance of slavery in American life.

We hear the blues on the *Pequod,* as on the plantation as described by Douglass, and the blues in this respect, as wise Pip clearly recognizes, portend no good for the nation. In thinking about slavery in the United States, as mediated through a reading of *Narrative,* Melville, like Douglass, recognized the conflicts at the heart of the American soul. Like Douglass, Melville was a great student of slavery and black culture in all their dimensions, and was able to plumb these contexts to imagine a funeral procession that speaks to the crisis of the time from an African perspective. With their blues metaphor for the nation's racial divide, it is hard to imagine more contemporary thinkers than Douglass and Melville.

A

NARRATIVE

OF

VOYAGES AND TRAVELS,

IN THE

NORTHERN AND SOUTHERN HEMISPHERES:

COMPRISING

THREE VOYAGES ROUND THE WORLD;

TOGETHER WITH A

VOYAGE OF SURVEY AND DISCOVERY,

IN THE

PACIFIC OCEAN AND ORIENTAL ISLANDS.

....

BY AMASA DELANO.

....

BOSTON:

PRINTED BY E. G. HOUSE, FOR THE AUTHOR.

1817.

CHAPTER XVI.

Description of the Coast of Chili—Chiloe Islands—Baldivia--Mocha
—Conception—Valparaiso—and Quoquimbo.

WHEN as far to the westward as longitude 78° 00' west, it will do to stand to the northward, by the latitude of Cape Pillar. The winds will not incline so much from the north west, after passing that cape as before; probably owing to the shape of the land, which runs from Cape Pillar to the south east a great distance, and no doubt causes the wind to blow in that direction. By standing to the northward by Cape Pillar, which is the south west cape, and Cape Victory the north west cape of the Straits of Magellan, on to the coasts of Chili, before obtaining a sufficient offing, there would be great danger of being driven on shore, or among the Chili islands, should a ship be caught in a gale of wind, so that she could not carry sail for any considerable length of time.

On the 12th of March, as has been before stated, we considered ourselves far enough to the westward of the cape, to stand to the northward with safety. We then found ourselves in latitude 49° 30' south, and longitude 86° 20' west, by account; which, after making all allowances for the easterly current and bad reckoning, led us to suppose we were to the westward of 80°; but on the 18th we obtained several sets of lunar observations, which placed us in longitude 77° 40' west, and at the same time, by reckoning, it was 86° 50'. The latitude was 41° south. Variation of compass 16° east. I would here remark, that it is very difficult to obtain observations for longitude, in making a passage round Cape Horn, on account of thick weather; and that all ships find a strong current setting constantly to the eastward. We found the winds blow chiefly from the south west, after getting to the northward of latitude 50° south, and as we advanced in this course it gradually hauled to the southward and eastward.

On the 26th, we saw the island of Juan Fernandez, and landed upon it; and on the 31st, arrived and landed at Massa Fuero. A particular description of these islands will be hereafter given. From this we continued our course to the northward, on the coast of Chili. We will here give a description of this coast, beginning at its southern extremity.

All the coast of Chili, from latitude 52° 00' south, or from Cape Victory down to latitude 41° 40' south, is one continued chain of islands, inlets, shoals, and dangers; and if driven in amongst them, there would be great danger of losing the ship, and all the crew perishing; as this coast is one of the worst that is known, for a ship to be cast away upon. I became very intimately acquainted with a Spanish commander by the name of Calminaries, who was with Malispeena, when he surveyed this coast. He informed me, that there were many good harbours amongst these islands; but were very difficult of access. Hair seals were to be procured; but it was hazardous for a vessel to go to look for them.

After passing down the coast below the last stated latitude; it is in general clear of dangers. The climate becomes mild, and the weather pleasant. In latitude 40° 5' south, and longitude 73° 20' west, lies the town of Baldivia. This is the most southern Spanish-settlement of any importance on the main coast of Chili. It is celebrated amongst the Spaniards in that part of the world, on account of the man whose name it bears, and because it is one of the strongest places on that coast. The next place of any consequence is Conception, which lies in latitude 36° 47' south, and in longitude 73° 6' west, and has a spacious bay. Valparaiso lies in latitude 33° 1' south, and longitude 72° 4' west. Coquimbo is in latitude 30° south, and longitude 71° 16' west. These four ports are all which the Spaniards have on the coast of Chili, of any consequence. There are other small ones; but none that are large enough to receive ships. The country, from the latitude 42° 00' south, is cultivated, and produces all kinds of provisions in the greatest plenty. They are most easily procured near Conception and Valparaiso.

The Spaniards have settled the island of Chiloe. Its northern extreme lies in latitude 41° 40' south. It is a great place for catching and curing fish. I have had several hundred weight of them. They exactly resemble the cod, which is caught in the bay of St. Loire, and are a very delicate table fish. It also abounds with very excellent timber, suitable for ships and other buildings, and common cabinet work. "Chiloe, a considerable island, being one of the governments of Chili, seated on its coast in the Southern, Pacific Ocean in the gulf of Chonos, or the Archipelago of Guaytecas, and separated in its southern part from the continent by a narrow sea, which forms a bay. It is about 140 miles in length, by 30 in breadth. It lies between 41° 40' and 43° 50' south latitude. The principal harbour of the island, on the north coast, is Chacao, which is said to be well fortified and capable of good defence; and at Culbuco, which is larger, resides a corregidor, nominated by the President of Chili, and also regidores and alcaldes, chosen annually. Besides the parish church, this place has two convents, and a college of Jesuits. The island is well peopled with Spaniards, mulattoes, and Indian proselytes."—*Rees' Cyclo. vol VIII. From* CHA to CHR.

In latitude 38° 28' south, and longitude 74° 4' west, lies the island of Mocha; famous amongst whalemen and sealers, for wild horses and hogs. They are numerous on it, and it is common to go on shore and shoot them for fresh provisions. I have eaten of the horse beef, which was very good. The island formerly had black cattle upon it; but either the ships' people which stopped there, or the Spaniards, have destroyed them. It lies about fifteen miles from the main land, has a tolerable harbour, or anchoring place, on its northerly part; is moderately elevated land; good soil, and would be valuable if settled and well cultivated. The longest way is from north to south, not more than eight or nine miles, and two-thirds of that distance in width. There is an island called St. Maria, in latitude 37° 00' south, and longitude 73° 34' west, which will be described hereafter.

In navigating this coast at any time between the months of October and April, the weather is pleasant, and the wind three fourths of the time from the south east, in moderate, steady breezes. I think I never witnessed such serene, pure air, as on this coast in summer; but in winter the winds are from the northward one half the time, from latitude 33° 00', to 40° 00' south, and blow at times very strong, when torrents of rain fall. Off from this coast lie Juan Fernandez, the famous place of Alexander Selkirk's exile, and Massa Fuero. To the north of them, lie St. Ambrose and St. Felix. These places will be hereafter described.

The country in the kingdom of Chili is remarkable for its mountains. A chain of them, of stupendous height, extends from near latitude 50° 00' south, down to the equator, with very few passes across them. Those which are farthest to the south are called the Andes, and this name is sometimes given to the whole chain, both those that run through Chili, as well as those that run through Peru. But the most common names given them at present are, those in Chili are called the Andes, and those in Peru the Cordelieras. They lie nearly parallel to the shore, from fifty to an hundred and fifty miles inland. I have seen them most part of the distance, from latitude 40° 00' south, to near the equator; having sailed along all that coast, frequently within five leagues of the land, and having an excellent opportunity of observing them. They sometimes are not visible in clear weather, when five or six leagues off shore. This is probably owing to their not being so high, or lying further back from the sea at some places than at others. They are sometimes to be seen partly covered with snow. Volcanos exist in the range, and particularly near the sea coast. There can be no doubt but they are the highest mountains in the world. The appearance of them is magnificent beyond description, when viewed from a ship's deck, eight or ten miles off shore; particularly when the sun is near setting, and the atmosphere clear; it then shines on their westerly side next the sea; in some places beautifully shaded, where one mountain stands a little in front of another, making the most interesting and splendid appearance that can be conceived of.

The next remarkable objects of this country are the mines of gold and silver, which have spread its fame over the four quarters of the world. In the kingdoms, as they are called, of Chili and Peru, there are great numbers of them; though but few that are profitable. I have seen a great quantity of copper at the port of Coquimbo, which was brought from these mines. It is valued much higher than the copper of Europe, being, as I understood, mixed with gold.

I was informed by the Spaniards when at Conception, that there were rich mines to the southward, in Chili, which they do not work, because the natives are so formidable in their vicinity, and are their enemies. I had it from undoubted authority, that there are natives in the southern interior of the kingdom of Chili, whom the Spaniards have never conquered, and to whom they are obliged to pay tribute, to keep peace with them; and that they had followed them over some parts of the Andes, where it was so cold that some of their men and horses were frozen to death, in crossing the mountain. After crossing it, they discovered one of the richest countries they had ever found in South America, for gold and silver; but the metals were not attainable, owing to the difficulty of crossing the mountains. The latitude of this rich country must be as high as 40°, or upwards, south. I will here remark, that I have spent nearly six months at one time in the port and city of Conception, always having the privilege of associating with the first class of people when I chose it. This gave me an excellent opportunity to get the most correct information of this country, which I improved to the best of my abilities, both at that time and at several other visits which I afterwards made, of from one to three months each.

The north head or westerly entrance of Conception bay is in latitude 36° 30' south, and in longitude 73° 25' west, from the best calculations we had an opportunity to make, subject however to an error of a mile or two, as we had no observation near it. In sailing into the bay or harbour, keep to the southward, when running for the port. This precaution is necessary also in making any harbour on the coast of Chili, especially in the summer season, as the prevailing winds are from the south east. In running along the coast there will be seen two remarkable hills, which lie to the south of the entrance of the bay, about four or five leagues distant. They are called the Maiden's Paps, or Dugs of Conception; resembling a woman's breasts, by which they have obtained their name. A bay makes in to the northward of the Paps, and a river to the southward; but after passing the small bay to the north of them, the coast trends about north, till coming up with the north head or westerly entrance into Conception, off which lie two small rocks, one white and the other black. The white one is the largest. The other lies to the north of it. When the head is passed, bring it to bear east, and then make an island, called Quiriquina, lying east from the head, in the middle of the passage into the bay. This island will not be opened distinctly till the head has been considerably passed; it will then be safe to haul in for its north end, and sail pretty near to it round to the eastward, and the bay will be open to the southward. The main land must not be kept too near on board when abreast the island, on account of some rocks that lie off the shore. After passing this island to the south a short distance, it will be best to keep the east side of the bay best on board, on account of some dangerous reefs, that lie on the west side above the island. When near the head of the bay, in six or seven fathoms water, it will be safe to stand westward, keeping the south shore on board; the reef will be left to the northward, and anchor in the same depth of water off the port of Talcaquana. This stands on the south west side of the bay, where will be found soft clear ground, sheltered from all winds except the north, and that much broken by the island before mentioned, which lies about three leagues distant, and forms one side of the bay. Its breadth is about two leagues from east to west. There are very regular soundings all the way from the island to the port, or anchoring place, decreasing from twenty fathoms near the island, to the depth laid down to anchor in. There is a passage to the westward of the island, but I should not recommend a ship to go that way, if it can be avoided. It is an easy place to go into, and is a good harbour, affording every kind of refreshment. The inhabitants are a kind and friendly people. The landing is very convenient, on a smooth gravelly beach, directly in front of the town, for landing and taking off a cargo, or stores. This place is healthy and handsomely situated. Its situation is low, being a skirt of land that lies between the mountains and the water. The land to the north and south of it is high. The houses are principally built of clay, which is baked in the sun, similar to the method that has been described in page 161, and covered on the roof with crooked tiles, made and baked in the shape of half a split reed, being twelve or fourteen inches long, and six inches wide. These crooked tiles are laid one end upon another, from the lower edge of the roof up to the ridge pole, in straight rows, so as to form troughs near enough together for the same shaped tiles to cover the edges of two; the tiles are then placed on them the other side up, one lying upon another as before. This of course turns all the water into the hollows, and it runs off the building in spouts. It is my opinion that it is the best and cheapest way that can be adopted to cover the roof of a house. The first cost of the tiles would not be any more, and perhaps not so much, as a roof of boards and shingles would be; and when they are well laid, and mortar at the same time put over the joints of the tiles, there would be no danger of their leaking. It is not necessary to have any more wood to form the roof than strong rafters, or pieces up and down, placed six feet distant from each other, and battens laid across them near enough together for the ends of the tiles to rest upon. They must be as near together as the length of the tiles. A roof made in this manner would not be very heavy, the tiles are not more than three quarters of an inch thick. If people should get into the way of making this kind of tiles, they could make them cheap, and regular as to size and shape.

The port of Talcaquana is nine miles from the city of Conception, in a north west direction, through a fine level plain. After leaving the port, there is a small hill to cross. The road then, for about three miles, runs parallel with and near the shore, where there is a beautiful beach on one of the branches of the harbour. It crosses near the head of several small creeks, between them and fresh ponds, which are drained into them. It is defended by two batteries, one lying on the easterly side of the port, on low ground. The guns are not more than fifteen or twenty feet above the level of the sea. The other is to the north west, on the side of a hill, between one and two hundred feet above the level of the water, and has seven or eight heavy guns in it, twenty-four or thirty-two pounders. They have a very commanding situation. That to the eastward has about the same number of guns; but is much better built. The two forts can cross each other's fires, when playing on a ship in the road. Their situation could not be better chosen to defend the place.

I shall here insert an affair, which I think will be amusing to the reader, that happened about the time I arrived here in February, 1805, carrying into port the Spanish ship Tryal, the particulars of which will be described hereafter. On our landing, we found all in confusion, the Spaniards having taken us for two English ships coming to revenge the injury which an English ship had sustained at that place about a week previous to our arrival. The circumstances were these: Two English whale ships came in to this place for refreshments, and to repair some damages; not knowing of the difficulties which existed at that time between the two countries, in consequence of the English having attacked four Spanish frigates that were going to Spain from the River of Plate with money on board, taking three of them, and sinking the other This had occasioned the Spaniards to stop all English ships. These two English whale ships were the Betsey, commanded by captain Richards, and the Thomas, commanded by captain Moody, who had his wife with him. They came in and anchored within a quarter of a mile of the forts. The Spaniards sent a guard boat on board, with the captain of the port, to offer any assistance they might stand in need of, and to invite them on shore. The two captains accepted their invitation, and ordered their first officers not to let any Spaniards come on board in their absence, (having some suspicions that the Spaniards were not sincere.) They went on shore with the captain of the port, and were very politely received on the beach by a number of officers, who, after escorting them to the captain of the port's house, and placing sentinels at each door, informed them of the existing difficulty, and that they should take possession of their ships. The English captains told them the ships would not be given up in their absence. Three or four large boats, filled with troops, attempted to go on board, and being refused, the Spaniards fired on them. The ships returned the fire. The two batteries then opened their fire upon them, and the Thomas soon gave up. The chief officer of the Betsey, whose name was Hudson, (a man of extraordinary bravery,) cut his cable, and his ship swung the wrong way, with her head in shore, passing within several Spanish ships, which, with every vessel in the harbour, that could bring a gun to bear, together with three hundred soldiers in boats and on ships' decks, and the two batteries, all kept up a constant fire upon him. The wind was light, nearly a calm. The shot flew so thick that it was difficult for him to make sail, some part of the rigging being cut away every minute. He kept men at the guns, and when the ship swung her broad side so as to bear upon any of the Spanish ships, he kept up a fire at them. In this situation this brave fellow continued to lie for three quarters of an hour, before he got his topsails sheeted home. The action continued in this manner for near an hour and a half. He succeeded in getting the ship to sea, however, in defiance of all the force that could be brought against him. The ship was very much cut to pieces, in sails, rigging, and hull; and a considerable number of men were killed and wounded on board.

Hudson kept flying from one part of the deck to the other during the whole time of action; encouraging and threatening the men as occasion required. He kept a musket in his hand most part of the time, firing when he could find time. Some of the men came aft and begged him to give up the ship; telling him that they should all be killed—that the carpenter had all one side of him shot away—that one man was cut in halves with a double headed shot, as he was going aloft to loose the fore topsail, and the body had fallen on deck in two separate parts—that such a man was killed at his duty on the fore-castle, and one more had been killed in the main top—that Sam, Jim, Jack, and Tom, were wounded—and that they would do nothing more towards getting the ship out of the harbour. His reply to them was, "Then you shall be sure to die, for it they do not kill you I will, if you persist in any such resolution." Saying at the same time, "Out she goes, or down she goes." Meaning that the ship should sink if she did not go out of the harbour. By this resolute and determined conduct, he kept the men to their duty, and succeeded in accomplishing one of the most daring enterprises, perhaps, ever attempted.

I had the above particulars from the two English captains, with whom I became acquainted after I arrived, and from many different persons who were at the place at the time; and also from some of the men who were on board the Betsey, whom I saw after I left this port. A Spanish, officer who commanded one of the batteries, told me, that they fired one hundred and thirty 32 pound shot from their battery at the Betsey, and the other battery as many, or more; besides what the ships and soldiers had done.

There is a great trade carried on between this port and Lima. Many ships are employed in carrying wheat from here. This country abounds with it for many degrees north and south. They also carry boards, spars, and timber; some wine, raisins, and other dried fruits; considerable of the herb of Paraguay, the production of the plains of that name, and is that which the inhabitants call *matte*. It is the tea of the country, and very much drank by all classes of people on the coast, and in all the country of Chili and Peru. The country here, like the other ports of Chili, is well cultivated, and abounds with the best of provisions. They make great quantities of very good wine; and have all the quadrupeds that are common to this country, and so plenty, that the people purchase them from one another at the following very low rate: for a good bullock, four dollars; a good horse, twenty, and common ones from four to eight dollars; sheep for half a dollar; and other flesh meat in the same proportion. Foreigners are charged more for what they purchase.

The feathered race of animals far exceed any thing of the kind I ever saw, particularly for those good to eat. The Spaniards here are not allowed to use fire arms in common, and as they have no Indians who hunt them, they are very plenty and tame. I have often gone out by permission on horse back, and shot a horse load in three hours; killing seven different kinds of ducks and teal, with various other sorts of fowls. The shores, water, and pastures in this vicinity, are covered with them. They have the finest fish, and in the greatest variety, of any place I ever visited. There are gold and silver mines near Conception; but not plenty enough to make much account of. The riches of this country consist in what is produced from the land, not from what is dug out of it. This city was founded two or three leagues further to the northward than it now stands, on the easterly side of the bay, and was called Pinko. It was removed to where it now is because of earthquakes; the old town or city being now quite deserted on that account.

The ladies of this place vie with any I ever saw in point of beauty. They are modest, mild, and very agreeable. Their dress is a little singular, as they wear the old fashioned hoop round the waist, of an extraordinary size; but to a gentleman who has been accustomed to travel, it would not be worthy of much notice. They are rather partial to the Americans and to Englishmen. I never can think it a crime to reciprocate their sentiments. The Spanish gentlemen are the noblest spirited men I ever was acquainted with. The idea that is entertained of their being a very jealous people, is not true. I never saw gentlemen more free from it.

In the city and port of Conception and its vicinity, there are about fifteen or twenty thousand inhabitants of all descriptions.

I shall here introduce the subject of Valparaiso, with Capt. Vancouver's remarks, which we found generally correct. He says—"ships destined to the port of Valparaiso, should endeavour during the summer months, to make the coast well to the southward of the bay, in order that a fair wind may be insured for entering it. The southerly winds, which in general extend sixty or seventy leagues from the coast, mostly prevail until the month of May; and from the middle of that month during all the months of June, July, August and September, I was given to understand the prevailing winds were from the north. These winds are commonly attended with great quantities of rain, and very foggy weather; but they do not often blow with much violence, as soon as the wind returns to the southward the dry season commences, and so it continues, with little variation, during the remainder of the year. These winds, however, frequently blow very strong, so as to break vessels adrift, though well secured by anchors on the shore near to the town of Valparaiso. Within four or five leagues of the point of Angels, which is the western point of the bay, is a low rocky point, near to which is a detached high barren rock. These points lie from each other north 51° east to the northward of the above low rocky point, are some scattered rocks, that lie about two miles from the point, and about a fourth of that distance from the shore, and to the northward of these rocks, is a sandy bay, on the north east side of which is a house. In this bay, I was led to believe that anchorage might be had, though the situation is certainly very much exposed.

"The point of Angels, (off which are also some rocks, lying very near to it,) may be approached by sailing at the distance of half a league from the shore, and as soon as the point is passed, the town of Valparaiso is instantly discovered. About seven miles to the northeast of this point, is a cluster of rocks, lying at some distance from the shore, on which the sea breaks violently; but we had no opportunity for ascertaining their situation with any degree of precision. The bay is about four miles wide, and about a mile deep. Apparently free from any sort of danger; but as it is greatly exposed to the northerly winds, the trading vessels constantly moor with two good anchors and cables in that direction, and with other cables fast to anchors on shore, in five or six fathoms water, soft sandy bottom, near the custom house; by which means it is expected that the officers of the revenue may be enabled to prevent any contraband trade, by vigilantly attending to their duty in the day time, and rowing guard during the night. The depth of the water gradually increases with the distance from the shore, to thirty six fathoms, and the bottom becomes more tenacious. In the depth of sixteen fathoms, in which we took our station, it is very stiff clay. Here we moored a cable each way to the northward, and to the southward; the point of Angels bearing by compass north 35° west. The fort in the town, north 86° west. The redoubt on the hill, south 5° east. The church of Almandrel, south 65° east. The east point of the bay, north 57° east, and the nearest shore south 7° west, a cable's length distant.

"On the top of a hill, on the east side of the bay is an open, or barbed battery, lately erected with stone and brick, and capable of mounting ten guns; this battery commands all that side of the bay, the beach , and the village of Almandrel. On the summit of another hill, is a stone redoubt, of a circular form, with embrasures. These command the beach and village of Almandrel to the eastward; the bay to the northward, and the town and harbour of Valparaiso, to the north westward. Although this fortification was in a most neglected and ruinous condition, we were given to understand, that the principal magazine was inclosed within its walls. The largest and most considerable fortification, is in the middle of the town, within which is the residence of the governor. It is situated on a small eminence, one side of which is open to the sea, and is separated from it by a very narrow pass. The height of the town wall, which is strong and well built with masonry, is about fifteen feet to the embrasures, of which there are six that point to the sea; two face the street to the eastward; and two look into the market place, to the westward. The upper part of the hill is surrounded by another strong wall, about ten feet in height; and half way up the hill a third wall crosses it, which shews three embrasures to the sea; immediately over the fort and governor's house. At the place where this wall terminates, which is near the summit of the eminence, the side of the hill falls perpendicularly down into a deep gully; by which the fort is encompassed, and which might be the means of rendering this fortification unassailable; and a place that might long be maintained, were it not for other hills within musket shot, which command every part of it. The space enclosed by the town wall, is about four hundred yards in length, and in some places about one hundred in breadth. Here are the barracks for the troops, and at the upper end is a building in which a court is held for the regulation of the police of the town. A door in that side of the wall, which points to the market place, is the only entrance; and leads by a winding staircase to the different parts of the fortification. There is another fortification about half a mile from the fort, situated on the west side of the bay, at the foot of a high hill, and but little elevated above the level of the sea. This shews a face of five embrasures to the east, and in that direction commands the west side of the bay; three embrasures, to the northward, are so disposed as to be able to open upon any vessel, the instant she passes round the point of Angels; whilst two others, to the southward, command the ships lying in the harbour, or the bay. We computed that these several places contained about seventy pieces of cannon, many of which were without proper carriages, and some were lying dismounted under the walls of the town battery, in the town.

"From the western fort, some rocks extend into the bay, and the bottom is too foul for vessels of any force to anchor nearer to this fortification, than about four hundred yards; but they may approach and anchor in a very eligible situation, within about two hundred and fifty yards of the garrison, or principal fortress: and in neither of these places, in their present situation, would be able to resist a well directed fire from two or three frigates."—*Vancouver's Voyage round the World.*

If intending to sail into Valparaiso, always make the land to the southward of the harbour, for in the winter, the south winds are much more prevalent than any other. It is best to make the land ten leagues to the southward of the harbour. The land there trends nearly north and south; but is indented with small coves and bays. If a ship falls in with the land, and the latitude is not exactly known, (if to the southward) it is not easy to miss the port. There is a kind of cove or bay, with a sand beach, about four or five miles to the southward of the rocky point, which captain Vancouver speaks of, lying to the south west of the point of Angels, with a ragged rock off it; but the coast does not trend much to the eastward until the ragged rock, above mentioned, is passed. We did not find the coast make so much to the eastward there, as captain Vancouver describes; neither do I think it so far from the ragged rock to the point of Angels, as he states it to be.

The reasons, why I differ from captain Vancouver, respecting the winds in the months of June, July, August, and September, (which are the winter months here,) and also in the courses and distances, are probably on account of my having entered, or been in the port of Valparaiso in nearly every month in the year; when he never was there but on one short visit of a month or two; and of course had not so good an opportunity of forming a correct judgment upon this subject, as I had.

It is not proper to sail out of Valparaiso with any but a fair wind; for should it blow from the westerly quarter, it will be difficult to keep clear of the land to the northward of the bay, as it makes out considerably to the westward, and the current is generally setting to the northward.

The harbour is very safe in summer; but in winter it sometimes blows from the northward strong gales; in which case the sea comes in so as to make it difficult riding. I do not believe the north winds ever affect vessels very much, as the land is so high to the southward, and so near to them, that it has a tendency to break its force. It is not considered a good winter harbour by the Spaniards. The productions of the soil here are like those of Conception, and it yields very plentifully. There are more fruit and vegetables in this market than at that place, such as peaches, apricots, oranges, lemons, melons, onions, and pumpkins. It is the port town of the capital of Chili, which is called St. James, or St. Jago. It has more trade than any port on this coast. The number of ships that lade here in the course of the season, with provisions of different kinds for Lima, and other ports, is considerable. There is considerable commercial intercourse by land between the River of Plate and this port. They march slaves over land, from Buenos Ayres, (to avoid carrying them round Cape Horn) and ship them again for the coast of Peru; as will be seen hereafter in the affair of the Tryal. There is one pass only that crosses the Andes, to go and come by. They transport from one coast to the other, many articles of merchandize across this pass. The herb of Paraguay is brought on the backs of horses, or mules, this way; and considerable quantities of gold and silver are carried in the same manner to be shipped for Spain. This kingdom is not so rich in mines as Peru; but there is a great number of them in the country. They have a mint at St. Jago, where they coin, as I was informed by good authority, two or three millions of dollars in gold and silver in a year. I have likewise been told, that there was more bullion carried out of this kingdom, than was coined in it. The air here is similar to that of Conception, neither hot nor very cold. I never saw ice in Chili, in latitude as low as 37° south, more than once or twice, and then not more than the thickness of window glass. Farenheit's thermometer is never higher than eighty-eight or eighty-nine degrees; commonly standing at about eighty at Valparaiso and Conception in summer. The distance from Valparaiso to St. Jago is about sixty miles. I have passed both winter and summer at Valparaiso and Conception, and made the coast of Chili and Peru my home for five years. This has given me an opportunity to obtain a correct knowledge of them, and enables me to render a just account of their manners and customs.

In the harbour of Valparaiso there are great numbers of the hump-backed and right-whale. Spermaceti whales are caught off this coast; but it is said they never come on soundings, the truth of which I have reason to doubt, however, as I have known them taken near this coast; and the squid, which they feed upon, is frequently found in this harbour. I often caught squid here, which were three or four feet long. This species of fish is said to be the only food the spermaceti whales ever eat.

I had frequent opportunities of being acquainted with many captains who are employed in the whale fishery on this coast. These men are possessed of a great share of courage and intrepidity in the pursuit of their business; but are in the habit of boasting of their superiority, when in company, and of exaggerating their exploits. While lying in the harbour of Valparaiso, captain George Howe was on board my ship, who had been frequently in company when the subject of killing whales was discussed, and one calm and very pleasant day, we discovered a large whale asleep within twenty rods of some of the ships. We thought this a good opportunity to try our skill in killing whales. We fitted out a whale-boat belonging to captain Howe, which was properly manned, and my boatswain, who had been in the business before, was to steer and direct the expedition. We prepared and rigged a lance, which was made for the purpose of killing sea elephants, having an iron shank about two feet long, with a pole to it, six or eight feet in length, and a small line attached to it, with the other end fastened to the stem of the boat, to prevent it being lost. Thus equipped we rowed up softly, within twenty feet of the whale, when I threw the lance into her, a little abaft the fore fin, which entered more than the length of the iron part. The whale, on feeling the hurt, raised its tail fifteen feet in the air, and brought it down with such force, within six feet of the boat, that it was half filled with water; and produced a most violent agitation in that element for a great distance around us. It may be considered a fortunate circumstance that we escaped injury; for had it hit the boat it would have been staved to atoms, and probably some of us been killed. Her head lay towards the shore, and she started in that direction, brought her head out of water, making the most terrible bellowing that can be imagined; turned herself round and went out of the bay, spouting blood till out of sight. Thus ended our first and last enterprise in killing whales. The experiment convinced us that it was a difficult and dangerous business, and ought never to be attempted by any, except those who have been bred up to and perfectly skilled in the art. The method we adopted was correct, excepting the first instrument thrown, which should have been a harpoon; which is an iron made with barbs to it, to prevent it from drawing out. To this should be a line or warp attached, three or four hundred fathoms in length; by which means we could have held on to the whale, and pulled the boat up so as to throw the lance with the most sure effect. The shank of a lance made use of by whalemen is four feet in length, with a pole fixed to it like the one we used. I have since had frequent opportunities of seeing whales killed by those who understood it, and was perfectly satisfied that it required courage, judgment, and activity.

Having mentioned the name of captain George Howe, who was my associate in the above described frolic, I shall for the satisfaction of his friends, give some account of him; some of the particulars of which are probably known to no one but myself. He was born in Stonington, state of Connecticut, and sailed out of the port of New London, in command of the schooner Oneco, on a sealing voyage. He arrived at Massa Fuero in 1800, and was compelled by misfortunes to go into Valparaiso and sell his vessel. Being disappointed in not receiving payment according to contract, he was obliged to go to St. Jago, the capital, before he could obtain justice. He got his money and returned to Valparaiso, and deposited upwards of twenty-two hundred dollars in the hands of a Spaniard, at whose house he resided, and was taken sick soon after. When I was at Valparaiso, in 1805, I made inquiry and found the house in which he lay sick. I was not a little surprised at finding him, and at the strange conduct of the people belonging to the house, as I had dined there several times since my arrival, yet they had neglected telling me of his being at the same time in the house; especially as it was well known to them we were friends, and had been particularly intimate, when in this port on a preceding voyage. I found him in a back room, no better than a hovel, in a most deplorable situation. He was lying on a miserable bed, or couch, in a very languishing state; his flesh wasted, till he was almost a skeleton; and no one near to afford him assistance, or friend to offer him a word of comfort. There was a well of water in the room adjoining, not more than twelve feet from his bed, from which was drawn all the water used by the family, with a door opening into his room, which was most of the time kept open. He had laid in this situation for five or six months. My feelings on the occasion can be better imagined than described. We had spent many happy hours together; and I could not help contrasting those times with what I now saw. I endeavoured to raise his spirits, and told him that I would take him on board my ship, and bring him home. I procured a barber and had him shaved, his clothes shifted, and dressed him in a decent manner, putting on his handsome Spanish cloak, and led him into the parlour, with an intention of giving him an airing; but the poor man was so reduced, that he fainted and was obliged to be placed on a sofa, and soon after carried back to his room, from which he never again was removed till a corpse. I visited him daily while I lay in this port, and each day sent him a kettle of soup; but I found he was too weak to be removed on board the ship. He died in about ten days after I left Valparaiso. Thus ended captain George Howe. He was a man of a noble mind; sincere in his friendships; honest and honourable in his dealings; and a remarkably pleasant companion: but his misfortunes broke his spirits.

The following particulars concerning captain Howe, which took place after I left him, I had from captain Bacon, whom I took with me when I left Lima, and who was with him most of the time after I sailed till he died. He informed me, that a short time before captain Howe died, the bishop, who was then at the port, had baptized him, and that he had received the sacrament; thus he died a Roman Catholic. This is made an important point with the priests of that religion. Just as he was dying, the man who kept the house, and with whom he had deposited his money, under-took to make a settlement with him. He brought forward his books, and made Howe acknowledge the different charges which he had prepared, when he was so far gone as to be just able to articulate, yes—without probably knowing what he said; thus defrauding him of his money, besides bringing him in debt. This transaction very much displeased the Spaniards here; and a remarkable accident happening to him about eight days after captain Howe died, caused them to make many remarks upon his conduct, and say, that it was a visitation of the judgment of God. There was a very high bank that was directly back of his house, which in consequence of a great rain, gave way, and fell on the very part where Howe had lain, and buried it under more than a hundred tons of earth.

The inhabitants here are similar to those of Conception. The ladies in general, however, dress rather more after the European or American fashion. I should calculate the inhabitants of Valparaiso and its vicinity to amount to fifteen or twenty thousand.

There is considerable of a military force kept on this coast, which is stationed at all places of any importance. It is well known that all this country is governed, as to its religious affairs, by Roman Catholics, and I found the inhabitants contented and apparently happy under those laws. Knowing but little concerning that part of the government, I can only say, that Conception is the see of a bishop, and has one residing in that city. I think Valparaiso is not, as the bishop who governs there resides at St. Jago.

The inhabitants of the coast of Chili are but a very small part of them Europeans, who are principally Spaniards. They hold themselves much higher in their own estimation than the Chilian born. As the Spaniards have mixed their blood with the aborigines so much, that there are but few born in the country, I believe, but what partake in a greater or less degree of it, on which account the European Spaniards undervalue them. The native Indians of South America are better featured than those of the northern part of the continent. They are treated in the south in the same manner as they have been in the north. The Spaniards have made war upon, harassed, and distressed them, till they have pretty much thinned them off near the sea coast. Some are made slaves by being taken prisoners in time of war, or by purchasing them from their enemies. I have been struck with horror to hear a Spanish priest call them brutes; telling me at the same time they were not Christians, and no better than cattle; when that same arrogant man's countrymen had robbed and despoiled the unfortunate Indian of all that was dear to him. Thus, "thinks I to myself," goes the world:—one man robs another of his country, his wealth, and his liberty; and then says he is a brute, and not a Christian. In such cases as these, I will say with the meritorious physician, to whom Bonaparte made the proposition to poison his soldiers at Jaffa, or Joppa: "If those be the requisites necessary to form a great man, I thank my God I do not possess them."

As I have remarked in another place, the dress of the ladies was not so graceful and becoming at Conception as at Valparaiso; at least, the extremely large hoops which are in general use at the former place did not strike me so pleasantly. I have been favoured with the sight of the hoop they wear underneath the outside petticoat. It is more than three feet in diameter, and is fastened higher than the hips, by some kind of linen or cotton cloth sewed around the hoop, leaving just room enough for the body. A string is reeved in the inner edge of the cloth, which draws it round the body above the hips, in the manner of a purse. This keeps the hoop in its place, and the body in the centre. As their petticoats are rather short, it gives them at first a very singular appearance; but any fashion in time becomes familiar, and its peculiarities are forgotten. The behaviour of the ladies was so delicate and pleasing, that a man must have more stoicism about him than I had, not to feel for them a strong partiality. Their dress was handsome, with gold and silver ornaments; such as gold hair combs, ear rings, bracelets for the wrists, chains round the wrist, and sometimes round the waist, and gold and silver shoe buckles. Many of these ornaments were inlaid with precious stones. Their head dress was the hair simply done up with four or five gold combs, tastefully disposed, which gave it a very charming appearance.

In horsemanship these people excel any men I have ever seen. Whether mounted on a well-broken, or untutored horse, they ride in the best manner, and shew great skill in the management of their steeds. It is seldom that the most vicious animal unhorses his rider. They, like the mamelukes, tutor their horses to start with astonishing quickness, and to stop suddenly. I have seen them ride with the geatest speed, till within six feet of the side of a house, and there stop as suddenly as if the animal had fallen dead on the spot. Sometimes I have seen them attempt to stop the horse in full career, when he would throw all his feet forward and slide perhaps more than four yards. Frequently the hinder feet would slip from under him, and seat him on his backside, in the position we sometimes see a dog.

The ladies also are fond of this exercise, and most of them ride extremely well. The better sort rode sidewise, like the women of this country. Their manner of mounting a horse was singular, and sufficiently ludicrous in the eyes of a stranger. At first I was unable to comprehend how the feat was performed. I soon, however, had an opportunity of receiving a lesson at a house where several ladies were assembled for the purpose of amusing themselves with a ride. When the horses were brought and all things ready, they prepared to mount. As a sailor is generally foremost when a lady is in the way, I offered my assistance, and the offer being accepted, one of them said, "Help me first." "O, yes," said I, with all the gallantry I possessed. She went to the side of a horse, held by a servant, and leaning her breast against his side, threw her arms over the saddle across his back, and stood in that posture, saying, "Help me." I stood awkwardly enough, not seeing any part, that delicacy would allow me to take hold of, in order to aid her ascent. The servant perceiving my embar-rassment, left his post, and taking one of her ankles in each hand, she gave a jump, and he assisted her *ascending node* with all his strength, till she was high enough to be seated. She then turned herself in the air, aided by the man, who, crossing his wrists, brought her into her seat, with the utmost grace and dexterity. In this manner the first ladies in the land are assisted in mounting a horse. I profited by the lesson, and was soon able to help a Spanish lady into her saddle, with as much grace, I suppose, as an ancient chevalier. Women of the inferior class sometimes ride with both feet on one side of the horse, and sometimes with both feet on the other side, and I have often seen them with a foot on either side; as to such affairs they seemed not to be very ceremonious. The furniture of their horses was different from what we had before seen; the reins of the bridle were worked in a manner resembling the lash of our whips, in a braid of four square made of some kind of skin; these were fastened to bits made according to our fashion, the reins long enough to come over the horse's neck, where they are united. The single part was extended six or seven feet, with a leathern tassel at the end, which was used as a whip. The saddle was first made something in the form of our saddle trees, then covered with a coarse skin, fitted to sit easy on the horse's back; these were covered with sheep skins, with the wool on, from four to six inches thick, painted with various colours and handsomely bound upon the saddle. This saddle looked well, and was easy to the horse and the rider. The most inconvenient part of the apparatus to an Englishman, was the stirrups. These were flat at the bot-tom, about a foot long, and six inches wide, the upper part making an arch highest in the middle, closed on the sides and fore part at the top, leaving an opening in the back part, large enough to admit the foot. They were fastened to the saddle with straps like ours, had a clumsy appearance, and in case of a fall might endanger the rider by confining his foot. Some ladies had saddles made in Europe, but for the most part they used those made in the country, which differed from the gentlemen's saddle chiefly by raising the tree on the off side, which made the top something in the form of a hollow bottomed chair. Both ladies and gentlemen are fond of equestrian amusements. Those of the higher ranks are rather indolent, having slaves and servants who per-form the greater part of the labour.

The ladies in some parts of the country have a cotton cloth, wove with stripes, very handsome, of different colours, about six or seven feet long and two thirds that width, which they form into something resembling a hammock on ship-board. This they suspend by small lines made fast to it through holes made for the purpose, two or three feet from the floors of their houses. On this they swing, sometimes sitting and sometimes lying, as best suits them. The dress of the gentlemen is very similar to the dress of the people of this country, only they have no outside coats in the manner of our countrymen. Some of them wear a cloak, made according to our fashion; they have also an outside garment called a poncho, which is much used. It is made of cloth similar to that of the ladies hammocks, of variegated colours, woven very thick, of a fine thread and curiously wrought. In weaving this cloth they use twelve or more treadles in the loom. It is usually from five to six feet square, handsomely fringed round the edges, having a slit in the middle of it just big enough to admit a man's head. This aperture was bordered with beautiful needle work. They put it over them, with their heads through the hole, and the garment hangs over them like a blanket. They are so thick and of so fine a texture, that they turn off water as well as leather, and are the most convenient garments to ride in, that could be contrived; the wearer having his legs and arms always at liberty, and his body completely defended from the rain.

In addition to what we have already said respecting the construction of their houses, we shall insert a few remarks, worthy of notice. They are mostly made of clay, and such houses have either tile or brick floors. The tile or brick being always laid on the ground, make these dwellings very unhealthy, more especially for women, on account of their dampness. The first class of people commonly build their houses of wood, with good wooden floorings, and are much more healthy. On one side of the sitting room the floor is raised about a foot, a little inclined from the wall, and about eight feet wide. This is covered with a carpet and mats, and next the wall are a number of small benches, like our ladies' crickets or stools, elegantly covered with cushions of crimson silk velvet or satin. This elevated place was the usual seat of the ladies. Their mode of sitting is cross-legged, in the Turkish fashion, or like a tailor on his shop-board, and near together. When a gentleman reclined on it, he drew one of these cushions under his arm for support. I was frequently in their parties, and found this a most agreeable resting place, especially when the ladies sat near me. Their prattle was innocent and lively; and they had a disposition to render the visits of their guests entertaining. Most of them sang well, accompanying the voice with the guitar, their favourite instrument. A customary compliment is for a gentleman to hand one of these instruments to a lady, who is ever ready to gratify him with her performance.

The employment of the men, other than amusements, is in laying out and planing their buildings, their vineyards, and their gardens, and transacting their mercantile affairs. A large proportion of them are employed in offices of government, either in a military or civil capacity. A great many are employed riding about the country transporting money, bullion, and all kinds of merchandize, most commonly conducted by convoys of horses and mules. These convoys sometimes consist of two or three hundred, laden with some kind of traffic. Many of these cross the Andes to and from the River of Plate. Some of the men are employed as mariners in the ships that are owned in the country. A few vessels are built on the coast, which give employment to numbers, in preparing cargoes, sawing boards and plank, and felling timber. They are very poorly provided with all kinds of good mechanics; medical men are likewise scarce. The ladies' employment is nothing more than sewing, or making their own clothes, some trifling embroidering and lace work, and in superintending their household affairs; they commonly, however, live pretty free from labour. I have been at almost all the ports on the coast of Chili repeatedly, and seldom but when I carried in more or less Spaniards who had been prisoners of war, or otherwise distressed. I have taken them off the Gallipagos Islands, after they have run away from English ships, and gone on shore to prevent being carried to England. I have also prevailed on several English captains to deliver some of their prisoners to me, whom I afterwards delivered to their friends in safety. On the other hand I have taken out of the different Spanish prisons on the coast of Chili and Peru, more than one hundred and fifty Englishmen at several times, and put them on board other ships, or kept them on board my own, until I arrived at some friendly port, or returned to America. My principal motive in such cases was always to relieve the unfortunate, and "grant the prisoner sweet release." Both the English and Spaniards, in the Pacific Ocean, have in general treated their prisoners with cruelty; but the conduct of the Spaniards has been most severe. I will relate a singular incident that happened in the year 1805. There was a captain Thomas Folger, a native of Nantucket, who commanded an English ship called the Vulture of London, on a whaling voyage. She mounted twelve or sixteen guns, and fell in with a Spanish ship, bound from the port of Conception to Lima, of equal force. The ships met not many leagues distant from the Spaniard's destined port, and a very severe action for small ships took place. Folger at last came off conquerer, captured his enemy, and gained himself much credit and honour; first, by fighting like a brave fellow, and then by treating the prisoners with humanity. He manned her and ordered her for St. Helena, putting six men on board, and leaving two Englishmen, who were on board when the Spaniard struck. One of them had been my gunner, and left Boston with me in 1803. He deserted from my ship in Conception, in

February, six months previously to his capture. The Spanish boatswain and two Spanish sailors, were likewise left on board. In two or three days after the ship was despatched, the Spaniards rose on the English, and put them all to death but two, one of whom had his hand half cut off. Some weeks after, the Englishman, or American, who had not been injured, whose name was Halsey, and the wounded Englishman, rose on the Spaniards and killed them. I saw Halsey and the Englishman afterwards, who related the above transaction, and the horrid barbarity which attended it. The three Spaniards took an opportunity, when part of the crew were asleep at night, and killed as many as they could before the rest awoke; and then dispatched the others as fast as they came on deck; having first determined to save Halsey alive, as he understood navigation, of which the Spaniards were ignorant. Having their plan thus arranged, they began their wicked work, and killed all the Englishmen on deck but the one who was wounded; he made a shift to go aloft as high as the foretop, and beg for his life. They then went below to the cabin, in which my unfortunate gunner lay, and told him to get out of his birth. He knowing what had happened, begged they would not kill him, and putting his hands over the side of his cabin, asked them to put irons on him, or do any thing but take his life. They then tied his hands and made him get out, when they struck him with a carpenter's axe and nearly cut him in two with the first stroke. This man was with captain Edward Edwards in the Pandora, when she was lost attempting a passage through Endeavour Straits. They spared the one in the foretop, as has been before stated. My gunner's name was Charles Spence; he had fought to save the lives of the Spaniards on board the ship Tryal, not six months before this unfortunate event. Then again came on the catastrophe of the three Spaniards, who had planned to hoist out the boat as soon as they should see land, to be ready to leave the ship should any vessel be discovered. Halsey had concerted with the Englishman a plan to go aloft, when it was expected they should draw near the coast, and whether he saw it or not, to call out, land. This being put in practice, two of the Spaniards went up to the fore top-mast head to view it. Halsey came down on deck, while the Spaniard, who was the former boatswain, was fixing tinder and fireworks in the caboose house, to be put in the boat. He took the cook's axe from beside the house, and as the boatswain turned to come out, gave him a blow on the back of the neck, which cut his head nearly off. The other two Spaniards came down, the first was killed, and the other wounded, who jumped overboard, swam to the rings of the rudder, and held fast till the wounded Englishman broke his hold by stabbing him with an iron ramrod. The two survivors kept the ship a number of days. They lost her in going into the harbour on the island of Mocha, by accidentally running her on shore.

The bay of Coquimbo lies in latitude 30° south, and longitude 71°16' west, as it is laid down in the Naval Gazetteer, which I found to be nearly correct. It is one of the finest harbours that nature ever formed. In going into it, make the land to the south of the harbour, and follow its course north, till you come near the north point of the bay, when the land trends off to the north eastward, turns round to the east, and then to the southward, and runs in to the south westward. When near the south point of the bay, a number of rocks and rocky islets will be seen lying off the point, which must be left on the right hand in going in; although I have been told that there was a good entrance between the rocks, and the south point; but it appeared to me too narrow for safety. I should by all means go in to the northward of the rocks, which passage is clear with sufficient room, if necessary to beat to windward, as it commonly will be, before getting up to the anchoring place, which is in the south west part of the bay, near some old warehouses. A ship may anchor in what depth of water they please abreast of these old houses, having nothing to fear from rocks or shoals. I never saw or heard that there were any in the bay. When at anchor you have the advantage of one of the best harbours, and, nearly all the year round, the best of weather; but with these advantages it is not a desirable place for a ship to visit, especially in time of war. Water cannot be had near the anchoring place, nor firewood at any time; and the inhabitants are so terrified at the idea of an enemy, that they prohibit all intercourse with strangers, during the existence of hostilities. This cautious and repulsive policy is owing probably to some *dog's tricks* which were successfully played on them, by some English privateersmen. The Spaniards here are generally well disposed towards Americans. The town of Coquimbo is three leagues north easterly from the port, and affords all kinds of provisions, which are to be found at Conception and Valparaiso.

The Bird Islands lie about six or seven leagues from the main land; and, I believe, have no dangers near them. The most southerly one lies in latitude 29° 36' south; and about west-north-west, seven or eight miles distant, lies the other. There are but two, both of a moderate height, but so high as to be seen four or five leagues; they do not afford any thing but birds, eggs, seal, and fish. I think there might be four or five thousand seals taken off those islands, in the course of two or three months; they are of both kinds, fur and hair. It is probable also that there would be some further chance of success to the northward; for in sailing in that direction, will be seen several more islands about the same distance from the coast as the Bird Islands; and all appear to have seals about them. My business, however, was of such a nature at that time, that I could not stop to take them. They are mostly of the hair kind.

The harbour of Coquimbo is a good place for a ship to lie at whilst the people are procuring seals off the islands in the Pacific Ocean; and it is a good place, in the proper season, for a ship to fill up with right-whale oil, as the whales come into this bay in great numbers.

The lofty Andes in the interior rise mountain over mountain as far as the eye can reach, with awful sublimity. The line, where vegetation ceases, seems but a short distance from their bases on account of the stupendous heights above. All the country below the latitude of Coquimbo has a sandy, barren, burnt appearance. In time of peace, and when the government happens to be composed of friendly, accommodating men, a traffick might be carried on to advantage. Gold and silver are very plenty in this place, brought from mines in the interior, and from those near the town. The place is much inferior to Valparaiso or Conception in point of inhabitants, trade, and produce.

"Coquimbo is one of the thirteen provinces of Chili, in South America. This is a rich, verdant, fruitful valley, not far from the coast of the South Sea, producing corn sufficient for considerable exportation to Lima, and abounding with various mines. One mine of copper is situated about five leagues north from the town of Coquimbo, on Mount Corro Verde, or Green Hill; it rises as a land mark to the port. The climate is singularly agreeable, being almost uniformly mild and serene."—*Rees' Cyclo.*

From Malham's Naval Gazetteer, vol. I, page 234, we extract the following.—"Coquimbo is a town of Chili, in South America, at the mouth of a river of the same name, near ninety leagues north from St. Jago, and has a good harbour."—"Get to windward, as the south and south west winds always prevail on the coast for nine or ten months. In the season which they call winter, they hang about north and north west, for two or three months. The Bird's Islands are north west from the bay of Coquimbo seven or eight leagues, and Guesco bay seven leagues farther."

"To go into Coquimbo, observe that the Herradura, or Horse Shoe Point, is to the windward of it, and forms the mouth of a small creek, of two cable's length over, where boats go in to procure fresh water. There are three or four rocks to the leeward side, of which the outermost is the largest, and two miles at north west by north from the main, or Point Tortuga, which is the south limit of Coquimbo port. There is a channel between this point and a small island to the south of the great rock, of seventeen fathoms, but very narrow; it is wholly unnecessary to go through here, as the port is two leagues and a half over at the entrance, and therefore affords abundant room to go in, after passing to the westward round the great rock, and so turning into the harbour, in which there is no danger. Keep the point of Tortuga as close aboard on the starboard as possible, as being to windward, otherwise it will not be easy to recover the road which is under the lee of the cape. The two islands or rocks just mentioned are under this point to the westward, which induces seamen sometimes to go through between them and the main, to keep to windward so as easily to make into the Road of Tortugas. The rocks are so clean and steep, the ships run within a boat's length of them, if possible, the easier to gain the road, where they ride in from six to ten fathoms near the Tortugas rock, which is about two fathoms long and one fathom above water. From twenty to thirty ships may ride in this part of the bay, which is the best part of the road, and sheltered from all winds; and in every other part of it there is plenty of water and a good bottom, but a little more open to the rolling of the sea, so that ships do not ride so easily or so safely."

"In coming out of the bay, if, as it may sometimes happen, a ship is be-calmed, avoid anchoring near the great rock above mentioned; for there is not only a depth of from forty to fifty fathoms, but the bottom is foul and rocky and will cut the cables, in which case it will be impossible to weigh the anchor by the buoy ropes. Though the town is opposite to the road, the surge is so great that there is no landing within two leagues of it; at which distance to the south-south-east boats go in easily, from whence seamen must walk over land to the town. The want of wood and water is also a more important inconvenience; as neither of them is to be had here. The port of Coquimbo has sometimes the name of Serena."

As I have said something respecting some *dog's tricks*, which the English privateers played upon them, I will here further explain myself. In the year 1805, a captain Cornelius Sole of Providence, a highly meritorious man, commanding the brig Tabor, was in these seas. He had been several times into Coquimbo for refreshments, and was always hospitably treated. He had been acquainted and intimate with the governor, and the first people of the place, who were in the habit of coming down from the town and visiting captain Sole on board his vessel, when she was in port. It happened that in his absence an English privateer brig, called the Antelope, of London, arrived there; and the governor and other gentlemen seeing from the town the vessel come into the harbour, they all repaired to the port thinking to meet their friend Sole; hailed the brig, and desired a boat might be sent for them; which was done, and the governor and all the party were on board, before they discovered their mistake. As soon as they were in the power of their enemy, demands were made for their ransom, which was agreed to, on the condition that some of them be allowed to go on shore to collect it. This liberty being granted, they selected from amongst themselves such men as they liked, and of course the governor was one. After they were gone, the privateer's men discovered his rank, which before they had not suspected. That they had lost such a good opportunity to make a great booty, greatly enraged them; for undoubtedly they would have received an extravagant sum for the ransom of such a personage. To wreak their vengeance they went on shore at the port, and did all the mischief they could to the few old buildings, before mentioned; and amongst other wanton acts of folly and villainy, tore to pieces a small mean building, which the Spaniards had converted into a church. They tore down and broke the images of the saints, fired pistol balls through the top of it, and made all the spoliation they conveniently could, and then went off. This act exasperated the Spaniards so much, that they would not allow any foreigner to obtain supplies. I was there soon after this transaction, and saw the havock that was made, and tried all in my power to get refreshments, but could not obtain the least favour of any kind.

The Antelope left Coquimbo, and after sailing down the coast, took her station off the port of Lima, which she blockaded for nine or ten days, when the ship Henry, from Cadiz, mounting about the same number of guns as the Antelope, (say eighteen,) came down the coast, bound in to Lima. The Henry was formerly of London, commanded by a captain Watson, and had been taken by the Spaniards several years previous. The Antelope saw her before night, and stood off shore on a wind with an intent to tack ship, as soon as she could fetch her. The Henry continued her course for the port, and when the Antelope concluded she had obtained a sufficient offing, she tacked ship, head on shore, and though she sailed much faster than the Henry, she did not come up with her till after dark, when they were within three or four miles of Calio. She run under the Henry's lee so near, that she got becalmed with the ship's sails, and the Henry fell on board. The brig thinking she was equal to the ship, hung on for a long time, keeping up a constant fire, but with less effect than the Spaniard. When the Englishman found he could not stay there any longer, and keep himself comfortable, he made the attempt to sheer off; but the Spaniard had grapnelled him, and would not dismiss him so readily. And there was nothing to be done but to fight it out. The Spaniard had the advantage, by being to windward, and much higher out of water. The Antelope fought till the captain was killed, the chief officer dangerously wounded, and thirty or forty men killed and wounded, when she struck her colours. The next morning the wounded were landed at Calio, put into carts and carried to the hospital. The Spaniards in the port attended as spectators, and, as several Englishmen and Americans who were present informed me, abused them, and when the wounded would cry out from the jolting of the cart, seemed to exult in their misery. The women were so exasperated that they threw stones at them, and called out to them, "Curse you English hereticks, what do you make all that noise for, do you remember Coquimbo." I saw the prisoners in Lima. They had little pity shown them, on account of the sacrilegious conduct, and foul deeds at Coquimbo.

The amusements of the people of the kingdoms of Chili and Peru, as before stated in part, are chiefly music and dancing. The instruments most in use are guitars, which nearly all the ladies play, accompanying them with their voices, which are very melodious. They likewise have harps, spinnets, harpsichords, and piano-fortes, which are very common, and on which they perform extremely well. The gentlemen play on flutes and clarionets. They dance with the most majesty and grace of any people I ever knew. Their dances are minuets, long dances, cotillions, and a very singular kind of dance, called fan-dango, which is common in old Spain. This graceful dance is usually performed by two persons, commonly a lady and gentleman, sometimes by two ladies. Gentlemen and ladies meet in parties at a friend's house at times, and the gentlemen form a party round a large table for cards. The game they generally play is similar to our game of loo. It is called banco; a game that is common in other nations. The ladies never join the party at table, but sit on their platform by themselves, playing on their guitars, and singing to amuse those engaged in play; and any gentleman who prefers their company to cards, has liberty to take a seat with them. Parties their company to cards, has liberty to take a seat with them. Parties formed to ride, both male and female, are very fond of concluding their diversion by going on board ships, or indeed of any excursion by water. The ladies are also very fond of receiving and paying afternoon visits.

When we left this place in February 1806, we steered off to St Ambrose and St. Felix; and found the coast from Valparaiso down to Coquimbo nearly straight, rather in a curve as you sail to leeward, making out to the westward a little from a north course, till you get near the latter place, where it trends faster to the eastward.

Notes

1. The work of two scholars, however, is very much related to my own. Fred Bernard, in a highly original essay, was the first to posit slavery, as I do in this work, as a major theme in *Moby-Dick;* and Joyce Adler suggests, with much prescience, creative riches, revealed and hidden, especially in *Benito Cereno.* The focus of both critics on hidden aspects of Melville's art resonates in unusual measure with the theme of this book. See Fred Bernard, "The Question of Race in *Moby-Dick*," *The Massachusetts Review* 43, no. 3 (Autumn 2002): 384–404; and Joyce Adler, *War in Melville's Imagination* (New York and London: New York University Press, 1981), especially page 89.

In a text that might be consulted, Eric Sundquist employs impressive erudition in his treatment of *Benito Cereno.* See Eric Sundquist, *To Wake the Nations* (Cambridge, Mass.: Harvard University Press, 1993), especially 139–175. In addition, for a beautifully crafted—and often searching—recent biography of Melville and his works, see Andrew Delbanco, *Melville: His World and Work* (New York: Alfred Knopf, 2005).

2. The fact that Melville did admire Dickens might have led critics to search harder for possible influences beyond those in "Bartleby," whose character sketches and peculiarity of style were thought to resemble closely work from the pen of Dickens. See Harrison Hayford, Alma A. MacDougall, G. Thomas Tanselle, et al., eds., *The Writings of Herman Melville: The Piazza Tales* (Evanston and Chicago: Northwestern University Press and the Newberry Library, 1987), 508.

3. Hershel Parker, *Herman Melville* (Baltimore and London: Johns Hopkins University Press, 1996), 609.

4. See Emory Elliott's series editor's preface to Richard H. Broadhead, ed., *New Essays on Moby-Dick* (Cambridge, UK: Cambridge University Press, 1986), vii. Regarding dance, African American novelist Paule Marshall represents a different tradition, presenting the very challenging "nation dances." In *Praise Song for the Widow,* sacred, circular dance has a flowering so richly complex that Douglass and Melville would have been intrigued. See Paule Marshall, *Praise Song for the Widow* (New York: G. P. Putman's Sons, 1984), 238–256.

5. Marshall Stearns writes the following about the Ring Shout:

> The dancers form a circle in the center of the floor, one in back of another. Then they begin to shuffle in a counter-clockwise direction around and around, arms

out and shoulders hunched. A fantastic rhythm is built up by the rest of the group standing back to the walls, who clap and stomp on the floor. Wave after wave of song is led by the shouting preacher, whose varying cry is answered by the regular response of the congregation. Suddenly, sisters and brothers scream and spin, possessed by religious hysteria . . . The continued existence of the ring-shout is of critical importance to jazz, because it means that an assortment of West African musical characteristics have been preserved, more or less, intact in the United States—from rhythms and blue tonality, through the falsetto break and the call-and-response pattern, to the songs of allusion and even the motions of the African dance. And an entire way of life has survived with it.

Marshall Stearns, *The Story of Jazz* (New York: Oxford University Press, 1956), 12 and 13.

6. See W.E.B. Du Bois, "The New Fatherland," in the Du Bois manuscript collection at the University of Massachusetts. I am indebted to German historian Kenneth Barkin for bringing the Du Bois essay to my attention. Barkin writes in a forthcoming paper that "Hegel's comments were shocking. He termed Africa as a 'land of gold and a land of children.'" We learn further from Barkin, quoting David Farrell Krell, that Hegel wrote that "the Negro represents . . . the natural human being in all its untamed nature and abandon." Further, Krell argues that Hegel thought that in the Negro's "character there is not a single intimation of the human." See David Farrell Krell, "The Bodies of Black Folk: From Kant and Hegel to Du Bois and Baldwin," in *Boundary 2, International Journal of Literature and Culture* 27, no. 3 (Fall 2000): 117.

7. History of religion scholar Charles Long responded to a query about Douglass and the dialectic in the following way:

First of all, let me say that dialectical thinking, very much like comparative thinking, is a generic aspect of all human thinking. Hegel gave specific meaning to the dialectic but he did not create dialectical thinking. This capacity in a formal manner can be seen early in Plato and Aristotle and, of course, in the rhetoric of the Apostle Paul in the New Testament. So, long before Hegel there was dialectical thought. It may be that other forms of dialectical thinking after Hegel might be attributed to Hegel while they in fact were not at all dependent upon him as an origin . . . My favorite and most profound dialectic is from the Buddhist thinker Nagarjuna (150 C.E.), however. So, I am certain that a person as smart as Douglass in his circumstances came upon dialectical thinking as an aid to his own thought—it may have been the Hegelian form or one of his own. For example, I could have invented the dialectic when I once said that "African Americans are a part of American culture by virtue of not being a part of it." I later found that Derrida had made a formulation that went something like this, "Presence must of necessity encompass absence for the full expression of presence."

The letter from Charles Long was received on June 3, 2006.

8. Harold Bloom, ed., *Narrative of the Life of Frederick Douglass* (New York: Chelsea House, 1988), 3. Douglass's discussion of his grandmother is found in *Narrative of the Life of Frederick Douglass, Autobiographies* (New York: Library of America, 1994), 48–49.

9. Ibid, 1. Bloom does not mention, when referring to James Baldwin and Douglass, musical resonances in their writings, or that Baldwin and Douglass treat the Ring Shout. What we get instead are unusually long, verbatim passages on the cruelties of slavery that threaten to overwhelm his commentary, which begins, "A rereading of the *Narrative of*

the Life of Frederick Douglass gives the impression that the book could have been called *A Slave Is Being Beaten*" (ibid., 1).

The dialectic—the unity of opposites—is said to have originated with Heraclitus thousands of years ago. As a mode of thought, the dialectic must have been employed by numerous thinkers over the centuries since Heraclitus rather than by a simple handful. Charles Long, quoted in endnote 7, is especially helpful here. Also see Howard Williams, *Hegel, Heraclitus and Marx* (New York: Harvester Wheatsheaf, 1989), chap. 1. Hegel's thought was mainly accessible by word of mouth in Douglass and Melville's time. In fact, Hegel was not particularly well known in the United States for quite some time. The formation of the St. Louis School of Hegelians did not occur until the 1860s, after the appearance of *Narrative of the Life of Frederick Douglass* and *Moby-Dick*.

10. The appendix, chapter 16, has pagination that follows consecutively after chapter 4 of this text. References in this book to other chapters and pages of Delano's *Voyages and Travels* carry the pagination found in the 1817 edition of that work.

11. Hayford's words are worth quoting, for they reveal that he had no doubt that *Benito Cereno* is mainly about slavery. But his words are so strong that they seem to discourage probing beneath the surface of the novella to determine how much Melville built on the historical account of the slave revolt. Hayford writes, "Melville owned a copy of Delano's *Narrative* . . . and he must have written 'Benito Cereno' with Chapter 18 constantly open before him." The reader will see, in these pages, that such was not so. Harrison Hayford et al., *The Piazza Tales,* 582.

12. Mungo Park, *Travels into the Interior Districts of Africa* (Durham, N.C.: Duke University Press, 2000 [1799]).

13. Frederick Augustus Ramsayer and Johannes Kuhne, *Four Years in Ashantee,* English trans. (New York: R. Carter & Brothers, 1975 [1875]); R. S. Rattray, *Religion and Art in Ashanti* (London: Oxford University Press, 1927).

14. Joseph Dupuis, *Journal of a Residence in Ashantee* (London: Frank Cass, 1966 [1824]); T. E. Bowdich, *Mission from Cape Coast Castle to Ashantee* (London: Frank Cass, 1966 [1819]); Willem Bosman, *A New and Accurate Description of the Coast of Guinea* (London, 1967 [1704]). Dupuis and Bowdich were British agents in Africa, Bosman a Dutch agent.

15. Mary K. Bercaw, *Melville's Sources* (Evanston, Ill.: Northwestern University Press, 1987). Also see Merton Sealts, *Melville's Reading: A Check-List of Books Owned and Borrowed* (Madison: University of Wisconsin Press, 1966), which makes no mention of the Ashantee sources.

16. R. P. Blackmur, *The Lion and the Honey-Comb* (New York: Harcourt, Brace and Company, 1955), 125, 126 (italics mine). A central argument of Blackmur's is, in fact, that Melville follows the "overt form of the novel." While he informs us of "the occasional particular spur" of a *rhythm* in Melville work, he has nothing to say beyond mention of the word. The context, sadly, is a vacuum. But rhythm is an aspect of Melville's aesthetic that has been greatly neglected. One could write at length on the subject, and it is explored in a variety of settings in this volume. A dancer himself, Melville was a master of rhythm and continually moves it to the printed page (ibid., 125). The insensitive nature of Blackmur's criticism is revealed even in dismissing a thought of his own about Melville: "It is not that his mind rotted," he writes in explaining Melville's alleged lack of creative energy following *Pierre* (ibid.).

17. Ibid, 132.

18. Herman Melville, *Moby-Dick, or The Whale,* The Writings of Herman Melville, vol. 6 (Evanston and Chicago: Northwestern University Press and the Newberry Library, 1988), 182.

19. Warner Berthoff answers Blackmur on "dramatic form," accusing Blackmur of raising "a certain conception of dramatic organization as an absolute standard of value for fiction." Berthoff finds that Blackmur's "craft of Herman Melville" "stands out," however, "as a uniquely stimulating inquiry into the actual character of Melville's performance as a writer." Warner Berthoff, *The Example of Melville* (Princeton: Princeton University Press, 1962), 139. One must reject Blackmur's exclusive standard of dramatic form because, with respect to Melville, unseen dramas are played out on multiple levels in both *Benito Cereno* and *Moby-Dick*. Melville's dramas, in fact, merit recognition as new forms of drama in creative literature. Blackmur, *Craft*, 268–274.

20. Newton Arvin, *Herman Melville* (Westport, Conn.: Greenwood Press, 1950), 77–78.

21. Ibid., 239.

22. Ibid.

23. F. O. Matthiessen, *American Renaissance* (London, Toronto, and New York: Oxford University Press, 1941), vii.

24. Lewis Mumford, *Herman Melville* (New York: Harcourt, Brace and Company, 1929), 178 and 195.

25. Elma Stuckey, *The Collected Poems of Elma Stuckey*, with an introduction by E. D. Hirschy Jr. (Chicago: Precedent Press, 1987).

26. The inscription is in a Modern Library edition of Herman Melville's *Moby-Dick*, introduction by Leon Howard (New York: Modern Library, 1950), 119.

CHAPTER I

1. Sterling Stuckey, *Slave Culture* (New York: Oxford University Press, 1987), especially chapters 1–4. An earlier version of this chapter was published in *The Cambridge Companion to Herman Melville*, edited by Robert S. Levine (Cambridge: Cambridge University Press, 1998).

2. For discussion of the religious origins of "secular" forms of art in black America, see Sterling Stuckey, "The Music That Is in One's Soul: On the Sacred Origins of Jazz and the Blues," *Lenox Avenue: A Journal of Interartistic Inquiry* 1 (1995): 73–88. Such transforming qualities are at the heart of an African aesthetic in which there is no apparent opposition between mind and body, emotion and intellect, the sacred and the secular. These qualities of culture, together with an extraordinary emphasis on improvisation, define African culture in this book. Great irony resides in the fact that slave artists did not regard themselves as American even as they defined for others, especially later generations, what is native to America in artistic terms.

3. Thomas F. De Voe, *The Market Book* (New York: Burt Franklin, 1969 [1862]), 344.

4. Bernhard, Duke of Saxe-Weimar Eisenach, *Travels in North America* (Philadelphia: Carey, Lea & Carey, 1828), 133. For a general discussion of celebrations and parades in the North, see Shane White, "It Was a Proud Day: African American Festivals and Parades in the North, 1741–1834," *Journal of American History* 81 (June 1994): 13–50.

5. James McCune Smith, *A Memorial Discourse, by Henry Highland Garnet* (Philadelphia: J. M. Wilson, 1865), 24.

6. For details on the Negroes' Burial Ground, see *The New York Times*, October 9, 1991.

7. Smith, introduction to *Memorial Discourse*, 24.

8. Ibid. We are just beginning to understand something of the richness of black music in New York City in the nineteenth century and earlier. Not only did the principal

mutual aid societies among blacks have their own bands, but there were "associations" of black musicians as well. In an "Oration Commemorative of the Abolition of the Slave Trade in the United States," delivered before the Wilberforce Philanthropic Association on January 2, 1809, Joseph Sidney outlined the procession, noting that it marched "through Broadway, down Pearl Street . . ." Dorothy Porter, ed., *Early Negro Writing* (Boston: Beacon Press, 1971), 363. Pearl Street was, of course, Herman Melville's birthplace and first residence in New York.

9. *New York Gazette and General Advertiser,* July 3, 1827.

10. *New York Statesman,* July 6, 1827.

11. Smith, *Memorial Discourse,* 24.

12. *New York Statesman,* July 6, 1827; *New York American,* July 6, 1827. Fifth of July and other parades of blacks to music in New York City were a well-established tradition by the 1820s, one that reached into subsequent decades, giving white New Yorkers ample opportunity to see and hear the celebration. Arfwedson writes the following of a parade in the mid-thirties: "A procession of blacks, accompanied by a band of music, passed through the principal streets. On the flanks of this procession rode Negroes dressed in white, with epaulets, sword, and cocked hat . . ." Carl David Arfwedson, *The United States and Canada in 1832, 1833, and 1834* (New York: Johnson Reprint Co., 1969 [1834]), 253.

13. Smith, *Memorial Discourse,* 24. I cite a half-dozen instances of such improvised dance/marching, drawn from as many states, in Stuckey, "Music in One's Soul," 79–83 (emphasis added).

14. Originally associated with the Dutch observances of Whitsuntide (the week following Pentecost), the day after Whitsunday was a holiday for slaves and servants, known as Pinkster Monday. Throughout the eighteenth century, the holiday grew in length and came eventually to be a week of celebration distinctly yet covertly expressing African spirituality on the grounds of the town commons, which became known as Pinkster Hill.

15. Edwin H. Miller, *Melville* (New York: George Braziller, 1975), 60. Herman Gansevoort, a maternal uncle of Melville's, married a Catherine Quackenboss or Quackenbush. Because more than one family in Albany and the surrounding area had Catherine's surname, her connection to Jackie remains, for now, a tantalizing possibility. Eleanor Melville Metcalf, back endpapers featuring the Ganesvoort family tree in *Herman Melville: Cycle and Epicycle* (Cambridge, Mass.: Harvard University Press, 1953). United States, Dept. of Commerce and Labor, Bureau of the Census, *Heads of Families at the First Census of the United States Taken in the Year 1790: New York* (Washington: Government Printing Office, 1908), 14, 43, 52.

16. James Eights, "Slave Holidays and Festivals," in Eileen Southern, ed., *Readings in Black American Music* (New York: W. W. Norton, 1971), 45–46 (emphasis in original). The essay originally appeared in 1867.

17. I discuss the theoretical basis of "spiritual recreation," first adumbrated by W. E. B. DuBois, in Stuckey, "Music in One's Soul," 76–77.

18. Joel Munsell, *Collections: History of Albany* (Albany, N.Y.: J. Munsell, 1867), 378–383.

19. The percentages cited for New York State and the Gansevoorts' Third Ward of Albany were calculated from U.S. Dept. of Commerce and Labor, Bureau of the Census, *Heads of Families . . . 1790,* 8, 9.

20. De Voe, *Market Book,* 344.

21. Munsell, *Collections,* 12. Emphasis added.

22. Munsell, *Collections,* 381.

23. Newton Arvin, *Herman Melville* (Westport Conn.: Greenwood Press, 1972 [1950]), 39.

24. Leon Howard, Herman *Melville: A Biography* (Berkeley: University of California Press, 1951), 12.

25. Herman Melville, *Moby-Dick, or The Whale,* The Writings of Herman Melville, vol. 6 (Evanston and Chicago: Northwestern University Press and the Newberry Library, 1988), p. 158 (hereafter pages cited parenthetically in the text). Here one suspects a play on words—that Melville was referring to Thomas Edward Bowdich (1791–1824), the African explorer, as well as Nathaniel Bowditch (1773–1838), author of *The American Practical Navigator.* Although the latter was essential for seamanship, that Melville depended as a writer on the former receives attention in this book.

26. Herman Melville, *Redburn: His First Voyage,* The Writings of Herman Melville, vol. 4 (Evanston and Chicago: Northwestern University Press and the Newberry Library, 1969), 155 (hereafter, pages cited parenthetically in the text, preceded by *R*).

27. The most extensive treatment of *Redburn* is William H. Gilman, *Melville's Early Life and Redburn* (New York: New York University Press, 1951), but perhaps its weakest aspect is its analysis, such as it is, of the Nelson sculpture, which Gilman argues inspired pleasant feelings in young Redburn. Of the long line of *Redburn* critics, only Carolyn Karcher, focusing on the chained figures, gives serious attention to the sculpture in relation to slavery and racism. See her *Shadow over the Promised Land* (Baton Rouge: Louisiana State University Press, 1980), 28–30.

28. Howard, *Melville,* 42.

29. James Fenimore Cooper, *Satanstoe* (New York: American Book Co., 1937 [1845]), 60–61.

30. Charles Dickens, *American Notes for General Circulation* (New York: Penguin Books, 1985 [1842]), 138–139.

31. Jean and Marshall Stearns, *Jazz Dance* (New York: Schirmer Books, 1979 [1964]), 46.

32. Munsell, *Collections,* 53.

33. Because De Voe's *Market Book* did not appear until 1862 and there is mention of springboard dancing in *Moby-Dick* and not in *American Notes,* for Melville to have a sailor remark, during the dance scene in "Midnight, Forecastle," that the *Pequod's* deck is too springy probably means that Melville personally visited Catharine Market, especially because it was a major dance center and dance a particular interest of Melville's.

34. Herman Melville, *Omoo: A Narrative of Adventures in the South Seas,* The Writings of Herman Melville, vol. 2 (Evanston and Chicago: Northwestern University Press and the Newberry Library, 1968), 241–242 (hereafter cited parenthetically in the text). Melville scholar Michel Imbert noted similarities between the Lory-Lory and the Ring Shout and brought them to my attention.

35. Amasa Delano, *Voyages and Travels* (New York: Praeger, 1970 [1817]), chap. 18.

36. Quoted in Metcalf, *Herman Melville,* 58–59 (emphasis mine.)

37. Herman Melville, *Benito Cereno,* in *The Piazza Tales and Other Prose Pieces, 1839–1860,* The Writings of Herman Melville, vol. 9 (Evanston and Chicago: Northwestern University Press and The Newberry Library, 1987), 104–105 (hereafter cited parenthetically in the text).

38. Mungo Park, *Travels in the Interior Districts of Africa* (London: W. Bulmer and Co., 1799), 196, 198, and especially chap. 21.

39. Ibid., 359.

40. Joshua Leslie and Sterling Stuckey, "The Death of Benito Cereno: A Reading of Herman Melville on Slavery," *The Journal of Negro History* 67 (Winter 1982): 301n.

41. I am grateful to Roediger for calling this reference to Hegel to my attention with the appearance of Herman Melville, *Journals,* The Writings of Herman Melville, vol. 15 (Evanston and Chicago: Northwestern University Press and The Newberry Library, 1989), 8. There are numerous references to Adler in the journals, suggesting that Melville and Adler, in the fall of 1849, spent many hours discussing German philosophers.

42. Edward Margolies, "Melville and Blacks," *CLA Journal* 18, no. 3 (March 1975): 364

43. Delano, *Voyages and Travels,* 328.

44. For a discussion of the uses of Ashantee dance in *Benito Cereno,* see Leslie and Stuckey, "The Death of Benito Cereno," 290.

45. The skeletal symbol of Lord Nelson's death, the foundation of Aranda's as figure-head, calls into question *Benito Cereno* criticism that depicts the New World as the source of energy in the novella and the Old World as largely drained of vital energy. See, for example, Max Putzel, "The Source and Symbols of Melville's 'Benito Cereno,'" *American Literature* 34 (1962): 191–206. Nelson's victories at the Nile and at Trafalgar laid the basis for more than a century of British supremacy at sea that greatly spurred imperialism and colonialism in Asia and Africa. Thus for Christopher Colon, as figurehead, to have been replaced by Aranda is emblematic of European brutality globally.

46. Delano, *Voyages,* 325.

47. Melville, *Journals,* 50.

CHAPTER II

1. Herman Melville, *Benito Cereno* in *The Piazza Tales and Other Prose Pieces, 1839–1860,* The Writings of Herman Melville, vol. 9 (Evanston and Chicago: Northwestern University and the Newberry Library, 1987), 48. Subsequent citations from *Benito Cereno* will be made parenthetically within the text, referring to the novella by its initials (*BC*) and providing a page number. An earlier version of this chapter appeared in *The Massachusetts Review* 46(3) (2005).

2. Herman Melville, *The Encantadas* in *The Piazza Tales and Other Prose Pieces, 1839–1860,* The Writings of Herman Melville, vol. 9 (Evanston and Chicago: Northwestern University and the Newberry Library, 1987), 46. Subsequent citations from *The Encantadas* will be made parenthetically within the text, referring to the novella by its initials (*EN*) and providing a page number.

3. Though we cannot prove conclusively that Melville as a teenager read Dupuis's *Journal,* first printed for and published by Henry Colburn of New Burlington Street, London, in 1824, it is not unlikely, considering that Newton Arvin writes, "The names of the great travelers indeed—Krusenstern, Captain Cook, Vancouver, Ledyard, Mungo Park—had scintillated before him like constellations during his whole boyhood, as the names of great soldiers do before other boys." Newton Arvin, *Herman Melville* (Westport, Conn.: Greenwood Press, 1976), 39.

4. Joseph Dupuis, *Journal of a Residence in Ashantee* (London: Frank Cass & Co., Ltd., 1966 [1824]), 82. Future citations from the *Journal* will be made parenthetically, referring to Dupuis and a page number.

5. Joyce Adler, *War in Melville's Imagination* (New York: New York University Press, 1981), 108. Carolyn Karcher has also addressed the "flawed bell" of the *San Dominick* and its relationship to the Liberty Bell in *Shadow over the Promised Land: Slavery, Race, and Violence in Melville's America* (Baton Rouge: Louisiana State University Press, 1980), 156–57.

One notes that Melville's choice of objects—the bells worn by Ashantee warriors, the silk cord around the king's neck, and the gold chain round his body—are all transmuted into art. Only now do we know how these objects came to his attention, making it possible for him to transform some into crucial symbols in *Benito Cereno*. But Joyce Adler first called those related to Atufal and others to our attention, practically setting forth a new research agenda for *Benito Cereno*. Brilliantly, she referred to "the symbolic implications that can be found in significant figures and objects: the skeleton, the black giant who may throw off his chains and will not ask pardon, the padlock and key, [and the] Spanish flag used as a rag" (104). As indicated earlier, Adler also noted the importance of the forecastle bell. She would not have been surprised to discover Melville's intense interest in Africa, but that cannot be said for most of us, for it has been practically unimaginable that America's greatest writer would have taken aspects of African culture, or of black culture elsewhere, seriously enough to make them major influences in his aesthetic.

6. Herman Melville, *Moby-Dick, or the Whale,* The Writings of Herman Melville, vol. 6 (Evanston and Chicago: Northwestern University Press and The Newberry Library, 1988), 120–121. Hereafter cited as *MD* with page number.

7. Melville must have noticed and pondered this information in a deposition in Delano's *Voyages and Travels*. The document reports that the deponent "spoke to them of peace and tranquility, and agreed to draw up a paper, signed by the deponent, and the sailors who could write, as also by the negroes, Babo and Atufal, who could do it in their language." Amasa Delano, *A Narrative of Voyages and Travels in the Northern and Southern Hemispheres* (New York: Praeger, 1970 [1817]), 337.

8. Awareness of the disparate levels of characterization and experience from which the Atufal we now know was created and the one-dimensional, defiantly quiet but immense Negro known to Delano enables us to know, once more, Melville's multifaceted process of characterization.

9. A trophy less important than Moby Dick catches our eye in "The Pequod Meets the Bachelor." Melville writes of a whale-boat suspended, "bottom down; and hanging captive from the bowsprit was seen the long lower jaw of the last whale they had slain" (*MD*, 493).

10. Melville's reference to *Benito Cereno* and *Moby-Dick* as tombs gives added weight to Fred Bernard's revolutionary thesis that slavery is at the heart of *Moby-Dick*. See Fred Bernard, "The Question of Race in *Moby-Dick*," *Massachusetts Review* 43, no. 3 (Autumn 2002): 384–404.

11. Delano's uncle's cannibalism of an Indian child is referred to in *Voyages and Travels,* 580. We know enough of Ashantee culture to know that Aranda's body was reduced to a skeleton not cannibalistically, as thought by some critics, but in accordance with Ashantee funeral practices. See "'Follow Your Leader': The Theme of Cannibalism in *Benito Cereno*," in Stuckey, *Going Through the Storm* (New York: Oxford University Press, 1994), 171–84. Discussions with Stafford Lewis, a student in the senior seminar on "American Social and Cultural Thought," led to the subtle connection above.

12. Melville decided to make use of this material while reading Delano's *Voyages and Travels*. Much of the shaving scene derived from this source, and in addition from other sources of Melville's inspiration.

13. It is an interesting formulation, for the Ashantee in the royal procession, after whom Atufal was modeled, was a carrier of objects, a porter as well. Melville thereby associates West Africans with Egyptians, just as in comparing Babo to a Nubian sculptor he associates the West African with an Egyptian neighbor that once conquered and ruled that great civilization.

14. Delano, *Voyages and Travels,* 496–497. This finding, rich in its implications, was made by graduate student Christian Trajano in the Nineteenth-Century American Research Seminar, History Department, University of California, Riverside, Spring 2002. The evidence of this passage argues that Melville, in *Benito Cereno,* relates the power of the ecclesiastical court, of the Inquisition, to slavery and trafficking in slaves, principal crimes of the modern era. The connection between church and state is found in this passage from *Voyages and Travels:* "The court consisted of priests, and sometimes a high officer or officers of state . . . This court does not meddle with any thing except infringements upon their holy religion. If, say they, these were to be passed over and let go with impunity, our church and state would fall to the ground" (497). Melville used the defiance of the authority of the church, which gave slavery its blessing, and the means of executing the heretic, to develop important parts of the novella related to Babo.

15. Delano is the prisoner in the jail-yard. "Though upon the wide sea," Melville writes at one point that he "seemed in some far inland country; prisoner in some deserted chateau, left to stare at empty grounds, and peer out at vague roads, where never wagon or wayfarer passed" (*BC,* 74).

16. I am indebted to Joshua Leslie for drawing my attention, many years ago, to the solution to this long-standing problem.

CHAPTER III

1. Herman Melville, *The Encantadas, or Enchanted Isles,* in *The Piazza Tales and Other Prose Pieces, 1839–1860,* The Writings of Herman Melville, vol. 9 (Evanston and Chicago: Northwestern University and the Newberry Library, 1987). Joseph Dupuis, *Journal of a Residence in Ashantee* (London: Frank Cass & Co., 1966 [1824]), 5. Subsequent citations to the *Journal* will be made parenthetically, referring to Dupuis and a page number.

2. Herman Melville, Benito Cereno, in *The Piazza Tales and Other Prose Pieces, 1839–1860,* The Writings of Herman Melville, vol. 9 (Evanston and Chicago: Northwestern University Press and the Newberry Library, 1987), 50. Subsequent citations from Benito Cereno will be made parenthetically within the text, referring to the novella by its initials (BC) and a page number.

3. Dupuis's discussion of Ashantee music is combined at one point with mention of an Ashantee god to whom one prays and makes offerings. We are therefore on the trail of how Queequeg was born in Melville's imagination. In the midst of attempting to account for the creation of Benito Cereno, we have another remarkable instance of material Melville used in creating *Moby-Dick,* this time Queequeg and his little Negro god Yojo. Melville, however, would have us believe that Yojo is a "Congo Idol." With gods as with characterizations in *Moby-Dick* and Benito Cereno, one might conclude that Yojo might well have been fashioned from Melville's knowledge of tutelary gods from the Congo and Ashantee. On close examination, however, we can say that Melville mainly has Ashantee gods in mind. Whereas an Ashantee offering to a god consists, according to Dupuis, of "a small calabash containing a little corn and plantain, steeped in fluid like blood," Melville writes that the offering to Yojo consisted of "a ship's biscuit," but reports

that Yojo did not "fancy such dry sort of fare at all; he never moved his lips," which suggests he preferred offerings of food more akin to what Ashantees provided. Moreover, what one finds in Dupuis's Journal and *Moby-Dick* with respect to prayer is similar. Praying is done aloud in each instance, the Ashantee uttering "certain mystical words in prayer" and Queequeg, before Yojo, praying "in a sort of sing-song" that also appears to have been mystical. Still more intriguing, considering that the Pequod travels highways of the sea, is this from Dupuis: "Like the Greeks, Syria, and Arabia, the Ashantees offered their gods 'highway suppers.'" Dupuis, Journal, 56.

4. The American College Dictionary (New York: Random House, 1963), 928. Melville noticed the sound of metal in the Galapagos chapter of Amasa Delano's Voyages and Travels, which he reimagines and presents in "Sketch Fourth" of The Encantadas. He discovered in Voyages that much of Albermarle Island is so heated by volcanoes. Delano explains that when he "walked over this clinker the tread of [his] feet would cause a remarkable sound, as if walking on bell metal" (383).

5. Within minutes after Dupuis is staggered by a "warlike mob" of Ashantees, he sights a giant Ashantee carrying the execution stool encrusted with blood, and hears him "howling the song of death" (Dupuis, 82). This passage suggests to Melville the wonderful strategy of bringing Atufal, as a symbol of danger and harbinger of death, into close proximity to Delano on several occasions in the novella.

6. Babo has had more than a dozen Spaniards brought to him and, distinguishing among them, determined that eleven must die. Although they begged for mercy, Babo, with Don Benito watching, ordered that they be thrown alive into the sea. One of them, the boatswain, Juan Robles, "who knew how to swim, kept the longest above water, making acts of contrition, and, in the last words he uttered, charged this deponent [Benito Cereno] to cause mass to be said for his soul to our Lady of Succour" (BC, 107). Thus Don Benito watched Robles die with a plea directed at him, which drove the death home in a highly disturbing sense. Don Benito knew that Babo had ordered that Aranda's body be taken below deck, where it was reduced to a skeleton. In the dark of the third night following Aranda's death, it was riveted to the bow. Don Benito knew that the Ashantee women wanted not only Aranda killed but him as well. And he knew that the women wanted personally to torture Aranda to death because the blacks made a point of so informing him. Was not the reference to torture directed, by implication, to Benito Cereno as well? Was he not being made repeatedly to feel the weight of his crimes against the Africans?

7. The effects of whiteness, under certain conditions, are revealed on Ashantee battlefields and in *Moby-Dick*. In describing the results of an Ashantee battle, Dupuis writes of "bleached human bones and skulls" forming "a distressing portrait of African warfare," and he observes that some involved in the battle "pointed to the relics, saying jocosely, they were Ashantee trophies: the Ashantees retorted the jest upon their fellow travelers with equal good-humour, and all parties were indifferent at the retrospection so paralyzing to humanity" (Dupuis, 9). On the subject of whiteness from Melville, "It was the whiteness of the whale that above all appalled me," Ishmael asserts. "But how can I hope to explain myself here; and yet, in some dim, random way, explain myself I must," he continues. Despite the color white's association with the honorable, in Ishmael's view, "there yet lurks an elusive something in the innermost idea of this hue, which strikes more of panic to the soul than that redness which affrights in blood" (MD, 272, 274).

8. T. Edward Bowdich, *Mission from Cape Coast Castle to Ashantee* (London: Cass, 1966 [1819]), 289. In revealing how Melville created Aranda's skeleton for literary purposes, we must bear in mind that the Ashantee Lecbe employed means indigenous to

his culture in the novella, using his repolished, sharp-edged hatchet to reduce Aranda's body to a skeleton by shaving off the flesh, after the fashion of the Ashantee in preparing the bodies of kings for funerals before placing them in the sacred mausoleum. With only three days to reduce the body to a skeleton, Lecbe had no choice but to shave the flesh from Aranda's body. Shaving is normally a sacred act unrelated to trophies, but in this instance the trophy principle is invoked because Aranda, having owned blacks, was a mortal enemy. Further citations from *Mission* will be made parenthetically, referring to Bowdich and a page number.

Willem Bosman, *A New and Accurate Description of the Coast of Guinea* (New York: Barnes and Noble, 1967 [1704]). It is evident that Melville went deep into Ashantee sources to create one of the most mysterious and stunning symbols in the novel.

9. While Delano is standing amid the decay of the ship, he thinks a white sailor—"from something suddenly suggested by the man's air"—is attempting to warn him that the blacks and Don Benito are in league against him. Tangled in that maze of Babo's making, he poses a question: "But if the whites had dark secrets concerning Don Benito, could then Don Benito be any way in complicity with the blacks? But they were too stupid" (*BC*, 75). Lost in his racist thought, Delano encounters a sailor whose hands are "full of ropes," and his mind, in transition, passes from "its own entanglements to those of the hemp." He had not seen such a knot before: "The knot seemed a combination of double-bowline-knot, treble-crown-knot, back-handed-well-knot, knot-in-and-out-knot, and jamming-knot" (*BC*, 76). The knotter was trying to tell him that the intricate knot was emblematic of the plight of whites on the ship.

Puzzled by what he was seeing, Delano addresses the knotter:

"What are you knotting there, my man?"
"The knot," was the brief reply, without looking up.
"So it seems; but what is it for?"
"For some one else to undo," muttered back the old man, plying his fingers harder than ever, the knot being now nearly completed.

As Delano watches, suddenly the knot is thrown to him, and the old man says, "in broken English—the first heard in the ship—something to this effect—'Undo it, cut it, quick.' It was said lowly, but with such condensation of rapidity, that the long, slow words in Spanish, which had preceded and followed, almost operated as covers to the brief English between" (*BC*, 76).

With Delano still holding the knot, an old Negro "with a pepper and salt head, and a kind of attorney air," approaches him. The Negro, in Spanish, with a knowing wink, informs him "that the old knotter was simple-witted, but harmless; often playing his old tricks." For such a statement—even for the wink—the old Negro might have been killed. He then displays greater boldness, sheathed in tact, concluding "by begging the knot, for of course the stranger would not care to be troubled with it." Melville notes, "Unconsciously, it was handed to him. With a sort of conge, the Negro received it, and turning his back ferreted into it like a detective Custom House officer after smuggled laces. Soon, with some African word, equivalent to pshaw, he tossed the knot overboard" (*BC*, 76). It is as though a scimitar has been waved a few feet from Delano without his being offended.

10. The Ashantee king brings his own unique perspective to European dress, so dramatically transforming it as to caricature himself. He is Melville's model for Don Benito as a "harlequin ensign." See Bowdich, 122, and *BC*, 87.

11. Hegel's entry into *Benito Cereno* is especially compelling and might be discussed at length in relation to Babo himself. Hegel's view that the consciousness of the slave is profoundly affected by the master's consciousness because the slave, choosing life over death, falls victim to conquest, is open to doubt in the case of Babo. One doubts, on the evidence, Babo was ever swayed by his master, Alexandro Aranda. The very thought that Babo seriously promised his initial master, or any master, absolute obedience seems almost absurd. In *Benito Cereno*, as in the historical account, Aranda is Babo's master. In the novella, Babo orders Aranda's death, that he be stripped down to a skeleton—to become the figurehead of the *San Dominick*, the ultimate symbol of oppression in the Americas. A great *master of consciousness* himself, Babo appears to have been biding his time from the moment of his enslavement but without hesitation chanced death by pursuing Benito Cereno into Delano's boat. As Melville writes, "Seeing all was over, he uttered no sound, and could not be forced to. His aspect seemed to say, since I cannot do deeds, I will not speak words" (*BC*, 116). Babo is made to order to test postulates from Hegel, including Hegel's conviction that Africans could hardly be taken seriously as makers of history. Is Melville, through his depiction of Babo, providing, in this respect, a critique of Hegel? For a discussion of Hegel on consciousness and slavery, see Charles Long, *Significations: Signs, Symbols, and Images in the Interpretation of Religion* (Philadelphia: Fortress Press, 1986), especially chapter 10: "The Oppressive Elements in Religion and the Religions of the Oppressed." For a fine discussion of Hegel, see David Brion Davis, *The Problem of Slavery in the Age of Revolution* (Ithaca, N.Y.: Cornell University Press, 1975), especially 561–564.

12. Although he argues that Melville made but one change in Delano's account of the historical revolt, H. Bruce Franklin should be read on Melville's characterization of Benito Cereno. See H. Bruce Franklin, "Apparent Symbol of Despotic Command:" Melville's *Benito Cereno, New England Quarterly* 34 (November 1961), 462–472.

CHAPTER IV

1. In this chapter I take into consideration the treatment of music in Douglass's *My Bondage and My Freedom* and *The Life and Times of Frederick Douglass*, published subsequent to the *Narrative*, as these works build on musical themes stated, or implied, in the *Narrative*. Frederick Douglass, *Narrative of the Life of Frederick Douglass, an American Slave; My Bondage and My Freedom;* and *Life and Times of Frederick Douglass* are found in *Autobiographies*, The Library of America, 1994 (hereafter pages are cited parenthetically after abbreviation of each text). The edition of *Moby-Dick* cited is Herman Melville, *Moby-Dick, or The Whale*, The Writings of Herman Melville, vol. 6 (Evanston and Chicago: Northwestern University Press and the Newberry Library, 1988); hereafter pages are cited parenthetically in the text.

This chapter is dedicated to Melvillean Viola Sachs, who asked me years ago if I didn't hear the blues in *Moby-Dick*.

2. Writing that the blues followed the spirituals in origin, the distinguished musicologist Eileen Southern comments, however, that "many of the spirituals convey to listeners the same feeling of rootlessness and misery as do the blues. The spiritual is religious, however, rather than worldly and tends to be more generalized in its expression than specific, more figurative in its language than direct, and more expressive of group feelings than individual ones." Even so, Southern writes that "it is often difficult to distinguish between

these two types of songs." See Eileen Southern, *The Music of Black Americans* (New York: W. W. Norton, 1971), 331.

3. Regarding the structure of the conventional blues, see Sterling A. Brown, Arthur P. Davis, and Ulysses Lee, eds., *The Negro Caravan* (New York: Dryden Press, 1941), 426. This volume, largely under Brown's influence, remains important for its views on the blues and spirituals, but Brown's position on balance is perhaps truer of the spirituals than of the blues, for it must come up against what no student of the blues has taken into account, Douglass's contention that words cannot do justice *to the anguish and bitterness* expressed in the blues. See especially, in *Caravan,* pages 412–421 (italics mine).

4. James Baldwin, a splendid student of folklore, absorbed the Ring Shout from his Harlem environment of the 1930s and 1940s. Moreover, as skilled as Charles Dickens in depicting dance, Baldwin writes of the blues and jazz, "White Americans seem to feel that happy songs are *happy* and sad songs are *sad* . . . I think it was Big Bill Broonzy who used to sing 'I Feel So Good,' a really joyful song about a man who is on his way to the railroad station to meet his girl. She's coming home. It is the singer's incredibly moving exuberance that makes one realize how leaden the time must have been while she was gone . . . This is the freedom that one hears in some gospel songs, for example, and in jazz. In all jazz, and especially in the blues, there is something tart and ironic, authoritative and double-edged." James Baldwin, *The Fire Next Time* (New York: Dell, 1962), 60–61.

Baldwin's collapsing of musical categories is brilliantly confirmed in "Bur Rabbit in Red Hill Churchyard," in which there is the union of blues with a form of jazz improvisation in sacred ring ceremony. Surrounded by others in a ring, Brer Rabbit uses his violin to invoke the ancestral spirits within a blues/jazz context that is as much of the twenty-first as of the nineteenth century. The violin, not the guitar, is the blues instrument of choice in the tale, and the dialect of the South Carolina storyteller is as thickly African influenced as the dialect heard by Douglass in Maryland. E. C. L. Adams, *Tales of the Congaree* (Chapel Hill and London: University of North Carolina Press, 1987), 235–236. That the violin is important in slave life is borne out by a comment from Douglass that on slave holidays, fiddling was "going on in all directions." Douglass, *My Bondage,* 289.

It is likely that holidays contributed to the blues becoming less and less sacred in Maryland slavery, for on holidays drinking left slaves sprawled out drunk. Slave masters encouraged drunkenness, pitting slave against slave in competitive drinking, placing bets. Douglass writes, "We were induced to drink, I among the rest, and when holidays were over, we all staggered up from our filth and wallowing." Holidays were "part and parcel of the gross fraud, wrongs, and inhumanity of slavery." Douglass, *My Bondage,* 291–93.

5. Conversation with French Melvillean Michel Imbert about *The Souls of Black Folk,* in Paris, France, in May 2005.

Douglass's interpretation of slave music gave W.E.B. Du Bois's *The Souls of Black Folk* its very name. Du Bois's treatment of the origins of slave song is consonant with Douglass's. He describes the process thus: "Sprung from the African forests, where its counterpart can still be heard, it was adapted, changed, and intensified by the tragic soul-life of the slave, until, under the stress of law and whip, it became the one true expression of a people's sorrow, despair and hope." Du Bois, *The Souls of Black Folk* (Greenwich, Conn.: Fawcett Books, 1961 [1903]), 141.

In an unusually ironic sense, then, DuBois introduced the world, as Melville did, to the blues of Frederick Douglass.

The all-but-crushed souls of blacks before last-ditch resistance led Du Bois to focus on the souls of blacks since slavery. From the divided souls of black intellectuals, artists, and artisans, we later learn in *Souls,* in "Of the Faith of the Fathers," chapter 10, that all blacks suffer from rending inner conflict, an argument based on a similar one in Douglass's *Narrative.* Thus the striving of the freedmen's sons is fraught with perils that recall those of their slave fathers, their travail of soul "almost beyond the measure of their strength" (Du Bois, 22). Nearly torn apart by the struggle between doubt and aspiration, blacks are burdened, in Du Bois's classic words, with "two souls, two thoughts, two unreconciled strivings; two warring ideals in one dark body whose dogged strength alone keeps it from being torn asunder" (DuBois, 17). The tragic spirit of the blues, which Du Bois joins Douglass in affirming, allows this almost hopeless depiction of the struggle in the souls of blacks.

The divided yet somehow held-together spirits of cheer and gloom are the warring ideals that Douglass heard in the singing of field hands. This DuBois knew from reading *Narrative of the Life,* which greatly interested him in the souls of his people, a subject about which he had thought deeply since the age of twenty while an undergraduate at Fisk.

More than fifty years later, in *Dusk of Dawn,* he writes, like Douglass, of "entombed" black souls. At the same time, recalling *The Souls of Black Folk,* he describes it as "a cry at midnight." And he writes that Albert Schweitzer should have tried "to heal souls of Europeans rather than the bodies of black Africa." W.E.B. DuBois, *Dusk of Dawn* (New Brunswick: Transaction, 1995 [1940]), xxix and 130–131. On either double consciousness or souls, DuBois was not as much in the tradition of European intellectuals as the conventional wisdom holds. Douglass most impressed him on questions of the soul and double consciousness. W.E.B. Du Bois, *Souls,* especially chapters 1 and 10. See W.E.B. Du Bois, "The New Fatherland," an unpublished undergraduate essay in German written in 1888 (W.E.B. Du Bois Manuscript Collection, University of Massachusetts). For Du Bois's comment on Albert Schweitzer, see "The Black Man and Albert Schweitzer," *The Albert Schweitzer Jubilee Book,* edited by A. A. Roback (Westport, Conn.: Greenwood, 1945), 126. Professor Kenneth Barkin, historian of Germany and one of the more interesting Du Bois specialists, brought Du Bois's Schweitzer comment to my attention.

Not unrelated to this, one thinks of Ralph Waldo Emerson's "The worst feature of this double consciousness is the two lives, *of the understanding and of the soul,* which we lead, really show very little relation to each other: one prevails now, all buzz and din; and the other prevails then, all infinitude and paradise." Ralph Waldo Emerson, "The Transcendentalist," in *Essays and Lectures* (New York: The Library of America, 1983), 205–206 (italics mine). But we see that understanding and the soul do meet in the life of the slave. Douglass thought the soul a source of understanding reflected in the singing of field hands. In fact, the soul for Douglass is the final seat of perception or understanding. His way of perceiving the soul certainly was an influence on Du Bois's conception of the soul, which was not an unqualified endorsement of philosophers of the West.

For a statement of the conventional wisdom on Du Bois, double consciousness, and the soul, see Henry Louis Gates, "Both Sides Out," *The New York Times Book Review,* May 4, 2003, 31.

One does not have to be a lover of the blues—Du Bois surely was not—to understand the circumstances of their birth and how they affected the souls of blacks, which is infinitely more important.

6. Hegel's treatment of extremes meeting is found in G. W. F. Hegel, *The Phenomenology of Mind* (New York: Harper Colophon Books, 1967), originally published in 1910, in chapter 4, "The True Nature of Self-Certainty." It is well to remember, however, Douglass's earlier assertion that whole volumes of philosophy on slavery could not do justice to the nature of the experience that slave song describes and analyzes.

7. We now know that in Maryland slavery the blues, although sharing certain qualities with the spirituals, were in full flower and deeply sacred. Sacred blues were undoubtedly created outside Maryland before and after Douglass heard them, but accounts of them have yet to be uncovered.

André Malraux draws attention to the blues in a form that is in some ways known to us both during and after Douglass's time in Maryland. Like Douglass, he brings Africa into focus: "Now observe this: the first great music of Africa does not sing of a lost or even of an unknown paradise, but of a very simple, very ordinary human happiness wrested forever from the unfortunate men who improvised on the banks of the Mississippi . . . [It] is the great lamentation, the eternal voice of affliction which, with its searing originality, entered European music as the blues." André Malraux, "Behind the Mask of Africa," *New York Times Magazine,* May 15, 1966, 30.

Both spirituals and blues, at an early stage, were probably sung at the same time, but largely by different groups of slaves: by those with some exposure to Christianity and by those with none. But it makes no sense to contend that slave Christians did not come under musical influence from field hands. Novelist Richard Wright writes of "those astounding religious songs known as the spirituals," which were created by slaves "closest to the Big House" who caught "whiffs" of Christianity. By contrast, according to Wright, "the field slaves were beyond the pale." See Richard Wright, foreword to Paul Oliver, *The Meaning of the Blues* (London: Cassell and Co., Ltd., 1960), 8. Wright's position is supported by what Douglass writes of life away from field work, where slaves whom he made a special effort to familiarize with the Bible sang spirituals with lines such as

O Canaan, sweet Canaan,
    I am bound for the land of Canaan (*B,* 308)

and a spiritual with the even more explicit double meaning of the North perhaps being the place to which one is bound:

I thought I heard them say,
There were lions in the way,
I don't expect to stay
Much longer here.
Run to Jesus—shun the danger—
I don't expect to stay
    Much longer here. (*B,* 308)

8. Adrienne Rich writes, "Frederick Douglass wrote an English purer than Milton's." Adrienne Rich, *Poems Selected and New,* 1950–1974 (New York: W. W. Norton, 1975), 151.

The exaggerations of white minstrels prevented them from truly representing any aspect of slave being—hair texture, skin color, features, and more—not just slave speech. But speech is the one attribute that can be changed to meet white standards.

Ellison's belief that the dialect of slaves and their descendants is "moribund" is false. How can the language in which the blues, spirituals, and Brer Rabbit tales were created be moribund? Moreover, slave songs largely fueled the Civil Rights movement of the 1960s. Ralph Ellison, *Going to the Territory* (New York: Random House), 281; see also Sterling Stuckey, "The Great Singing Movements of the Sixties," in S. Stuckey, ed., *Going through the Storm* (New York: Oxford, 1994), 265–281.

The language of dialect can be as nuanced and subtle, as powerful and revolutionary as analogous features of any language in existence. (Listen to recordings of Paul Robeson singing in dialect.) But one must not be ashamed and willing to deal with slavery to appreciate this. Apart from vague excursions along the margins of the institution, Ellison avoids the subject and yet arrives at the thesis, never before argued, that the "Americanized" slave artist, cooperating with whites in the creative process, functioned in a "democratic culture." In this manner, he would have us ignore the dangerous conditions under which slaves created. With unintended irony, however, he writes, "I must say that our pluralistic system is a difficult system under which to live" (Ellison, *Territory,* 142–143, 281–282).

Finding little in common culturally between Africans and their descendants in America, Ellison nevertheless claims understanding of Melville, "We took to dialect at a time when *Benito Cereno, Moby-Dick,* and *Leaves of Grass* were at hand to point a more viable direction for a people whose demands were revolutionary." Ellison does not understand that the blues are a revolutionary force—an emblem of modernity—in Douglass's *Narrative* and in *Moby-Dick.* Under strong African influence, as described by Douglass, the blues inform Melville's creative process *on multiple levels of craft* (Ellison, *Territory,* 281).

9. An example of a Ring Shout that is a near duplicate of the one Douglass saw in Egypt was observed by Fredrika Bremer in an all-black New Orleans Church in the 1850s: "And as they leaped," she writes, "they twisted their bodies round in a sort of corkscrew fashion, and were evidently in a state of convulsion; sometimes they fell down and rolled in the aisle, amid loud, lamenting cries and groans . . . Whichever way we looked in the church, we saw somebody leaping up and fanning the air." Fredrika Bremer, *America of the Fifties: Letters of Fredrika Bremer,* edited by Adolph B. Benson (New York: Oxford University Press, 1924), 129. Similar leaping by blacks in a nineteenth-century Philadelphia church is described by a Reverend Daniel: "Those forming the ring joined in the clapping of hands and wild and loud singing, frequently springing into the air, and shouting loudly . . . This continued for hours, until all were completely exhausted, and some had fainted and been stowed away on benches or the pulpit platform." Commenting on this description of the Ring Shout, Du Bois writes, "The writer hardly does justice to the weird witchery of those hymns sung thus rudely." See W.E.B. Du Bois, *The Philadelphia Negro* (New York: Shocken Books, 1967 [1899]). I thank historian Jermaine Archer for calling to my attention the Egyptian reference.

10. Some examples of "Indian-file" involve universal application of the designation. Describing a procession among Ashantees, Joseph Dupuis writes, "A number of women and girls, whose employment consisted in attending upon their husbands . . . closed the order of the march, which from the nature of the path was necessarily in Indian file," Joseph Dupuis, *Journal of a Residence in Ashantee* (London: Frank Cass & Co., Ltd., 1966 [1824]), 10. A similar reference, from Melville after the publication of *Moby-Dick,* appears in his *Journals* under the heading "Voyage from Liverpool to Constantinople": "Peddlers of all sorts & hawkers. Confectionary carried on head. A chain of malefactors with iron rings about their necks—Indian file." Herman Melville, *Journals,* The Writings of Herman Melville, vol. 15 (Evanston and Chicago: Northwestern University Press and the Newberry Library, 1989), 65. Another example of circularity that does not involve Indians was used by white missionaries in referring to the Ring Shout, equating it with dance "Indian file." Ezra Ely describes a camp meeting in which blacks and whites were "commingled" while "wheeling around in Indian file." Rev. Ezra Stiles Ely, "Review of Methodist Error," *The Quarterly Theological Review* 2 (April 1819), 226, 228.

11. Frank Moore, *Anecdotes, Poetry, and Incidents of the War, North and South, 1860–65,* 146–147 (italics mine). Though perhaps not as free of stereotyping as she might have been, Constance Rourke, with minstrelsy a factor, brings together extremely agile dance

like that found in *American Notes*, and the circular movement of dance introduced by Melville in "Midnight, Forecastle."

> The climax of the minstrel performance, the walkaround, with its competitive dancing in the mazes of a circle, was clearly patterned on Negro dances in the compounds of the great plantations, which in turn went back to the communal dancing of the African. The ancestry was hardly remote. Many who heard the minstrels in the Gulf States or along the lower Mississippi must have remembered those great holidays in New Orleans early in the century when hundreds of Negroes followed through the streets a king chosen for his youth, strength, and blackness. License ran high, and the celebrations ended in saturnalia of barbaric, contortionist dancing. Often the walkarounds of minstrelsy were . . . accompanied by strident cries.

See Constance Rourke, *American Humor* (Tallahassee: University Press of Florida, 1959).

12. Jean and Marshall Stearns write that "Lane's dancing had an authenticity. He was apparently swinging—relatively speaking—naturally and effortlessly. At a time when white men in black face were making a fortune imitating the Negro, the real thing must have been a revelation." They argue that "Negro historians have ignored him, perhaps because . . . he did not excel at an art which had prestige." Jean and Marshall Stearns, *Jazz Dance* (London: Schirmer Books, 1964), 44 and 47.

13. Douglass provides the definitive example of Jubilee beating: "It supplies the place of the violin, or of other musical instruments, and is played so easily, that almost every farm has its 'Juba' beater. The performer improvises as he beats and sings his merry song, so ordering the words as to have them fall pat with the movement of his hands" (*B*, 290).

14. Samuel Floyd Jr., *The Power of Black Music* (New York: Oxford University Press, 1995), 83. The swaying motions of dance, flowing out of and resembling the Ring Shout, might be visualized at sea (on the ocean floor) as ships sail high above.

15. William Dunlap, *Diary of William Dunlap, 1766–1839* (New York: New York Historical Society, 1930), 505–506. On land, the swaying motions of dance accompany the return from the cemetery.

16. Samuel Floyd Jr. has done the most work on the funeral procession and port cities. Floyd reveals the following: "There can be no mistaking the fact that the beginnings of jazz in the ring—as partial as it may have been—was a direct result of the transference of the structure and character of the shout to the funeral parades of black bands and community participants." See *Black Music*, 21 and 83.

Mahalia Jackson, the gospel singer, says of New Orleans funeral processions, "When the body would come out, the drums would hit up these sad songs, and they would march behind the hearse of the deceased all the way . . . to the cemetery close to the community." After the burial, she notes, "The bands would strike up these religious songs and people from all over would meet at the cemetery and come back and dance in the streets . . . would all get into the *jubilant* feeling of this jazz music." *The Life I Sing About,* Caedmon Records TC 1413. Jackson's reference to jazz and funeral procession takes us back to Pip's scatting of "Rig-a-dig, dig, dig!" just before he promises to beat a funeral march.

See Sterling Stuckey, "The Music That Is in One's Soul: On the Sacred Origins of Jazz and the Blues," *Lenox Avenue, A Journal of Interartistic Inquiry* 1 (1995): 80–83.

Though Melville could not possibly have known of the connection to jazz, he prefigures its partial origins in the Ring Shout on the *Pequod* with the funeral procession itself representing the blues, a major ingredient of jazz in the postslavery era.

Index

Acushnet (ship), 29
Adams, E. C. L., 137n4
Adler, George, 10, 36, 131n41
Adler, Joyce, 125n1, 132n5
African Americans, 18
African Circle Dance, 18
African culture. *See also* Ashantees;
    black music; burial rites
  Bakongo faith, 25–26
  Benito Cereno influences, 33–34
  blues music, 19
  funeral processions, 94–95
  and Melville, 20, 27–28, 31, 43
  mutual aid societies, 23–24
  Negroes Burial Ground, 23
  Pacific Islands dance, 33
  Pinkster festivals, 26–27
  Satanstoe, 30
  spirituality of, 21–22, 128n2
  work skills, 35
Ahab, 50, 95–97. *See also Moby-Dick*
Albany
  arson, 26
  Melville schooling, 27
  Pinkster festivals, 25–26
  slave music, 6–8
  slave population, 26
Albermarle Isle, 61, 134n4
Almandrel, 109
American Notes for General Circulation.
    See also Dickens, Charles
  Catharine Market, 19
  circular dance, 7, 140–41n11

"Master Juba," 7, 91–92
  and *Moby-Dick*, 6
The American Practical Navigator, 130n25
Andes Mountains, 102, 120
Antelope (ship), 122–23
Aranda, Alexandro. *See also Benito Cereno*
  Ashantee burial rites, 14, 43–44,
    132n11
  and Don Benito, 44–46, 48, 68
  as figurehead, 49–50, 60, 71, 134n6,
    134–35n8, 136n11
  and the hatchet-polishers, 57
  master-slave relationship, 136n11
  Nelson statue, 38, 77, 131n45
  slave revolt, 34
  St. Bartholomew's church, 71
Archer, Jermaine, 140n9
Archipelago of Guaytecas, 101
Arfwedson, Carl David, 129n12
Arvin, Newton, 16–17, 27, 131n3
Ashantees. *See also* Dupuis, Joseph;
    Journal of a Residence in Ashantee
  in *Benito Cereno*, 13–14, 33–34, 39,
    56, 60–62, 133n13
  burial rites, 14, 57, 71, 132n11,
    134–35n8
  execution stool, 59
  Four Years in Ashantee, 14
  harlequin ensign, 74, 135n10
  hatchet-polishers, 35, 68
  Indian-file, 140n10
  and Melville, 13–14
  in *Moby-Dick*, 13, 49–50

Ashantees (*continued*)
    music, 65–69, 133–34n3
    Narrative of Voyages and Travels, 12
    Religion and Art in Ashanti, 14
    royal adornments, 46–47, 132n5
    spirituality of, 133–34n3
    war dance, 45–46
    war trophies, 49, 134n7
Atufal. See also *Benito Cereno*
    and Amasa Delano, 44, 48–49, 134n5
    appearance, 44–45
    Arvin critique, 16
    and Babo, 49
    chains symbolism, 132n5
    and Daggoo, 47–49, 79, 132n8
    death imagery, 134n5
    death of, 61
    and Don Benito, 44–46, 48, 68
    execution stool, 47
    literacy, 46
    pardon for, 55–56
    plans deception, 41
    Spanish heretic, 79

Babo
    and Aranda's skeleton, 44
    attack on Don Benito, 38–40, 60, 74
    and Atufal, 49
    execution of, 5, 76
    as executioner, 134n6
    literacy, 46, 48
    as mastermind, 10
    master-slave relationship, 35–37, 43,
        52–53, 78, 136n11
    model for, 76
    as Nubian sculptor, 55, 73, 133n13
    plans deception, 41
    shaving scene, 54–55, 71–75, 77–78
    slave revolt, 34
    Spanish heretic, 133n14
    trial of, 61
Bachelor (ship), 95–97. See also
    Moby-Dick
Bachelor's Delight (ship), 39, 41, 58, 60.
    See also *Benito Cereno*
Bacon (Captain), 113
Bailey, Betsey, 11, 83
Baldivia, 101

Baldwin, James
    blues music, 85
    and Douglass, 11–12, 126–27n9
    jazz, 97, 137n4
    Ring Shout, 137n4
Banna, 69
Barkin, Kenneth, 126n6, 137–38n5
Batama, 71
Battery, 23–24
The Bell Tower, 36
Benito, Don. *See* Don Benito
Benito Cereno. See also hatchet-polishers;
        Moby-Dick
    African culture influences, 27, 33–34
    Ashantee influence, 12–13, 47, 56,
        60–62, 133n13
    Babo's execution, 5
    burial rites, 14
    clothing and illusion, 78–79
    "Coast of Chili," 70
    dance, 13–14, 33–34
    death imagery, 51–52, 59, 132n10
    The Encantadas, 4–5, 40, 43, 60–62,
        133n16
    and the Encantadas Islands, 41–42
    Hegelian influences, 9–10, 136n11
    Journal of a Residence, 14–15, 45–46,
        65–70
    master-slave relationship, 36–37
    Matthiessen critique, 17
    mourning weeds, 38
    Mumford critique, 3
    music themes, 6
    Narrative of Voyages and Travels, 8, 12,
        75–79, 118–19
    Nelson statue, 29, 131n45
    and Park, 13
    Redburn, 5, 37
    shaving scene, 47, 54–55, 132n12
    slavery themes, 52–55
    Spanish heretic, 56, 133n14
    Sundquist critique, 125n1
Bercaw, Mary K., 14
Bernard, Fred, 9, 125n1, 132n10
Berthoff, Warner, 127–28n18
Betsy (ship), 105–7
Big Bill Broonzy, 137n4
Bird Islands, 120–21

black music. *See also* blues music; jazz;
    Ring Shout; spirituals
  black marching bands, 7, 23, 141n16
  and Charles Dickens, 137n4
  Fifth of July parades, 129n12
  and Frederick Douglass, 8, 82
  juba beating, 7
  and Melville, 22–26, 33
  in *Moby-Dick*, 92–93
  in New York City, 21, 128–29n8
  slave song, 82–88
  Wilberforce Society, 22–24
Blackmur, R. P., 15–16, 127n15,
    127–28n18
Bloom, Harold, 11–12, 126–27n9
blues music. *See also* black music
  and Adams, 137n4
  African culture, 19
  and Baldwin, 85
  and dance, 19
  dialectic, 10
  and Douglass, 137n3, 139n7
  jazz, 19
  and Malraux, 139n7
  "Midnight, Forecastle," 89–90
  Moby-Dick, 9, 19, 82, 93–94, 97–98
  "The Music That Is in One's Soul,"
    128n2, 141n16
  Narratives, 11, 82, 84, 97–98
  "The Pequod Meets the
    Bachelor," 97–98
  Pip's tambourine, 93
  ring dancing, 19
  and Sachs, 136n1
  slave song, 84, 86, 137–38n5
  and slavery, 81
  spirituals, 19, 81, 136–37n2, 137n3
  violin playing, 137n4
Bosman, Willem, 14–15, 28, 71,
    134–35n8
Bowdich, Nathaniel, 130n25
Bowdich, Thomas Edward
  Ashantee procession, 74
  burial rites, 71
  and Melville, 28, 40, 130n25
  *Mission from Cape Coast Castle to
    Ashantee*, 14–15
break-down, 31

Bremer, Fredrika, 140n9
Broadhead, Richard H., 125n4
Broadway, 22, 128–29n8
Brown, Sterling A., 20, 82, 137n3
Buenos Ayres, 111
"Bur Rabbit in Red Hill
    Churchyard," 137n4
burial rites
  Ashantees, 14, 57, 71, 132n11,
    134–35n8
  Negroes Burial Ground, 23
  and the Ring Shout, 19–20
  skeletonizing of bodies, 37

calabash rattles, 68
Calio, 123
Calminaries, 101
cannibalism, 51, 132n11
Cape Horn, 73, 100
Cape Pillar, 100
Cape Victory, 100–101
castanets, 65–66, 68, 72
Catharine Market
  dance contests, 18, 26, 130n33
  juba beating, 31
  and Melville, 29, 31, 130n33
  tap dancing, 18–19
Cereno, Benito. *See* Don Benito
Chacao, 101
Chesapeake Bay, 84
Chili
  Andes Mountains, 102
  "Coast of Chili," 70
  mines, 103
  music of, 123–24
  navigation problems, 100–101
  St. Jago, 111
Chiloe Islands, 101
China Sailor, 33. See also *Moby-Dick*
Christianity, 139n7
circular dance, 7
City Hall, 23
Civil Rights movement, 139–40n8
Civil War, 89
"The Clarkson Benevolent Society," 24
"Coast of Chili," 70
Colburn, Henry, 131n3
Colon, Christopher, 131n45

Colonel Lloyd, 82, 87–88

Commons, 23, 30

Conception
 location, 101
 Maiden's Paps, 103–4
 mines, 103, 107
 population of, 108
 Talcaquana, 105

Cook (Captain), 27, 131n3

Coomassy, 68

Cooper, James Fenimore, 29–30

Coquimbo
 attack on, 122–23
 and Delano, 124
 location, 101
 mines, 103
 navigation of, 120–21

Cordelieras, 102

Cortlandt Street, 23

Covey, 86

cowrie shells, 19

Culbuco, 101

cutting sessions, 18

Daggoo, 47–49, 79, 92, 132n8. See also
  Moby-Dick

dance. See also music
 Bakongo faith, 25–26
 Benito Cereno, 13–14, 33–34
 and the blues, 19
 break-down, 31
 Catharine Market, 18, 26, 130n33
 circular dance, 7, 140–41n11
 cutting sessions, 18
 double shuffle, 30–31, 90–92
 Emancipation Day, 24–25
 Indian-file, 90–91, 140n10
 Irish jig, 91
 jazz, 9
 Lory-Lory, 33, 130n34
 "Master Juba," 30–31, 141n12
 and Melville, 6, 127n15
 "Midnight, Forecastle," 89–90,
   140–41n11
 minstrelsy, 140–41n11
 Moby-Dick, 13, 18, 29, 32, 81
 nation dance, 125n4
 Pacific Islands dance, 33

"The Pequod Meets the Bachelor," 96

Pinkster festivals, 7, 26–27
 ring dance, 31–33, 140n10
 Ring Shout, 19–20, 82–83, 88–89,
   140n10, 141n14
 slavery, 6–7, 28, 82–83, 87
 in South America, 123–24
 South Carolina Ring Shout, 90
 springboard dancing, 130n33

Davis, Arthur P., 137n3

Davis, David Brion, 136n11

De Voe, Thomas F., 31, 130n33

death imagery
 and Atufal, 134n5
 Benito Cereno, 51–52, 59, 132n10
 Daggoo as death warrior, 48
 execution stool, 134n5
 forecastle bell, 44–45, 47–48, 55, 72,
   132n5
 funeral procession, 94–95
 Moby-Dick, 132n10, 134n7
 oakum-pickers, 70
 and slavery, 57–58
 whale jaw bone, 50

Delano, Amasa, 104–5. See also Delano,
  Amasa (fictional); A Narrative of
  Voyages and Travels in the Northern
  and Southern Hemispheres
 Africans, 10, 37
 and Calminaries, 101
 cannibalism, 51, 132n11
 "Coast of Chili," 70
 Conception, 103
 Coquimbo, 123–24
 and Don Benito, 49, 52–54
 Galapagos Islands, 118, 134n4
 and George Howe, 112–14
 and Halsey, 119
 and Melville, 12, 136n12
 Nelson statue, 38
 shaving scene, 132n12
 and Spence, 119
 and Valparaiso, 110–11, 124
 whaling, 112

Delano, Amasa (fictional). See also Benito
  Cereno; Delano, Amasa
 and Atufal, 44, 48–49, 134n5
 death imagery, 51–52

and Don Benito, 52–54
and the Encantadas Islands, 42–43
forecastle bell, 59, 79
and the hatchet-polishers, 75
literacy of the slaves, 48
and the oakum-pickers, 70
as prisoner, 133n15
sailor's knot, 135n9
and the *San Dominick*, 41–42
Delbanco, Andrew, 125n1
Derrida, 126n7
Dett, R. Nathaniel, 18
dialectic
  blues music, 10
  and Douglass, 126n7
  and Hegel, 88, 126n7, 126–27n9,
    138n6
  Heraclitus, 126–27n9
  and Melville, 10–11
  Narratives, 11
  slave song, 93, 139–40n8
Diamond, John, 7, 31
Dickens, Charles
  *American Notes for General
    Circulation*, 7, 30
  black music, 137n4
  and Melville, 5–6, 90–91, 125n2
dig, 32
Divine Comedy, 17
Don Benito. See also *Benito Cereno*
  and Amasa Delano, 49, 52–54
  and Aranda's skeleton, 44, 71, 134n6
  Arvin critique, 17
  and Atufal, 44–46, 48, 68
  and Babo, 38–40, 60–61, 74
  empty scabbard, 74
  forecastle bell, 49
  and George Howe, 77–79
  as harlequin ensign, 77–78, 135n10
  and Infelez, 61
  and Joseph Dupuis, 79–80
  master-slave relationship, 35–37, 43,
    52–53, 78, 136n11
  model for, 76
  shaving scene, 16, 54–55, 71–75
  slave revolt, 34
double shuffle, 30–31, 90–92
Dough-Boy, 93. See also *Moby-Dick*

Douglass, Frederick. See also *Narrative of
    the Life of Frederick Douglass*
  and Baldwin, 11–12, 126–27n9
  and Betsey Bailey, 11, 83
  black music, 8, 82
  Bloom critique, 11
  blues music, 137n3, 139n7
  dialectic, 126n7
  Hegelian influences, 10
  juba beating, 141n13
  Life and Times, 83, 85–86
  and Melville, 15, 80, 93–94
  on music, 81–82, 136n1
  My Bondage, 84
  Ring Shout, 88–89, 140n9
  slave song, 82–88, 97, 137–38n5,
    139–40n8
  on slavery, 81
  spirituals, 139n7
Du Bois, W.E.B., 9, 126n6, 137–38n5,
    140n9
Dugs of Conception, 103
Dunlap, William, 95
Dupuis, Joseph. See also *Journal of a
    Residence in Ashantee*
  Ashantee attack on, 69, 134n5
  Ashantee culture, 48–49
  Ashantee music, 69, 133–34n3
  Ashantee reception, 67–68, 75
  Ashantee war trophies, 134n7
  hatchet-polishers, 63–65
  and Melville, 28, 40, 65, 131n3
  as model for Delano, 79–80

Edwards, Edward, 119
Egypt, 89, 140n9
Elliott, Emory, 6, 125n4
Ellison, Ralph, 88, 139–40n8
Ely, Ezra, 140n10
Emancipation Day, 22–24, 128–29n8
Emerson, Ralph Waldo, 137–38n5
The Encantadas
  Benito Cereno, 4–5, 40, 43, 60–62,
    133n16
  and Delano, 12
  "Sketch Fourth," 63–64, 68, 73,
    134n4
Encantadas (Galapagos Islands), 41–42

Endeavour Straits, 119
execution stool, 46, 47, 59, 134n5

fan-dango, 124
Fifth of July parades, 129n12
Five Points district, 30
Floyd, Samuel, Jr., 94–95, 141n14, 141n16
Folger, Thomas, 118–19
Follow Your Leader, 39, 71
forecastle bell. See also *Benito Cereno*
    and Amasa Delano, 59, 79
    death imagery, 44–45, 47–48, 55,
        72, 132n5
    and Don Benito, 49
    Liberty Bell, 47, 132n5
    oakum-pickers, 44, 47, 70
    and the ocean breeze, 52, 55
    shaving scene, 72
Four Years in Ashantee, 14
Fourth of July celebrations, 23
Franklin, H. Bruce, 136n12
French Sailor, 90–92
funeral processions, 94–95, 98, 141n14,
    141n16

Galapagos Islands, 12, 41–42, 118, 134n4
Gansevoort, Leonard, 26
Gansevoort, Maria, 25
Gates, Henry Louis, 138
Gilman, William H., 130n27
gloomy-jolly, 93, 95
Great House Farm, 85, 89
"The Great Singing Movements of the
    Sixties," 139–40n8
Green Hill, 121
guitars, 117, 123–24
gulf of Chonos, 101

Halsey, 76, 119
Hardenburgh, Samuel, 23–24
harlequin ensign, 74, 77–78, 135n10
hatchet-polishers. See also *Benito Cereno*
    and Amasa Delano, 75
    Aranda's skeleton, 57
    artistic influences, 13
    Arvin critique, 16
    and Ashantees, 68
    "Coast of Chili," 70

and Joseph Dupuis, 63–65
and the oakum-pickers, 64–65
"Sketch Fourth," 63–64, 68
slave revolt, 34–35
Hayford, Harrison, 12, 125n2
Hegel, G. W. F.
    Benito Cereno influences, 9–10, 136n11
    dialectic, 88, 126n7, 126–27n9, 138n6
    and Du Bois, 126n6
    master-slave relationship, 36–37
    and Melville, 9–11
Henry (ship), 123
Heraclitus, 126–27n9
Herradura (Horse Shoe Point), 121
Highlander (ship), 37
Highlanders, 74, 77
Horse Shoe Point, 121
The House of the Seven Gables, 17
Howe, George, 77–79, 112–14
Hudson (Officer), 106–7

Iceland Sailor, 32. See also *Moby-Dick*
Imbert, Michel, 87, 130n34, 137–38n5
Indian-file, 90–91, 140n10
Infelez, 61
Inquisition, 61, 133n14
*Interior Districts. See Travels into the Interior
    of Districts of Africa*
Irish jig, 91
Ishmael, 93–94, 134n7. See also
    Moby-Dick

Jackson, Mahalia, 141n16
jazz. *See also* black music
    and Baldwin, 97, 137n4
    and the blues, 19
    funeral processions, 141n16
    Jazz Dance, 141n12
    "The Music That Is in One's Soul,"
        128n2, 141n16
    scat singing, 32
    and slavery, 9
Journal of a Residence in Ashantee. See also
    Dupuis, Joseph
    and *Benito Cereno*, 14–15, 45–46,
        65–70
    execution stool, 59
    Indian-file, 140n10

and *Moby-Dick*, 14–15, 65
music themes, 79–80
Journals, 36, 131n41, 140n10
Juan Fernandez Island, 100, 102
juba beating
"Master Juba," 7, 83, 90–91, 141n12
in *Moby-Dick*, 91–92
ring dance, 31–33, 130n33
slave music, 7, 141n13

Kant, 36
Karcher, Carolyn, 130n27, 132n5
Karfa, 35
King Charley, 7, 25–26, 31
knotting problem, 135n9
Krell, David Farrell, 126n6
Krusenstern, 27, 131n3
Kuhne, Johannes, 14

Lane, William Henry "Master Juba"
Jazz Dance, 141n12
and Melville, 30–31
Pinkster festivals, 7
and the Ring Shout, 83, 90–91
Leaves of Grass, 17
Lecbe, 134–35n8
Ledyard, 27, 131n3
Lee, Ulysses, 137n3
Leslie, Joshua, 36, 133n16
Lester, Freeman, 18
Lewis, Stafford, 132n11
Liberty Bell, 47, 132n5
Life and Times, 83, 85–86
Lima, 76, 107, 111, 123
Liverpool, 28–29, 37, 40
Long, Charles, 26, 126n7, 136n11
Long Island, 18
Long Island Negroes, 96. See also
Moby-Dick
Long Island Sailor, 92. See also
Moby-Dick
Lory-Lory, 33, 130n34

MacDougall, Alma A., 125n2
Maiden's Paps, 103–4
Malispeena, 101
Malraux, André, 139n7
Maltese Sailor, 92. See also *Moby-Dick*

Manhattan Island, 22
Manx Sailor, 32, 94. See also *Moby-Dick*
Mardi, 21
Margolies, Edward, 37
Marshall, Paule, 125n4
Maryland, 137n4, 139n7
Massa Fuero, 100, 102, 113
"Master Juba." *See* Lane, William Henry
"Master Juba"
master-slave relationship. *See* slavery
Matthiessen, F. O., 17
Melville, Allan, 29
Melville, Herman. See also *Benito Cereno;*
The Encantadas; Moby-Dick; Redburn
abolition, 21
and Adler, 10, 36, 131n41
African culture influences, 20, 27–28,
31, 35
Albany Academy, 27
Albany residence, 6–8
The American Practical Navigator, 130n25
Arvin critique, 16–17
Ashantee influence, 12–14, 39
The Bell Tower, 36
Berthoff critique, 127–28n18
black music influences, 22–26
blues music, 9, 97–98
and Bosman, 134–35n8
and Bowdich, 40, 130n25
Catharine Market, 18–19, 29,
31, 130n33
"Ciceronian baboon," 28
and Cooper, 29–30
dance lessons, 26, 32
and Delano, 12, 136n12
Delbanco biography, 125n1
and Dickens, 5–6, 30, 90–91, 125n2
and Douglass, 15, 80, 93–94
and Dupuis, 28, 40, 65, 131n3
early life, 21, 128–29n8
Elliott critique, 6, 125n4
and Hegel, 9–11, 36, 78
intertextuality, 5, 40, 43
Journals, 36, 131n41, 140n10
and Kant, 36
Mardi, 21
and Margolies, 37
and Eleanor Melville Metcalf, 129n15

Melville, Herman (*continued*)
  "moral Ethiopian," 28
  Mumford critique, 17
  music themes, 6
  Narrative of the Life of Frederick Douglass, 81
  Narrative of Voyages and Travels, 10, 46, 56, 132n12
  Nelson statue, 28–29, 40
  Omoo, 5, 33, 130n34
  and Park, 13, 28, 40
  Pierre, 15–17, 127n15
  Pinkster festivals, 29
  and Schlegel, 36
  sea life, 29
  sources for, 3–4, 14
Memphis, 18–20
Merchant's Exchange, 21
Metcalf, Eleanor Melville, 129n15
middle passage, 29
"Midnight, Forecastle." See also *Moby-Dick*
  and blues music, 89–90
  circular dance, 89–90, 140–41n11
  Dickens' influence, 6
  Ring Shout, 89–90, 94
  springboard dancing, 130n33
  whaling, 81
Miller, Edwin H., 129n15
minstrelsy
  and dance, 140–41n11
  Moby-Dick, 32
  and the Ring Shout, 90
  slave song, 88, 139–40n8
  walkaround, 141n12
Mission from Cape Coast Castle to Ashantee, 14–15
Moby-Dick. See also *Benito Cereno*; "Midnight, Forecastle"
  and African American culture, 18
  African culture influences, 27–28, 32–33
  American Notes for General Circulation, 6
  Ashantee influence, 13, 49–50
  and *Benito Cereno*, 17–18, 20, 48–51, 132n10
  black music, 92–93

blues music, 9, 19, 82, 97–98
cannibalism, 51
Daggoo, 47–48
dance, 13, 18, 29, 32, 81, 83, 130n33
death imagery, 132n10, 134n7
Divine Comedy, 17
funeral processions, 98
Hegelian influences, 10–11
Journal of a Residence, 14–15, 65
juba beating, 91–92
minstrelsy, 32
Mumford critique, 3
music themes, 6, 13, 16, 81
Odyssey, 17
Omoo, 5
"The Pequod Meets the Bachelor," 95–98, 132n9
Pip's tambourine, 21
publication of, 17
Queequeg and Yojo, 133–34n3
Ring Shout, 18, 32–33, 83
"The Ship," 49
slavery themes, 7–9, 31–33, 80, 97–98, 125n1, 132n10, 139–40n8
springboard dancing, 130n33
"The Try-Works," 51
"The Whiteness of the Whale," 11, 134n7
whale jaw bone, 50
Mocha Island, 102, 119
Moody (Captain), 105–7
Moore, Frank, 140–41n11
Mount Corro Verde (Green Hill), 121
mourning weeds, 38
Mumford, Lewis, 3, 17
Munsell, Joel, 27, 31
music. *See also* black music; dance
  Ashantees, 60, 65–68
  and Douglass, 136n1
  Journal of a Residence, 79–80
  in Melville works, 6
  Moby-Dick, 13, 16, 81
  "The Music That Is in One's Soul," 128n2, 141n16
  Pinkster festivals, 25–26
  scat singing, 32
  South American instruments, 117, 123–24

tambourine, 30–32
try-pot drums, 95–96
mutual aid societies, 23–24, 128–29n8
My Bondage, 84

Nagarjuna, 126n7
Nantucketer, 92–93. See also
      Moby-Dick
Narborough Isle, 61, 68
Narrative of the Life of Frederick Douglass
      Benito Cereno, 8
      blues music, 82, 84, 97–98
      and Melville, 81
      Ring Shout, 18, 83
*A Narrative of Voyages and Travels in the
      Northern and Southern Hemispheres.*
      See also Delano, Amasa
      Benito Cereno, 8, 12, 75–79, 118–19
      Bloom critique, 11–12, 126–27n9
      Coast of Chili navigation, 100–105,
            108–10
      Galapagos Islands, 12, 118
      ladies of Chili, 107, 114–17
      and Melville, 10, 46, 56
      mines, 103, 107
      music of South America, 123–24
      slavery in South America, 111–12
      slaves murdered, 74–75
      Talcaquana kidnapping, 105–7
      whaling, 112
nation dance, 125n4
Naval Gazetteer, 120–21
Negroes Burial Ground, 23
Nelson statue
      and Aranda, 38, 77, 131n45
      description, 37–38
      and Melville, 28–29, 40
      Redburn, 29, 37–38
      satyr figure, 76
      slavery, 130n27
*A New and Accurate Description of the
      Coast of Guinea*, 14–15, 134–35n8
New Guinea, 54, 73, 77–78
New Jersey, 18, 26
New Orleans, 140n9, 141n12, 141n16
"The New York African Society for
      Mutual Relief," 24
New York American, 24

New York City
      black music, 21, 128–29n8, 129n12
      Catharine Market, 18–19
      Dickens' visit, 6, 30–31
      slave music, 6–7
*New York Gazette and General
      Advertiser*, 24
New York State, 21–22, 26
New York Statesman, 24, 129n12
Norfolk, 95

oakum-pickers. See also *Benito Cereno*
      forecastle bell, 44, 47, 70
      and the hatchet-polishers, 64–65
      shipboard attack, 53, 69–70
Odyssey, 17
*Omoo: A Narrative of Adventures in the
      South Seas*, 5, 33, 130n34
Oneco (ship), 113
"Oration Commemorative of the
      Abolition of the Slave Trade in the
      United States," 128–29n8

Pacific Islands dance, 33
Pandora (ship), 119
Paraguay, 107, 111
Park, Mungo
      African work skills, 35
      and Melville, 27–28, 40, 131n3
      *Travels into the Interior of Districts
            of Africa*, 13–14
Parker, Hershel, 6
Pearl Street, 22, 128–29n8
Pequod (ship). See also *Moby-Dick*
      Ashantee influence, 49–50
      Ashantee revolt, 13
      black music and, 8
      Journal of a Residence, 15
      "The Pequod Meets the Bachelor,"
            95–97, 132n9
      slave song and, 84
      springboard dancing, 130n33
      as tomb, 51
Perseverance (ship), 39
Peru, 102–3, 111
Phaedon (ship), 28
Philadelphia, 140n9
Pierre, 15–17, 127n15

Pinko, 107
Pinkster festivals
    Albany, 7, 25–26
    and Melville, 29
    in New York City, 21, 23
    origins of, 129n14
    ring dance, 31–33
Pinkster Hill, 26, 27
Pip. See also *Moby-Dick*
    black artist, 7
    funeral march, 141n16
    "The Pequod Meets the
        Bachelor," 96
    and Queequeg, 94
    and the Ring Shout, 90–93
    tambourine, 21, 32–33, 93–95
point of Angels, 108–10
Point Tortuga, 121
Pomp, 26
Porter, Dorothy, 128–29n8
Preston Pans, 37, 74, 77
Putzel, Max, 131n45

Quackenboss, Catherine, 129n15
Quackenboss, Jackie, 25–26, 129n15
Queequeg, 94, 133–34n3. See also
    Moby-Dick
Quiriquina Island, 104

Ramsayer, Frederick Austus, 14
Rattray, Robert S., 14
Redburn
    Benito Cereno, 5, 37
    Gilman critique, 130n27
    Merchant's Exchange, 21
    Nelson statue, 29, 37–38
    slavery, 29, 37
Religion and Art in Ashanti, 14
Representative Men, 17
Rhode Island, 30
Rich, Adrienne. *See also* Douglass,
    Frederick
Rimac Bridge, 5, 61
ring dance, 18, 32–33, 83
Ring Shout
    African Circle Dance, 18
    and Baldwin, 137n4
    and black music, 9

burial rites, 19–20
and dance, 18–20, 82–83, 88–89,
    140n10, 141n14
description, 125–26n5, 140n9
funeral procession and, 94–95
Lory-Lory, 130n34
and "Master Juba," 83, 89–91
"Midnight, Forecastle," 94
minstrelsy, 90
and slave song, 33, 88–89
River of Plate, 118
Road of Tortugas, 121–22
Robeson, Paul, 139–40n8
Robles, Juan, 134n6
Roediger, David, 36
Rourke, Constance, 140–41n11
Rover (boat), 51, 69

Sachs, Viola, 136n1
Saint Lawrence (ship), 28–29
San Dominick (ship). See also
    Benito Cereno
    African revolt, 13, 68
    and Amasa Delano, 41–43, 60
    Aranda as figurehead, 38, 40, 60, 71,
        134n6, 134–35n8, 136n11
    forecastle bell, 47, 132n5
    navigation problems, 72
    oakum-pickers, 69–70
    slave revolt, 34
    as tomb, 51
Santa Maria, 41–42
Satanstoe, 30
satyr figure, 76
The Scarlet Letter, 17
scat singing, 32
Schlegel, 36
Schweitzer, Albert, 137–38n5
Selkirk, Alexander, 102
Sequid vuestro jefe, 38
Serena. *See* Coquimbo
Shakespeare, 80
shaving scene. See also *Benito Cereno*
    Arvin critique, 16
    Benito Cereno, 47, 54–55, 132n12
    and Don Benito, 16, 54–55, 71–75
    forecastle bell, 72
    and George Howe, 77–78

New Guinea material, 54, 73
Preston Pans, 74, 77
Spanish flag, 47, 54–55, 73–74,
    132n5
"The Ship," 49
shotgun houses, 19
Sidney, Joseph, 128–29n8
"Sketch Fourth," 63–64, 68, 73, 134n4.
    See also *The Encantadas*
slavery. *See also* black music; Douglass,
    Frederick
  abolition, 21–22
  African work skills, 28
  Ashantee burial rites, 71
  Benito Cereno, 52–55
  and the blues, 81
  Covey, slave breaker, 86
  dance, 28
  death imagery, 57–58
  economics of, 28
  Emancipation Day, 22–24
  forecastle bell and death
      imagery, 47
  funeral processions, 95
  and the Inquisition, 133n14
  juba beating, 141n13
  living conditions, 26
  master-slave relationship, 35–37, 43,
      52–53, 78, 85–86, 136n11
  Melville theme, 5, 80
  middle passage, 29
  Moby-Dick, 9, 97–98, 125n1, 132n10,
      139–40n8
  music and dance, 6–7, 82–83
  Nelson statue, 130n27
  "Oration Commemorative of the
      Abolition of the Slave Trade in the
      United States," 128–29n8
  Pinkster Monday, 129n14
  Redburn, 29, 37
  revolt in *Benito Cereno*, 34
  Ring Shout, 33
  slave song, 82–89, 93, 137–38n5,
      139–40n8
  in South America, 111, 114–15
  and spirituals, 81
  violin playing, 137n4
Sole, Cornelius, 122–23

South America, 42–43, 70, 72–73
South Carolina Ring Shout, 90
South Sea, 120
South Street waterfront, 22
Southern, Eileen, 82, 136–37n2
Southern Road, 20
Spanish flag, 47, 54–55, 73–74, 132n5
Spanish heretic, 56, 61, 79, 132n12
Spanish Sailor, 92. See also
    Moby-Dick
Spence, Charles, 76, 119
spirituals. *See also* black music
    and the blues, 19, 81, 136–37n2,
        137n3, 139n7
    and slavery, 9, 81
springboard dancing, 130n33
St. Ambrose, 102, 124
St. Bartholomew's church, 71
St. Felix, 102, 124
St. Helena, 118
St. Jago (St. James), 111, 113
St. Louis School of Hegelians,
    126–27n9
St. Maria, 73
St. Maria Island, 102
Stearns, Marshall and Jean, 125–26n5,
    141n12
Straits of Magellan, 100
Stuckey, Elma, 18, 19
Stuckey, Sterling
    African American music, 18–20
    Ashantee burial rites, 132n11
    "The Great Singing Movements
        of the Sixties," 139–40n8
    master-slave relationship, 36
    "The Music That Is in One's Soul,"
        128n2, 141n16
    Southern Road introduction, 20
Sundquist, Eric, 125n1

Tabor (ship), 122
Talcaquana, 104–5
tambourine, 21, 30–33, 90–94
Tanselle, G. Thomas, 125n2
Tashtego, 50, 92. See also *Moby-Dick*
Taylor, 36
Thomas (Captain), 105–7
Thomas (ship), 105–7

Trajano, Christian, 133n14
*Travels into the Interior of Districts
of Africa*, 13, 28
Tryal (ship), 105–7, 111, 119
try-pot drums, 95–96
"The Try-Works," 51

Valparaiso
   and George Howe, 77, 113
   location, 101
   navigation of, 108–10
   whaling, 111
Vancouver, 27, 131n3
Vancouver (Captain), 108, 110
violin, 137n4
volcanoes, 134n4

Voyages and Travels. See *A Narrative of
Voyages and Travels in the Northern
and Southern Hemispheres*
Vulture (ship), 118–19

Walden, 17
walkaround, 141n12
Watson (Captain), 123
whaling, 112
"The Whiteness of the Whale," 11, 134n7
Whitsuntide, 129n14
Wilberforce Society, 22–23, 128–29n8
Williams, Howard, 126–27n9
Wright, Richard, 133–34n3

Yojo, 133–34n3